China's Contained Resource Curse

As a country rich in mineral resources, contemporary China remains surprisingly overlooked in the research about the much debated 'resource curse'. This is the first full-length study to examine the distinctive effects of mineral resources on the state, capital and labour and their interrelations in China. Jing Vivian Zhan draws on a wealth of empirical evidence, both qualitative and quantitative. Taking a subnational approach, she zooms in on local situations and demonstrates how mineral resources affect local governance and economic as well as human development. Characterizing mining industries as pro-capital and anti-labour, this study also highlights the redistributive roles that the state can play to redress the imbalance. It reveals the Chinese state's strategies to contain the resource curse and also pinpoints some pitfalls of the China model, which offer important policy implications for China and other resource-rich countries.

JING VIVIAN ZHAN is Associate Professor in the Department of Government & Public Administration at The Chinese University of Hong Kong. She specializes in comparative political economy, contemporary Chinese politics, intergovernmental relations, local governance and development studies.

China's Contained Resource Curse

How Minerals Shape State–Capital–Labor Relations

JING VIVIAN ZHAN
The Chinese University of Hong Kong

Shaftesbury Road, Cambridge CB2 8EA, United Kingdom

One Liberty Plaza, 20th Floor, New York, NY 10006, USA

477 Williamstown Road, Port Melbourne, VIC 3207, Australia

314–321, 3rd Floor, Plot 3, Splendor Forum, Jasola District Centre, New Delhi – 110025, India

103 Penang Road, #05–06/07, Visioncrest Commercial, Singapore 238467

Cambridge University Press is part of Cambridge University Press & Assessment, a department of the University of Cambridge.

We share the University's mission to contribute to society through the pursuit of education, learning and research at the highest international levels of excellence.

www.cambridge.org
Information on this title: www.cambridge.org/9781009048989

DOI: 10.1017/9781009049757

First published 2022
First paperback edition 2024

A catalogue record for this publication is available from the British Library

Library of Congress Cataloging-in-Publication data
Names: Zhan, Jing Vivian, 1978- author.
Title: China's contained resource curse : how minerals shape state-capital-labor relations / Jing Vivian Zhan, The Chinese University of Hong Kong.
Description: Cambridge, United Kingdom ; New York, NY, USA : Cambridge University Press, 2022. | Includes bibliographical references and index.
Identifiers: LCCN 2021033286 (print) | LCCN 2021033287 (ebook) | ISBN 9781316511268 (hardback) | ISBN 9781009048989 (paperback) | ISBN 9781009049757 (epub)
Subjects: LCSH: Mines and mineral resources–Political aspects–China. | Mineral industries–Labor productivity–China. | Natural resources–China. | BISAC: POLITICAL SCIENCE / Political Economy
Classification: LCC HD9506.C62 Z36 2022 (print) | LCC HD9506.C62 (ebook) | DDC 338.20951–dc23
LC record available at https://lccn.loc.gov/2021033286
LC ebook record available at https://lccn.loc.gov/2021033287

ISBN   978-1-316-51126-8   Hardback
ISBN   978-1-009-04898-9   Paperback

To Jiji, Feifan, and Chufan,
for your unending love, unfailing support, and unceasing distractions

Contents

Figures

Tables

Acknowledgments

This book would not have been possible without the financial support of the General Research Funds (14601915 and 456712) provided by the Hong Kong Research Grants Council, and the institutional support of the Chinese University of Hong Kong (CUHK). Over the course of the past few years, the financial support helped me to travel widely across China, visit interesting places, and talk to people from all walks of life; these experiences constantly left me awestruck and puzzled and pushed forward my research. I also had the luxury to think and write quietly and freely on the beautiful campus of CUHK and to exchange ideas with fantastic colleagues and postgraduate students in the Department of Government and Public Administration (GPA). I am indebted to the incredible collections, visiting scholar schemes, and amazing staff at the Universities Service Centre for China Studies (USC), which not only provided crucial data sources for my research but also became an important source of inspiration for my academic pursuit.

Writing a book is a lonely journey. But I was fortunate to receive priceless intellectual and moral support from my long-term collaborator Zeng Ming and wonderful colleagues in the GPA Department, especially Chen Xi, Pierre Landry, and Li Lianjiang. Meanwhile, I greatly benefited from the comments from Michael Ross, Daniel Treisman, Hiroki Takeuchi, Chen Xi, James Kung, Cai Yongshun, Jean Hong, Xiao Yang, Ma Rong, Hill Gates, and three anonymous reviewers at various stages of this research. I am also grateful to Li Fangchun and Zhu Tianbiao for inviting me to visit Chongqing University and Zhejiang University in 2017 and 2018, respectively, which allowed me to concentrate on my research and engage in stimulating and inspiring discussions with the scholars in these two institutions. In addition, I thank Chen Chuanmin, Chen Xiaoyan, Dong Jiang'ai, Duan Haiyan, Fan Hongmin, Liao Jinying, Ma Fenglian, Andy Wong, Xi Keke, Xie Ting, Zeng Ming, Zhang Huiteng, Zhou

Haoyue, and Zhuang Yuyi for their valuable assistance to this research, especially during my fieldworks in China. Finally, I am truly thankful to Editor Joe Ng at the Cambridge University Press for his professional guidance and tireless support throughout the publication process.

Last but not least, I would like to dedicate this book to my husband, Zhang Jiji, for his love, encouragement, and critique from a philosophical perspective, and to my sons, Zhang Feifan and Zhang Chufan, for brightening up my gloomy days and making me a supermom who can overcome any difficulty. I am also thankful to my parents, Zhan Zhengguo and Liu Youfen, for their unconditional love and care throughout these years, without which I could not have come this far.

Abbreviations

CASS	Chinese Academy of Social Sciences
CCP	Chinese Communist Party
CLB	China Labour Bulletin
CNOOC	China National Offshore Oil Corporation
CPPCC	Chinese People's Political Consultative Conference
FDI	foreign direct investment
GDP	gross domestic product
IT	information technology
MENA	Middle East and North Africa
NPC	National People's Congress
OECD	Organization for Economic Cooperation and Development
PISA	Programme for International Student Assessment
PPP	provincial people's procuratorate
SOE	state-owned enterprise
VAT	value-added tax

1 | *Minerals and the State–Capital–Labor Triad*

Men of a fat and fertile soil are most commonly effeminate and cowards; whereas contrariwise a barren country makes men... careful, vigilant, and industrious.

— Jean Bodin (Six Books of a Commonwealth, 1967)

China: An Atypical Resource-Rich Country

After the wave of independence movements swept Africa and the Middle East in the 1950s and 1960s, the newly independent countries in the region were acclaimed and assumed to have a bright prospect of development ahead. One important reason for the optimistic outlook was that these countries are endowed with abundant oil and mineral resources, which were believed to provide raw materials and start-up funds crucial for industrialization and economic takeoff (Spengler, 1960). However, half a century later, the world has realized that instead of promoting growth, natural resources are oftentimes associated with sluggish economic development (Auty, 1993; Sachs & Warner, 1995) and low levels of human development (Blanco & Grier, 2012; Gylfason, 2001a). Moreover, resource-rich developing countries tend to suffer weak, nondemocratic political institutions (Collier & Hoeffler, 2005; Jensen & Wantchekon, 2004; Ross, 2015) and to experience high risks of civil conflicts (Fearon & Laitin, 2003; Klare, 2001; Ross, 2015). Scholars and policymakers have thus tried to unravel the paradoxical effects of mineral resources and embarked on a decades-long debate on the so-called curse of natural resources since the notion was first proposed in the 1990s (Auty, 1993, 1994).

Little noticed in the debate is that China, the world's largest developing country that has undergone remarkable economic growth in the past four decades or so, is also a resource-rich country. As Chinese

1

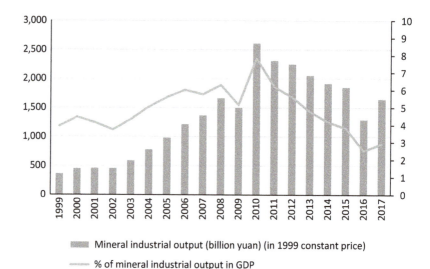

Figure 1.1 National mineral industrial output (1999–2017)

Source: Figure compiled based on statistics from *China Land and Resources Statistical Yearbook 2000–2018*, *Statistical Yearbook of China 2020* and World Bank database (https://data.worldbank.org.cn/indicator/FP.CPI.TOTL.ZG?locations=CN)

Note: The bars stand for the inflation-adjusted annual mineral industrial output (with 1999 as the base year); the line is the percentage of mineral industrial output in national GDP. Mineral industrial output data include all provinces and offshore oil fields but exclude Hong Kong, Macao, and Taiwan.

children are proudly taught in school, China is a grand country with a vast territory and abundant natural resources (*dida wubo* 地大物博). Although internationally not known as an economy heavily dependent on resource exports, China is actually a major producer and consumer of a large variety of mineral resources, including fuels such as coal, oil and natural gas, metals such as iron and copper, and other nonmetallic minerals such as limestone. Since the turn of the millennium, China has experienced a sustained resource boom of more than one decade. As Figure 1.1 shows, the real mineral industrial output (in 1999 constant price) rose substantially between 1999 and 2017, the period under this study. At the peak of the resource boom, China's mineral industrial output accounted for 7.84% of the national gross domestic product (GDP) in 2010. In resource-rich regions such as Shanxi Province, Qinghai Province, and Xinjiang Uyghur Autonomous Region, mineral industrial outputs constantly accounted for 20%–30% of the provincial GDP throughout the 2000s and 2010s,[1] which makes these regions comparable to typical oil-rich countries such as in the Middle East and North Africa (MENA).[2] Mineral resources not only prove crucial for the local economy of resource-rich Chinese localities, but are also indispensable for China's overall industrialization and modernization.

Ironically, while generating national pride and economic dividends, mineral resources are often associated with negative news in China. For instance, a massive riot broke out in 2008 in Weng'an County in Guizhou, an underdeveloped province in southwest China. The riot involved more than twenty thousand participants and led more than one hundred government offices to be smashed and torched and the Chinese Communist Party's (CCP) county headquarters to be completely burnt down.[3] While triggered by rumors, this incident was later found out to be caused by the strong popular grievance accumulated during the chaotic exploration of rich phosphorus deposits in the county (Liu, 2009; Zhan, 2013). Such resource-triggered social conflicts and mass protests have broken out in other Chinese localities as well.[4] By scouring three datasets on mass protests in China, including China Labour Bulletin (CLB) "Strike" dataset,[5] the "Collective Incidents" dataset collected by the Chinese Academy of Social Sciences (CASS),[6] and the "China Strikes" dataset (Elfstrom 2017),

---

[1] The national and provincial percentages are calculated based on statistics from *China Land and Resources Statistical Yearbook (Guotu Ziyuan Tongji Nianjian) 2000–2016* and *Statistical Yearbook of China (Zhongguo Tongji Nianjian) 2018.*

[2] According to the World Bank data, the share of oil rents in GDP in MENA fluctuated between 11.7% and 32.6% from 1990 to 2018. Statistics are obtained from https://data.worldbank.org/indicator/ny.gdp.petr.rt.zs?end=2017&name_desc=false&start=1973, accessed on January 14, 2021.

[3] Wang Weibo, 2008. "Weng'an Guanyuan Fangkai Xinwen Baodao Yingdui Xinren Weiji (Weng'an County Officials Opened Media Reports in Response to Trust Crisis)." *Zhongguo Xinwen Zhoukan (China News Weekly)*, July 9, http://news.sina.com.cn/c/2008-07-09/040015896433.shtml, accessed on November 4, 2019.

[4] See, for example, Yan Dingfei, 2014. "Shifang houyizheng (In the aftermath of Shifang)," *Nanfang Zhoumou (Southern Weekend)*, October 30, www.infzm.com/content/105194, accessed on March 24, 2020.

[5] China Labour Bulletin. https://maps.clb.org.hk/, accessed on January 11, 2021.

[6] I am grateful to Jiang Junyan for generously sharing this dataset. For detailed information about this dataset, see the supporting information of Jiang et al. (2019).

I identify a total of 436 mining-related mass protests between 2005 and 2020, which are widely distributed across Chinese provinces. This suggests that the extraction of mineral resources has become an unneglectable source of social unrest in China.

Mineral resources also appear to be closely associated with corruption. For instance, since President Xi Jinping launched a high-profile anti-corruption campaign in 2012, Shanxi Province, the largest coal producing province in China, stood out as an exceptional hotbed of corruption. Thousands of Shanxi officials, including dozes of high-level cadres at the provincial and prefecture levels, were investigated and disciplined for corruption. The corruption cleanup led to a serious crisis for Shanxi local governments in 2014, as they scrambled to find suitable replacements for hundreds of suddenly vacated offices.[7] Although many speculated on the power struggle behind the political earthquake in Shanxi,[8] there is clear evidence linking the coal and related industries and revealed corruption cases.[9] Similarly, Inner Mongolia, another major producer of coal, also discovered a large number of corruption cases in its coal mining industry between 2000 and 2020. Of its five provincial-level officials investigated for corruption since 2018, four of them are closely related to the coal industry.[10]

Apparently mineral resources have generated devastating sociopolitical impacts in China, similar to those plaguing many other resource-rich developing countries. But interestingly, China has not seen the outbreak of large-scale violent conflicts or pervasive decay of political institutions, some common symptoms of the resource curse. Moreover,

[7] Fan Jianghong, 2017. "'Tafangshi Fubai' de Shanxi, Rujin Zhili de Zemeyang le? (After Collapsing Corruption, How Is Shanxi Governed Now?)" *Shangguan News*, January 5, www.jfdaily.com/wx/detail.do?id=41369, accessed on November 4, 2019.
[8] The downfalls of former top officials Zhou Yongkang and Ling Jihua as well as their associates are believed to have triggered the investigation of corruption cases in Shanxi Province.
[9] Duowei News, 2018. "Shanxi Meitan Fubai Xianru Guaiquan, Beihou Ancang Zhengshang Guanxi (Official-business Ties behind Coal-related Corruption in Shanxi)." September 25, http://news.dwnews.com/china/news/2018-09-25/60087095.html, accessed on November 4, 2019.
[10] Guo Xing, 2021. "Neimonggu Tiewan Zhengzhi Shemei Fubai, Chuli Chufen 14000 Yu Ren (Inner Mongolia Cracks Down Coal-related Corruption with An Iron Hand, Disciplining over 1400 Officials)," *Central Commission for Discipline Inspection*, March 6, www.ccdi.gov.cn/yaowen/202103/t20210306_237234_m.html, accessed on March 7, 2021.

the Chinese economy has grown continuously and strongly for decades, including in those resource-rich localities. These contradictory pictures thus raise intriguing and important questions: Why does China suffer some symptoms of the resource curse but not the others? Does the endowment of mineral resources affect local development and governance in China in similar ways as in other resource-rich countries that suffer the resource curse? If yes, at what levels and through which channels does the resource curse take place? If not, how does China contain the adverse impacts of natural resources and cope with the resource curse?

The Exploration of Mineral Resources: What Has It Brought to China?

Mineral resources have long played important roles in China's industrialization and modernization since the Maoist era, providing over 90% of China's primary energy, 80% of industrial raw materials, and 70% of agricultural inputs (Information Office of the State Council, 2003). After the start of the post-Mao reforms, the Chinese central government further encouraged the utilization of mineral resources by launching the policy of "speeding up the water flow (*youshui kuailiu* 有水快流)" in 1983, allowing non-state-owned enterprises to explore mineral resources that had been strictly controlled by the state under the planned economy (Dong, 2016, p. 33). While state-owned companies continued to control the larger, richer mines and oil fields and those of strategic importance, the smaller and strategically less significant ones were opened up to collective and private investors. With the flush of market forces, mineral production started to grow rapidly, and mineral prices were no longer artificially suppressed but gradually converged to market prices. Starting around the turn of the millennium and especially after 2003, the Chinese resource market experienced a "golden decade" with both demands and prices rising sharply. The national mineral production increased sharply from 357.3 billion yuan in 1999 to the peak of 3,231 billion yuan in 2010. Although mineral production declined slowly in the following years, it still remained at 2,428 billion yuan in 2017, according to the latest statistics.[11]

---

[11] Statistics are based on *China Land and Resources Statistical Yearbook 2000–2018 and Statistical Yearbook of China* 2018.

At the national level China does not heavily rely on mineral production for its economy or exports, however, at subnational levels many
Chinese localities produce massive amounts of minerals and are heavily reliant on the resource sector for their economic development and
fiscal incomes. As Figure 1.2 shows, there exists wide cross-regional
variation in resource endowment and exploration. While all provinces
are engaged in mineral production to certain extents, the magnitude
varies widely across provinces, with the major producers concentrated
mostly in inland areas and the northern part of China. Between
1999 and 2017, the average share of mineral industrial output in

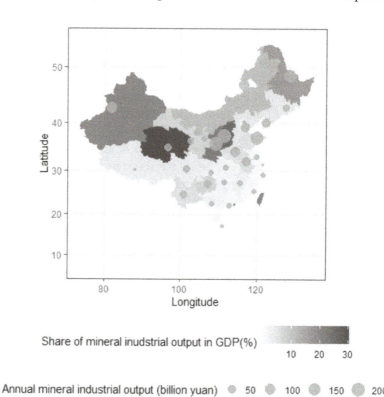

Figure 1.2 Regional mineral production in China (1999–2017)
Note: Map drawn based on statistics from *China Land and Resources Statistical
Yearbook 2000–2018* and *Statistical Yearbook of China 2000–2018*. The button size
in each province indicates the average annual mineral industrial output (including oil,
gas, and solid minerals) between 1999 and 2017. The shade of each province demonstrates the average share of mineral industrial outputs in provincial GDP between
1999 and 2017. Data exclude Taiwan, Hong Kong, and Macau.

provincial GDP ranged between 0.4% and 30.4%,[12] indicating vastly different levels of resource dependence across Chinese provinces as well. In the resource-rich regions, mining industries contribute significantly to local economic development and revenue generation. Moreover, mineral products are exported to other Chinese regions to meet their insatiable needs for energy and raw materials. Certain minerals, such as coal and oil, are also exported to other countries. Due to their important roles in the Chinese economy, mineral resources are indispensable for China's remarkable economic growth and rapid industrialization in the post-Mao reform era.

However, the extraction and consumption of the mineral resources have generated profound socioeconomic and political consequences as well as serious environmental damages. Numerous journalistic reports have revealed mining-caused air, water, and soil pollution, health problems, labor disputes, mining accidents, popular protests against mining companies and local governments, etc. While environmental problems such as pollution, land loss, and depletion of resources have attracted worldwide attention in media, academia, and policy circles, the socioeconomic and political consequences, which involve constant contentions, negotiations, and compromises between different stakeholders, have not drawn sufficient attention from scholars or policymakers in and outside China.

Since the mid-2000s, some Chinese scholars have taken the first steps to assess the risks of the resource curse in China (e.g., Xu & Wang, 2006; Yang & Niu, 2009; Zhang et al., 2007). These scholarly efforts largely focus on the economic side of the story, namely the impacts of resource endowment on local economic performance. For example, some statistical analyses have revealed negative correlations between resource endowment and economic growth at provincial and prefecture levels (Fu & Wang, 2010; Xu & Wang, 2006) and in certain areas (Shao & Qi, 2008). Some have identified a subnational variant of the Dutch disease (Corden & Neary, 1982) in China and shown that resource boom suppresses per capita consumption growth by driving up local prices of non-tradable goods and damages the competitiveness of local firms (Zhang et al., 2007). However, the empirical evidence

---

[12] The percentages are calculated based on statistics from *China Land and Resources Statistical Yearbook 2000–2018* and *Statistical Yearbook of China 2018*.

remains ambiguous as to whether there exists a resource curse in China in economic terms (Zhang & Brouwer, 2020).

On the other hand, looking beyond the economics discipline, scant scholarly attention has been paid to the far-reaching and multifaceted political and social impacts of resources, such as corruption, political decay, and social conflicts, which have been well documented in other resource-rich countries and thoroughly examined by the comparative literature. With a few notable exceptions (e.g., Ho & Yang, 2018; Hong & Yang, 2018; Yang et al., 2017), there have been very limited efforts to examine, for example, how resource endowment affects the quality of political institutions, state–society relations, and social conflicts in China.

The massive resource boom since the turn of the millennium makes China an intriguing case to study the impacts of mineral resources on the society. Moreover, as Figure 1.2 shows, mineral resources are widely but highly unevenly distributed across Chinese localities. The cross-regional variations in resource endowment and dependence function as a natural experiment for researchers to investigate the socioeconomic and political effects of mineral resources through subnational comparison. By controlling for national-level institutional factors such as political regime, bureaucratic structure, and economic system, we can more closely and clearly examine the causal channels through which resources affect socioeconomic and political outcomes.

How Do Resources Affect Human Society? Existing Debates

In the past four decades or so, a growing body of literature has advanced numerous arguments on how mineral resources affect human society and why they appear to be counterproductive and even detrimental for the host countries, the vast majority of them being developing countries. After Corden and Neary (1982) proposed the Dutch disease theorem as a pioneering economic explanation of the resource curse, this paradoxical phenomenon started to attract growing scholarly attention from multiple disciplines. Auty (1993) first clearly proposed the resource curse thesis, and he further elaborated the ideas in his subsequent publications (Auty, 1994, 2001). Following the footsteps of Auty's seminal works, scholars in economics, political science, and other disciplines have increasingly joined force and proposed a large number of theories from different perspectives to explain the counterintuitive phenomenon. With the remarkable progresses since the 1990s, the discourse on the resource curse has by now gone far beyond purely economic theories, and has tapped on the rich intellectual reservoirs of different disciplines.

In the economic arena, Corden and Neary (1982), as the pioneers, argue that resource abundance gives rise to the so-called Dutch disease, which undermines the non-resource sectors through direct and indirect deindustrialization and thus hurts the long-term prospect of development. Since then a voluminous literature in economics has empirically tested the effects of mineral resources, especially petroleum, on economic performance and advanced multiple causal mechanisms for the resource curse,[13] which often go beyond economic factors such as deindustrialization, exchange rate and trade and are intertwined with political factors such as the quality of political institutions, corruption, and civil conflicts, as will be discussed below. However, controversies persist regarding whether or not natural resources pose a curse on economic performance. Different studies, all with supporting empirical evidence, show contradictory findings about whether resource endowment hampers economic development (e.g., Alexeev & Conrad, 2009; Brunnschweiler & Bulte, 2008; Butkiewicz & Yanikkaya, 2010; Lederman & Maloney, 2008; Michaels, 2011; Sachs & Warner, 1995) and whether the effects vary between different time periods in history (Andersen & Ross, 2014; Gerelmaaa & Kotani, 2016). And looking at the short- versus long-term effects of resources may also lead scholars to arrive at different conclusions (Allcott & Keniston, 2018; Michaels, 2011). Therefore, no consensus has been reached on the effect of natural resource abundance on economic development and the underlying mechanism (Havranek et al., 2016).

Political scientists pay more attention to the political foundations of the resource curse, such as weak political institutions, lack of democracy, and epidemic corruption in resource-rich countries.[14] The rentier state theory argues that as rentier states derive a dominant share of their revenue from resource rent rather than taxation on productive activities, they have less obligation to respond to citizens' demands (Brautigam et al., 2008; Mahdavy, 1970); the citizens also have less

---

[13] For some detailed reviews of the economic literature on the resource curse, see Wick and Bulte (2009) and van der Ploeg (2011).

[14] For an excellent survey of the political science literature on the resource curse, see Ross (2015).

incentive to create mechanisms of accountability and to closely monitor the government and public officials (Ross, 1999, 2001). Thus
rentier states commonly suffer weak political institutions based on
patronage instead of electoral competition, scrutiny, and civil rights
(Collier & Hoeffler, 2005), and experience enduring autocratic rule
and difficulty in democratic transition (Aslaksen, 2010; Barro, 2009;
Tsui, 2011). Resource-rich countries also tend to lack socially intrusive
and elaborate bureaucracies (Fearon & Laitin, 2003), state capacity to
provide public goods to the general population (Ross, 2003), and the
ability to maintain law and order and resolve social conflicts (Karl,
1997; Reno, 1998). However, these arguments are empirically con-
tested. For example, some studies find that resource discovery or boom
can strengthen regime stability and capacity (Côte & Korf, 2018;
Smith, 2004) and fasten democratization under certain conditions
(Dunning, 2008; Markus et al., 2012), while some statistical studies
find no correlation between oil wealth and democracy (Haber &
Menaldo, 2011). Therefore, resource does not necessarily undermine
political institutions or democracy, which is rather contingent on the
power, incentive, and strategy of relevant social and political actors.

Another stream of research on resources and political institutions
argues that resource windfalls create both economic opportunities and
temptations for corruption (Bulte et al., 2005; Caselli & Michaels,
2013; Franke et al., 2009; Karl, 1997; Leite & Weidmann, 1999;
Robinson et al., 2006). Meanwhile, the fierce competition for powerful
political positions that control the resource rents fuels political corruption in such forms as vote buying in elections and patronage networks
(Caselli & Cunningham, 2009; Franke et al., 2009; Kolstad & Søreide,
2009; Vicente, 2010). But other studies dispute the linkage. For instance,
Bhattacharyya and Hodler (2010) argue that resources feed corruption
only in countries without democratic institutions, and good-quality
democracies appear immune to this problem. Treisman (2000) finds
that countries where fuel, metals, and minerals take up larger shares in
exports tend to have higher corruption, but when economic development and democracy are controlled for, this effect disappears.

Socially speaking, resource abundance is believed to arouse civil
conflicts due to grievance and greed.[15] The resource economy often
creates grievance among local population due to unequal distribution

---

[15] For a careful review of the relevant literature, see Ross (2015).

of wealth, income instability due to price shocks, or negative externalities during resource extraction such as land expropriation and environmental hazards (Klare, 2001; Switzer, 2001). Even worse, resource rents provide motivation as well as start-up funds for violent competition for the control of resources among social groups (Collier & Hoeffler, 1998; Collier, 2003; Englebert & Ron, 2004). In general, resources are believed to make armed conflicts more likely and civil wars last longer (Bannon & Collier, 2003; Collier & Hoeffler, 1998, 2004; Fearon & Laitin, 2003; Fearon, 2004; Lujala et al., 2005). However, it is debatable whether resource-dependent countries are bound to suffer higher tendency of social conflicts. As some scholars point out, when rentier states redistribute their windfall revenues or invest them in building state institutions, including repressive apparatuses, a natural resource, oil in particular, actually lowers the likelihood of civil war and anti-state protest (Basedau & Lay, 2009; Cotet & Tsui, 2013; Smith, 2004; Wright et al., 2015).

Finally, some scholars debate the cognitive effects of resource endowment on people's mindsets. Development scholars have long ago suggested that resource boom can induce either myopic sloth or exuberance in policymakers (Ross, 1999). As Bodin (1967) puts it, "men of a fat and fertile soil are most commonly effeminate and cowards; whereas contrariwise a barren country makes men... careful, vigilant, and industrious." However, other scholars challenge the fundamental assumption of the cognitive effect, arguing that human beings are revenue maximizers instead of revenue satisficers and thus resource booms should not discourage other means to promote development (Ross, 1999). Meanwhile, some contend that resource-rich states are typically advised by international organizations such as the World Bank, which should alert them about the negative consequences of resource booms (Varangis et al., 1995).

Overall, the exisiting studies have greatly enhanced our understanding about the adverse socioeconomic and political impacts of natural resources. However, controversies persist regarding the existence and causal mechanisms of the curse of natural resources. We are yet to reach agreements on many of the abovementioned arguments and there are still numerous unanswered questions. Given the state of the art, I believe there are different approaches and promising directions to further advance the research on the resource curse. For example, most existing researches focus on oil and natural gas and, to a lesser extent, on precious gemstones as the subject of study, but have neglected many other types of mineral. The extraction of widely used solid minerals such as coal could also generate important consequences and deserves to be examined systematically.

Meanwhile, the resource curse literature has been predominantly cross-national statistical analysis or country-level case studies, with individual country as the analytical unit. In recent years, scholars started to zoom in on single countries and examine the effects of resources at subnational levels (Allcott & Keniston, 2018; Caselli & Michael, 2009; Cust & Poelhekke, 2015; James & Aadland, 2010; Johnson, 2006; Libman, 2013; Zhan, 2013). The notion of the local resource curse, which focuses on how natural resources affect the local, rather than national, economic and political conditions and the welfare of local citizens, has attracted growing scholarly attention (Aragón et al., 2015; Sexton, 2020). Within-country studies are indeed a fruitful approach, as they can control for broad institutional settings such as political regime and sociohistorical contexts, and they allow scholars to disaggregate causal mechanisms and examine them more closely (Cust & Viale, 2016; Ross, 2015).

The resource curse discourse can also benefit from some new perspectives. In particular, the extant literature has not paid sufficient attention to the state, which is an important stakeholder and can play crucial roles in shaping socioeconomic and political outcomes. In much of the existing discourse, the state is either curiously missing or present as merely a victim that passively suffers the adverse effects of resource endowment and extraction on its own capacity. Actually, political institutions can generate major intervening effects on the socioeconomic impacts of natural resources. Scholars have recently started to examine the conditioning effects of political institutions, such as regime type, constitutional arrangements, and state ownership of resources, on the existence or extent of the resource curse (Ahmadov, 2014; Andersen & Aslaksen, 2008, 2013; Bhattacharyya & Hodler, 2010; Dauvina & Guerreiro, 2017; Luong & Weinthal, 2010; Treisman, 2000). However, these studies largely take institutions as exogenous and static instead of being malleable and responsive to resource-triggered socioeconomic happenings. Only a handful of studies realize the active roles that a state can play to alter the impacts of the resources on social outcomes and determine whether resources pose a blessing or a curse (e.g., Dunning, 2005; Englebert & Ron, 2004). For example, when resource-rich states invest their windfall revenues in building state institutions and political organizations, natural resources may enhance regime durability and decrease civil conflicts (Basedau & Lay, 2009; Cotet & Tsui, 2013; Smith, 2004; Wright et al., 2015). Therefore, it is necessary to bring the state in as an active player, to examine what roles it plays with regard to natural resources and to assess the impacts of the state's strategies.

Moreover, the existing studies commonly treat individual countries or subnational regions as the analytical unit and take an undifferentiating approach toward the unit as a whole, but the divergent impacts of resources on different stakeholders and during different time periods have not received much attention. For instance, the economic studies typically try to identify the correlation between natural resources and the overall economy as manifested by GDP or GDP growth rate.[16] However, resource endowment may generate divergent impacts on different sectors and stakeholders in the economy, and we need to disaggregate the effects on different parties and look into them separately. An obvious reason is that the resource economy must have positive impacts on certain social groups and during certain periods of time, otherwise there would be little incentive for human beings to explore and utilize natural resources. But mineral resources also generate various problems and impose the costs on other groups, such as the local communities that suffer from the environmental damages associated with mineral extraction, and mineral extraction may bring about negative consequences in the long run for future generations. Therefore, when examining the impacts of natural resources, one needs to distinguish the targets of such impacts and the time frame during which the impacts take place.

Minerals and State–Capital–Labor Relations: A Refined Theory

In view of the lacunae in the existing literature, this book aims to contribute to the debate on the resource curse by conducting a subnational study on China and disaggregating the society into three major players, the state, capital, and labor. It proposes a refined theory about

---

[16] For example, see Auty (2001) and Sachs and Warner (1995). The majority of existing studies on the impacts of resource abundance/dependence follows the practices of these seminal works.

the impacts of mineral resources on each of the three players as well as the triangular relationship between them, which altogether determine the socioeconomic and political outcomes in resource-rich regions. This theory explains why China has experienced some symptoms of the resource curse as in other resource-rich developing countries but has largely contained the resource curse to limited scales and isolated cases.

I identify the state, capital, and labor as the three major players in the resource economy. This is determined by the particular character-istics of the mining industry that set it apart from other industries. First of all, the mining industry operates under strong state intervention. As the mining industry extracts natural resources which are normally owned by the state, at least nominally, it gives the state legitimate reasons to sanction and monitor the operation of mining activities. In the Chinese context, all mineral resources, regardless of the ownership of the land to which the mineral resources are attached, belong to the state.[17] Once mineral reserves are discovered and exploration proved feasible, mining enterprises need to obtain permission from the gov-ernment to start operation. Mineral exploration and extraction are extensively regulated by various government departments such as the land and resources, taxation, work safety, environmental protection, industry and commerce departments. Therefore, the state is involved in the whole process from the prospecting of mineral reserves to the production, processing, transportation and transaction of mineral products. Especially in an authoritarian country where the Communist Party-state has a strong presence and deeply penetrates into the econ-omy and the society, the Chinese local state is deeply embedded in the resource sector. Local governments and officials make various policies to regulate the mining industry, but at the same time their economic and political interests, on both organizational and personal levels, are closely intertwined with resource interests.

Second, the mining industry is highly capital-intensive,[18] which makes capital another major actor in the scene. Capital is the interest

---

[17] Land in China is publicly owned by the state or by village collectives (for rural areas).

[18] Depending on the types of mineral, mining industries may have varying degrees of capital intensiveness. For example, oil and gas industry may be more capital intensive than coal industry (Ross, 2012, pp. 45–46), but overall mining is considered as highly capital-intensive.

group running mining companies and related businesses. The capital intensiveness of the mining industry gives capital strong bargaining power vis-à-vis labor, owing to the limited demand for labor in the increasingly mechanized mining industry. Under the Chinese legal and fiscal systems, mining rights can be obtained upon the payment of some modest prospecting and mining fees and last for up to 30 years, and minerals extracted are taxed at very low rates that are negligible compared with mineral prices. Such settings make capital the biggest winner of the resource boom, who accumulates huge resource wealth and constantly seeks opportunities for further investments and returns. Meanwhile, under the local state corporatism that has underpinned China's economic miracle in the reform era (Oi, 1992; Unger & Chan, 1995), capital is subject to extensive state regulation and control, and is embroiled in a symbiotic relationship with local state that features close collaboration and incessant negotiations between the two parties.

Third, mining activities generate considerable externalities and profound implications for citizens working in the mining sector and living in surrounding areas, which calls in labor as the last major player in resource-rich regions. In this research, labor is broadly defined to include not only workers in the mining industries but also common citizens living in mining areas. I regard common citizens as labor because they compose the labor force for mining and other industries in a regional economy. Their employment and income are determined by the local economic structure, demand for labor, and profitability of various industries. Meanwhile, their welfare is influenced by the state's provision of public goods such as education and health care that develop human capital and cultivate the labor force. Thus, local citizens as labor interact with both the state and capital on multiple fronts, with both shared and conflicting interests in different aspects.

Resource endowment not only affects the interests and behaviors of each of the abovementioned three actors, but also shapes the triangular relationship between them. This research tells a threefold story. To begin with, resource endowment does not impose a universal curse on the host region, but rather generates divergent impacts on different parties in the economy. In particular, resource boom exerts unequal and unfair effects on capital and labor. As a capital-intensive industry, mining highly favors capital by boosting capital accumulation. Contrary to the sweeping claim that resource endowment presents a curse and inevitably undermines economic growth, this research finds that resource boom not only generates massive capital accumulation in the resource sector, but also has a positive spillover effect by enhancing capital investment in other industrial sectors, especially low-tech ones such as construction and manufacturing. In this sense, mineral resources are helpful for economic growth, at least from the perspective of short-term capital formation and industrial diversification. Nevertheless, the long-term effects of resource-boosted investment are questionable. First, the spillover effect does not boost capital investment in high-tech industries such as information technology (IT) and finance, which means that resource-rich regions have dimmer prospect for industrial upgrading and transformation and may be stuck in low-tech industries and low-quality growth. Moreover, resource revenue induces considerable flow of investment into speculative industries such as real estate, leading to housing bubbles that threaten financial stability and hurt long-term economic development. Therefore, the impacts that mineral resources generate on the economy are rather mixed.

Meanwhile, the boom of the resource sector suppresses labor income and leads to welfare losses of local citizens. Despite the slightly higher wage level in mining industries than in other labor-intensive industries, the demand for labor from the mining sector is limited due to the increasing mechanization of mineral extraction and processing. Moreover, with inadequate protection of labor rights and substandard working conditions in Chinese mines, mine workers often encounter work-related injuries and diseases such as pneumoconiosis and frequently get into labor disputes with mining companies about compensations, wage arrears, pensions, etc., making the mining industry a highly dispute-prone sector. More broadly, resource boom diminishes employment opportunities in other industrial sectors, even though it boosts capital investment in them. Thus, resource boom hardly benefits labor as it does to capital. Meanwhile, the resource sector generates considerable negative externalities to surrounding areas including environmental hazards, public insecurity, and economic disputes. As a result, local citizens in mining areas shoulder heavy financial and health costs and become the victims of the resource economy. Statistical analysis shows that both urban and rural citizens in resource-rich regions receive notably lower incomes than their counterparts in non-resource regions. The imbalanced distribution of the benefits and costs between capital and labor thus makes the resource economy an unfair game. It breeds widespread popular grievance and

frequent conflicts between the mining businesses and local communities, a serious consequence that threatens regime stability and calls
the state into play.

The Chinese state finds itself caught between the conflicting interests
of resource capital and labor. The resource wealth significantly shapes
the state–capital relations in resource-rich regions. Driven by the top-
down pressure to promote economic and fiscal growth (Landry, 2008;
Li & Zhou, 2005), the local state in resource-rich regions zealously
promotes the development of mining industries and forges a symbiotic
relationship with the resource capital. Unfortunately, the heavy
state intervention in the resource sector creates both incentives and
opportunities for state employees to engage in corruption. Empirical
evidence reveals that resource-rich Chinese localities tend to suffer
significantly higher corruption rates than non-resource regions. In a
sense, the resource wealth magnifies the loopholes in the Chinese
political economic system and encourages the capture of the local
state by resource interests.

At the same time, the resource economy changes the state–labor
relations in terms of public goods provision. On the one hand, the
reliance on mining industries seriously weakens the local state's incentives to cultivate human capital. Due to the diminished need for healthy
and well-educated labor force in the resource as well as other sectors,
local governments in resource-rich regions tend to spend less on human
capital-developing public goods including education and health
services, which further hurts the welfare of labor who already suffers
suppressed income. On the other hand, due to the widespread popular
contention between local communities and mining businesses, local
governments in resource-rich regions are pressured to step up
redistribution so as to address the unequal and unfair distribution of
the resource wealth and alleviate the tension between the resource
capital and labor. As a result, resource-rich Chinese localities tend to
spend more generously on social security welfares to appease the
aggrieved citizens and prevent them from turning against the regime.

Overall, this research finds that the benefits and costs of the resource
economy are unevenly distributed between capital and labor. Whereas
mining businesses as capital benefit hugely from the inflow of resource
wealth, local citizens as labor do not benefit much from resource boom
but bear heavy financial and health costs due to the negative
externalities of mining activities. The unfair game and increasing

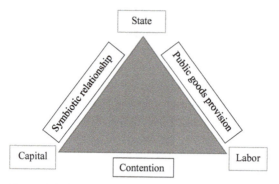

Figure 1.3 State–capital–labor relations in resource-rich regions
Source: drawn by author

inequality arouse widespread popular grievance and social conflicts in mining areas. In response, the Chinese state actively mediates between the conflicting parties and devises various strategies to promote the development of the resource economy on the one hand and preserve regime stability on the other hand. This triangular relationship is presented in Figure 1.3.

Interestingly, while the local state may be carried away by resource boom, captured by resource interests, and bombarded by resource conflicts, the existence of a higher layer of government contains the abovementioned maladies to limited scales and helps China escape the resource curse at large. Thanks to the limited representation and influence of resource interests at the national level, the Chinese central state can design countermeasures and induce local governments to treat the malaises in resource-rich localities. The centralized and tight personnel management system of the Communist Party-state plays a decisive role here. The cadre evaluation system, with heavy emphasis on economic development and stability maintenance as two key targets, forces local agents to maintain a delicate balance between capital and labor. While local governments and officials tend to side with resource interests in order to promote economic development, they have to respond to the citizens' demands in certain ways to prevent resource-triggered conflicts from escalating into major social unrests that threaten regime stability; and the top-down monitoring of local officials also curbs the collusion between the local state and resource capital to a certain extent. The top-down pressure has driven Chinese local governments and officials to devise a variety of innovative policies to avert some of the adverse effects of the resource economy. In this sense, the state is not, as some resource curse literature assumes, merely a victim that passively suffers the resource curse, but can be an active player to cope with the curse. In this sense, the resource curse is not really a curse by nature, but rather due to human ignorance and policy failures. What it takes to mitigate or even break the resource curse is well-functioning political institutions, farsighted policymaking, and corrective measures to address the unequal and unfair distribution of the benefits and costs of the resource sector.

Plan of the Book

This book is organized as follows. After a brief introduction about the general situtations of mineral resource distribution and exploration in China, Chapter 2 examines the impacts of resource endowment on local economic development, with a focus on capital accumulation and investment. Through qualitative studies on mining entrepreneurs and statistical analysis on Chinese provinces, it shows that resource boom in general benefits capital by not only boosting capital accumulation in the mining industries but also generating positive spillover effects on other industrial sectors, especially those labor-intensive ones. However, resource-generated capital tends to impede the investment in high-tech industries and induce speculative investment in real estate, which may discourage industrial upgrading and undermine economic growth in the long run. Therefore, resource boom has rather mixed effects on local economic development.

In contrast to the benefits that capital enjoys, Chapter 3 shows in detail the largely negative impacts of mineral extraction on labor. Based on qualitative evidence on the working conditions and employment opportunties in mining industries, it reveals that resource boom in general does not benefit common citizens as the labor force. Moreover, mining industries generate serious negative externalities to local communities, which impose heavy financial and health costs on local citizens. Statistical analysis corroborates the empirical observations and shows that resource abundance and dependence diminish employment opportunities in not only high-tech but also labor-intensive industrial sectors and repress labor income in both urban and rural areas. The findings suggest that the resource sector can be characterized as pro-capital and anti-labor, which generates profound implications for social equality and stability.

Chapter 4 analyzes how mineral resources shape the state–capital relations in resource-rich regions. It argues that the symbiotic relationship between local state and resource capital can easily become collusive under the resource boom. Through studies of resource-related corruption cases, it shows how the state's regulation and interference in the resource sector create structural opportunities for rent-seeking and collusion between the regulators and regulatees, and how the resource windfalls turn local government departments into hotbeds of corruption. The panel data analysis on the corruption rates of Chinese provinces further testifies that resource-rich regions are indeed more corrupt than other regions. This chapter suggests that mineral resources amplify the existing loopholes in the Chinese political economic system and highlights the danger of local state capture by resource capital.

Chapter 5 moves on to analyze how mineral resources affect local provision of public goods. Through case studies and statistical analysis, it shows that local governments in resource-rich regions tend to spend less on human capital-developing public goods, including education and health care, due to the diminished demand for labor, the myopic decision-making of both citizens and officials, and the shedding of government responsibilities onto mining enterprises. On the other hand, wary of the tension between mining industries and local citizens and driven by the pressure to preserve social stability, the local governments in resource-rich regions spend more fiscal revenue on social security benefits for disadvantaged citizens. The redistribution of the resource wealth from resource capital to labor partially compensates for the latter's welfare losses. Overall, while resource-rich regions have weak incentives to invest in human capital development, they do spend more on redistributive policies to redress popular grievance and ameliorate resource-triggered social conflicts.

Based on the findings of the earlier chapters, Chapter 6 recapitulates the multifaceted impacts that rich mineral resources generate on the state–capital–labor triad in China. It analyzes in detail the Chinese state's coping strategies to mitigate the resource curse at local levels. Moreover, it explains why the Chinese state is able and willing to take the observed strategies to contain the resource curse. The key lies in the Chinese Communist Party-state's strong capacity to penetrate into the economy and the society and also in its top-down monitoring and tight control of the local agents. In the end, this chapter critically evaluates the successes and pitfalls of the China model of resource management, which can provide important policy implications for not only China but also other resource-rich countries.

Research Methods and Data Sources

This research examines mineral resources including fuels such as oil, natural gas, and coal, and nonfuel minerals such as metals and non-metallic minerals. Among the more than 200 types of mineral resource actively explored and extracted in China, coal is by far the largest component. Hence a large part of the story in this book is about coal. This research focuses on mineral resources located on land within the Chinese border under the regulation of the Chinese government, mainly at the local levels. This qualification excludes maritime resources within the Chinese territory such as oil and natural gas in the East China Sea and South China Sea, which are primarily controlled by the Chinese central government via several central state-owned companies such as China National Offshore Oil Corporation (CNOOC). This research also excludes resources located in other countries but explored by Chinese or Chinese-invested companies. Nor does it consider the externalities of China's practices that affect other countries or regions. Therefore, this book mainly discusses the political economy of the resource sector in the domestic context in China, although the external repercussions of China's mineral exploration and production are important issues that deserve careful examination in separate projects.

In terms of time span, this research examines the post-Mao reform era, with an emphasis on the period between 1999 and 2017. This is a period when China witnessed a massive expansion of mineral production and rise of mineral prices, followed by a notable decline in the 2010s. The fluctuations in the mineral market have brought about profound changes to the Chinese economy as well as local governance that are acutely felt by all the stakeholders including the mining businesses, local governments, and citizens in mining areas. The boom and bust of the resource sector create ample opportunities for us to compare and assess its multifaceted impacts.

This research adopts mixed research methods combining qualitative study and quantitative analysis. Qualitative study mainly consists of detailed case studies of resource-rich localities and mining companies based on in-depth fieldwork and secondary information sources including media reports, government policy papers, gazetteers, memoirs, and scholarly publications. The qualitative observations serve to reveal the causal channels through which resource endowment and exploration affect local state–capital–labor relations. They also provide the empirical basis for the definition and measurement of key variables. However, solely focusing on resource-rich areas risks the methodological problem of selection bias. We need to put the observations in mining areas into the general picture of local governance and development in China by comparing them with less resource-abundant regions. Therefore, cross-regional and longitudinal statistical analyses are conducted to test the qualitative findings. The qualitative and quantitative methods complement each other in the sense that the qualitative analysis reveals the micro-foundations for the large-N statistical studies, while the quantitative analysis serves to cross-validate and generalize the findings from the qualitative research.

This research takes a subnational approach to examine the impacts of natural resources on Chinese localities. As scholars point out, subnational comparative analysis can be a very useful approach to advance the study of the resource curse (Cust & Viale, 2016; Ross, 2015). An important benefit of the subnational approach is that it helps alleviate, though may not completely eliminate, the institutional heterogeneity issue in cross-national comparisons. Because although regional variations exist within countries to certain degrees, the localities within a country share largely the same regime type, legal system, bureaucratic structure, economic institutions, etc. By controlling for the potentially intervening factors of national institutional settings, we can discern the effects of natural resources on social outcomes with greater clarity and more confidence. Moreover, studying the local conditions within one country allows more accurate examination of the causal mechanisms and how they work on the ground.

This book focuses on the Chinese provinces as its unit of analysis for the statistical analysis, primarily due to the availability of data. Although statistics at sub-provincial levels would allow us to examine the empirical details more clearly, such statistics are scanty and often inaccessible to the public. Therefore, I conduct quantitative analysis based on provincial-level statistics, which are the most comprehensive and complete data available. Fortunately, the qualitative analysis is not confined to the provincial level but goes down to grassroots levels, where causal mechanisms can be more clearly discerned. As I shall explain below, I have visited city, county, township, and village levels to conduct in-depth fieldwork and closely observed the operation of the resource sector and its interaction with local governments and citizens. The extensive fieldwork in multiple regions in China reveals many untold stories and nuanced pictures. The subnational analysis proves to be a fruitful approach to reveal the micro-foundations of the observed socioeconomic and political impacts of natural resources.

In terms of data sources, I draw on extensive field research in different mining areas across China for qualitative data. Between 2010 and 2016, I visited dozens of localities in Shanxi Province, Jiangxi Province, Henan Province, Inner Mongolia Autonomous Region, and Xinjiang Autonomous Region for focused fieldwork, some of which I visited multiple times. These localities were not randomly sampled but were selected for three reasons. First, all the field sites host sizable reserves of mineral resources such as coal, copper, zinc, limestone, and rare earth, among which coal is the most commonly seen mineral. And mining-related industries play major roles in the economy of these localities. Second, they cover eastern, central, and western regions of China, and arguably can represent the cross-regional discrepancies in China. Third, these localities differ considerably on multiple dimensions, including size of territory and population, level of economic development, degree of urbanization, amount of mineral reserves, stage of resource extraction (established versus emerging mines), and ownership and scale of mining companies. The common patterns observed in these divergent cases are likely to be generalizable to other resource-rich regions as well. Last but not least, my contacts in the city, county, and township governments of the field sites enabled me to find reliable information sources and conduct candid interviews with multiple stakeholders to accurately assess the real situation on the ground.

During the field trips, I conducted face-to-face interviews with more than 100 local officials in the Chinese Communist Party county, township, and village branches and government departments such as the Department of Land and Resources, the Department of Finance, Taxation Bureau, the Department of Civil Affairs, the Department of Public Security, the Office of Letters and Petitions, Development and Reform Commission, and Work Safety Supervision Department; managers and employees of state-owned and private mining companies of both large and small scales; and local citizens who frequently interact with the mining companies and/or local governments (see Appendix 1.

A for the list of field sites and interviewees). Although individual sources of information may carry certain bias and withhold part of the truth, the multiple sources can cross-validate each other and allow me to generate relatively reliable pictures about these field sites.

The interviews were semi-structured, following pre-designed lists of questions according to the professions and positions of the interviewees (see Appendix 1.B for the interview questions). Depending on the contingencies, extra questions were also asked so as to extract as much information as possible from the interviewees. As researchers versed in field research may well recognize, contingent questions are crucial for warming up with the interviewees and opening the gate to candid and fruitful interviews. And detours in interviews that diverge from the preset plan of questions can often lead to unexpected and exciting findings as well as inspirations for new research directions.

I have also obtained through the field visits a large collection of official documents and statistics that are not easily accessible through public channels but provide detailed information about local conditions and official policies. Overall, the extensive fieldwork reveals the complicated situations in mining areas and the multifaceted impacts of the resource economy on different players in the economy and society. The field research proves instrumental for me to acquire a deep understanding about the complexity of local governance and the politics of the resource economy. The findings from the fieldwork serve to both test existing theories and generate new hypotheses that can be tested against statistical analyses in this book and future works.

In addition to the field research, I have collected and scoured a vast amount of secondary information sources, including official documents, laws and regulations, gazetteers, media reports, memoirs of mining entrepreneurs, and scholarly works. These secondary information sources serve to provide background information about the general situations of mineral exploration and the legal structures that govern the mining industries in China, and they also cross-validate the information collected through the abovementioned fieldwork.

Nevertheless, realizing that the qualitative case studies are limited to only select resource-rich regions, this research also conducts a series of cross-regional and longitudinal statistical analysis on the Chinese provinces to test and generalize the qualitative findings. The dataset, which contains a wide array of environmental, socioeconomic, and political variables, spans from 1999 to 2017.[19] Major statistical data sources include *China Land and Resources Statistical Yearbook, China Industry Statistical Yearbook/China Industry Economy Statistical Yearbook,*[20] *Statistical Yearbook of China, Procuratorial Yearbook of China, Finance Yearbook of China, China Population Statistics Yearbook, China Population and Employment Statistics Yearbook, Statistical Yearbook of the Chinese Investment in Fixed Assets, China Commerce Yearbook, China Real Estate Statistics Yearbook, China's Ethnic Statistical Yearbook, China Energy Statistical Yearbook, China Price Statistical Yearbook,* and *China Data Online.* Other provincial, city, and county yearbooks and gazetteers have also been consulted for detailed information on certain variables.

---

[19] One reason I focus on this time span is that the Ministry of Land and Resources (*Guotu Ziyuan Bu*) was established in 1998, combining the Ministry of Geology and Mineral Resources (*Dizhi Kuangchan Bu*), State Land Administration (*Guojia Tudi Guanli Ju*), State Oceanic Administration (*Guojia Haiyang Ju*), and State Bureau of Surveying and Mapping (*Guojia Cehui Ju*). It started to release comprehensive, systematic statistics of mineral exploration at the provincial level in 1999. The Ministry of Land and Resources was reorganized into Ministry of Natural Resources in 2018, which disrupted the release of the abovementioned statistics. Therefore, the majority of my data analysis covers the period of 1999–2017.

[20] Both *China Land and Resources Statistical Yearbooks* compiled by the Ministry of Land and Resources and *China Industry Economy Statistical Yearbook* (1986–2012)/*China Industry Statistical Yearbook* (from 2013 onward) compiled by the National Bureau of Statistics provide national- and provincial-level statistics on mineral resource exploration in China. Although the latter data source provides a longer time span, there are missing data in various years and in different categories. Moreover, the statistics from the two data sources, such as the gross industrial output values and sales income of the mining industries by province, are not consistent with each other. In general, statistics reported by the National Bureau of Statistics tend to be larger than those reported by the Ministry of Land and Resources, though the two are highly correlated with each other. This discrepancy may be due to the reporting methods employed by the two systems. The Ministry of Land and Resources relies on its subordinate departments to fill in, audit, and submit reports on mineral-related statistics (See "Rules on Land and Resources Statistical Reporting (Guotu Ziyuan Tongji Baobiao Zhidu)," http://f.mnr.gov.cn/201703/t20170329_1447133.html); while the National Bureau of Statistics relies on the self-reporting of individual companies, including those in mining industries, to collect information on their economic activities. The practice of self-reporting by companies may give rise to inaccuracies and make the statistics less reliable than those collected and processed by the Department of Land and Resources. Taking into consideration the pros and cons, this research mainly relies on the statistics reported in *China Land and Resources Statistical Yearbooks* for resource-related variables and use those from *China Industry Economy Statistical Yearbook/China Industry Statistical Yearbook* as supplementary data sources.

APPENDIX 1.A List of Field Sites and Interviewees

The author interviewed a total of 120 interviewees in 20 cities/counties in Shanxi Province, Jiangxi Province, Henan Province, Inner Mongolia Autonomous Region, and Xinjiang Uygur Autonomous Region. The anonymized interviewees are listed below according to their locations and the time of interviews.

Jiangxi Province, May 2010

1. Township Party secretary, Z Town, D City (county-level city)
2. Official, County Bureau of Finance, D City (county-level city)

Shanxi Province, May 2012

3. Former owner of private mining company, T City
4. Official, Committee of Politics and Law, T City
5. Former government official, T City
6. Official, Department of Finance of Shanxi Province, T City
7. Official, Bureau of Finance, T City
8. Official, Bureau of Finance, T City
9. Lawyer, T City
10. Official, Bureau of Coal, T City
11. Official, Research Center of T City Government
12. Employee, a state-owned coal trading company, T City
13. Employee, a private mining company, T City
14. Official, State Taxation Bureau, Y City
15. Official, Bureau of Finance, Y City
16. Official, Bureau of Finance, Y City
17. Official, Local Taxation Bureau, Y City
18. Director, Bureau of Coal Industry, Y City

Inner Mongolia Autonomous Region, August 2012

19. Secretary, Committee of Politics and Law, A Banner, A League
20. Party secretary, Bureau of Land and Resources, A Banner, A League
21. Director, Mineral Resource Management Office, A Banner, A League
22. Official, Bureau of Land and Resources, A Banner, A League
23. Director, Bureau of Finance, A Banner, A League
24. Official, Bureau of Finance, A Banner, A League
25. Official, Township Government, Y Banner, E City
26. Party secretary, B Village, Y Banner, E City
27. Party secretary, M Village, Y Banner, E City
28. Official, Bureau of Land and Resources, Y Banner, E City
29. Official, Bureau of Land and Resources, Y Banner, E City

Shanxi Province, October 2013

30. Director, Development Research Center of T City Government, T City
31. Official, Development Research Center of T City Government, T City
32. Official, Development Research Center of T City Government, T City
33. Official, Development Research Center of T City Government, T City
34. Official, Development Research Center of T City Government, T City
35. Official, Development Research Center of T City Government, T City
36. Researcher, Development Research Center of T City Government, T City
37. Researcher, Development Research Center of T City Government, T City
38. Researcher, Development Research Center of T City Government, T City
39. Researcher, Development Research Center of T City Government, T City

40. Researcher, Development Research Center of T City Government, T City
41. Researcher, Development Research Center of T City Government, T City
42. Researcher, Development Research Center of T City Government, T City
43. Former official, T City
44. Former official, T City
45. Former official, T City
46. Former official, T City
47. Director, Committee of Economic Information, T City
48. Official, Bureau of Coal, T City
49. Official, Bureau of Coal, T City
50. Official, Bureau of Coal, T City
51. Deputy director, State Assets Administration Committee, T City
52. Deputy director, Bureau of Commerce, T City
53. Official, Bureau of Science and Technology, T City
54. Official, Office of Financial Services, T City
55. Official, Local Taxation Bureau, T City
56. Official, Administration of Work Safety, T City
57. Official, Development and Reform Commission, T City
58. Manager, a state-owned mining company, T City
59. Official, Q County Government
60. General manager, a private mining company, Q County
61. Mine manager, a private mining company, Q County
62. Employee, a private mining company, Q County
63. Employee, a private mining company, Q County

Jiangxi Province, June 2014

64. Chinese Communist Party secretary of J Town, X County
65. Deputy director, Bureau of Letters and Petitions, X County
66. Official, Bureau of Finance, X County
67. Official, Bureau of Geology and Mineral Resources, X County
68. Official, Bureau of Environmental Protection, X County
69. Official, Non-tax Revenue Administration, X County
70. Official, Bureau of Public Security, X County
71. Deputy director, Bureau of Civil Affairs, X County

72. Chinese Communist Party secretary of T Town, X County
73. Official of T Town Government, X County
74. Mine manager of a private coal company, X County

Xinjiang Uygur Autonomous Region, October 2014

75. Manager of a private mining-related company, F City
76. Manager of a private coal company, F City
77. Chinese Communist Party secretary of a coal chemical company, also a former official, F City
78. Manager of a private coal company, F City
79. Official, Bureau of Coal, F City
80. Official, Bureau of Environmental Protection, F City
81. Director, Bureau of Land and Resources, C County
82. Official, Bureau of Land and Resources, C County
83. Director, Bureau of Environmental Protection, C County
84. Deputy director, Bureau of Civil Affairs, C County
85. Manager of a state-owned mining company, C County
86. Official, Bureau of Human Resources and Social Security, N County
87. Official, Bureau of Coal, N County
88. Manager of a state-owned mining company, N County
89. Employee of a state-owned mining company, N County
90. Employee of a state-owned mining company, N County

Jiangxi Province, May 2015

91. General manager of a state-owned mining-related company, N City
92. Worker of a state-owned mining company, G City
93. General manager of a private mining company, C County
94. Manager of a private mining company, C County
95. Vice general manager of a private mining company, C County
96. Manager of a private mining company, also former government official, C County
97. Manager, a mining-related company, D County
98. Owner and manager of a private mining company, D County
99. Manager of a private mining company, D County

100. Mine manager of a private mining company, D County
101. General manager of a private mining company, D County

Henan Province, November 2015

102. Party secretary, Political and Legal Affairs Commission, R City
103. Party secretary, Bureau of Coal, X City
104. Deputy director, Bureau of Finance, X City
105. Deputy director, Bureau of Letters and Petitions, X City
106. Political commissar, Bureau of Public Security, X City
107. Deputy director, United Front Work Department, X City
108. Director, Office of Letters and Petitions, L Town, X City
109. Official, L Town Government, X City

Shanxi Province, July 2016

110. Official, Development and Reform Commission, L City
111. Local citizen (driver), L City
112. Village cadre, D Village, X County, L City
113. Official, Commission of Rural Affairs, L City
114. Official, Commission of Rural Affairs, X County, L City
115. Scholar, S University, T City
116. Scholar, S University, T City
117. Official, W District, X City (county level), L City
118. Official, Commission of Rural Affairs, X City (county level), L City
119. Party secretary, N Village, X City (county level), L City
120. Village head, N Village, X City (county level), L City

APPENDIX 1.B *Interview Questions*

The following list includes the staple questions of the semi-structured interviews with the interviewees listed in Appendix 1.A. The question list was followed as much as conditions allowed, and additional questions were asked spontaneously depending on the contingencies during the interview processes.

1. General Questions for Local Governments

- What are the general economic conditions in your city/county/town, such as the weight of different industrial sectors, urban and rural residents' income levels, consumer goods prices, housing prices, and land revenues?
  (请介绍一下本地的经济发展水平：工业和第三产业发展、城市/农村居民收入水平、物价水平、房地产价格、土地收益等)
- What contributions do different types (by scale, ownership and administrative level if state-owned) of mining industries make to local economy and public finance?
  (不同类型（规模、所有制、级别）的矿企对地方经济和财政有什么贡献？)
- How do the changes in demands for and prices of mineral products affect local economy and fiscal income? How do you deal with the impacts?
  (资源需求和价格变化对地方经济及财政有何影响？有何应对措施？)
- What environmental protection measures are adopted?
  (环境保护方面有哪些举措？)

2. Questions for Fiscal Departments Including Bureau of Finance, State Taxation Bureau, and Local Taxation Bureau

- How much annual fiscal revenue and expenditure did you have in the past few years? How much revenue was generated from mineral resources?

（地方财政收支状况如何？有多少来自矿产资源的收入？）

- Which kinds of taxes are collected from mining industries? How are the taxes divided between the central and local governments? How important are these taxes for local public finance?
  （与矿业相关税收收入有哪些？中央和地方各级政府所占比例？对地方财政的重要性？）
- What kinds of nontax revenues are collected from mining industries? How are the revenues divided between the central and local governments? How important are these revenues for local public finance?
  （与矿业相关的非税收入有哪些？非税收入在各级政府间如何分配？对地方财政的重要性？）
- How did the Resource Tax Reform affect local fiscal conditions?
  （资源税改革对地方财政有何影响？）
- Who collects mining prospecting fees, mining rights user fees, mineral resource compensation fees, etc.? How important are these fees for local public finance?
  （探矿权、采矿权使用费、价款和矿产资源补偿费等由谁收？对地方财政的贡献有多大？）
- Do land revenues play an important role in local public finance?
  （土地收益对地方财政重要吗？）
- How many fiscal transfers do you receive annually? Where do they come from?
  （财政转移支付的来源、规模如何？）
- Does your local government face debt issues?
  （地方政府债务严重吗？）
- How do you spend local fiscal revenue and transfers?
  （财政自有收入和转移支付的支出去向?）
- Roughly how much do you spend on education, health care, social security, environmental protection, and public security annually?
  （地方政府公共服务支出：教育、医疗、社保、环保、公共安全）
- How are fiscal expenditures on the police, procuratorate, and court determined? Are the expenditures influenced by crime rates?
  （公检法的财政支出如何决定？会受犯罪率影响吗？）
- How many and what types of fiscal expenditures are for stability maintenance? How are stability maintenance funds budgeted?
  （地方用于维稳方面的支出情况如何？维稳基金如何预算？）
- How are fiscal reserves determined and expended?
  （财政预备费如何确定和使用？）

3. Questions for Bureau of Land and Resources, Bureau of Coal, and Bureau of Environmental Protection

- What types of mineral resources does your region host? How many reserves have been identified? How are they explored and utilized?
(请介绍一下当地的矿产资源状况：储量规模、开采情况等)
- How many mining enterprises are there in your region? How about their scales, types of ownership, sources of investment, number of employees, and taxes and profits?
(本地矿企的规模、类型、数量、矿企的资产构成、从业人员、利税情况如何？)
- Do mining enterprises provide public services such as schools and health services?
(矿企还管理学校、医院等公共事业吗？)
- What policies and measures have been adopted to consolidate the mineral resources? When did the consolidation start? How much progress has been made? Are there any difficulties in the process?
(有没有资源整合的政策和措施？何时开始？进度如何？有何难点？)
- How are lands appropriated and compensated in mining areas?
(矿区征地拆迁的补偿情况如何？)
- What environmental protection measures are adopted in mining areas? How are mined out areas treated? Are there any restoration measures?
(矿区中有哪些环保措施？采空区、塌陷区的复垦情况如何？
- How do you maintain stability in mining areas? Have there been collective incidents triggered by resource exploration? How do you deal with them?
(矿区维稳的主要工作方式有哪些？如何应对因矿产资源开发引起的群体性事件？)

4. Questions for Bureau of Public Security, Procuratorate and Court

- Are there any illegal exploration or mining activities in your region? How do you treat these problems?
(非法探矿、采矿现象严重吗？如何管理？)

- How is the general public security situation in your region? What kinds of crimes are often observed? What measures do you adopt to treat these problems?
  (矿区的治安状况如何？什么类型的犯罪比较常见？有何应对措施？)
- How are expenditures on the police, procuratorate, and court decided? Are they influenced by crime rates?
  (公检法的财政支出如何决定？会受犯罪率影响吗？)
- Are there any usuries and/or illegal fundraising activities in your region? Where do the funds come from? What impacts have such activities generated on local financial market and social stability?
  (目前非法集资或高利贷情况如何：这类资金的主要来源？对金融市场和社会稳定造成什么的影响？)
- Do you have any funding specifically designated for stability maintenance? How do you use the fund?
  (有无维稳经费，如何安排使用？)

5. Questions for Office of Letters and Petitions

- Could you please tell us about the general situation of social stability (such as the petitions you receive) in your region, especially in relation to mineral resources?
  (目前维稳的形势如何？特别是和自然资源有关的维稳情况怎么样？)
- What working mechanisms and measures do you adopt to maintain stability and treat the petitions?
  (你们主要的工作机制和措施是什么？)
- How do you use the stability maintenance fund, if any?
  (维稳经费如何安排使用？)
- How many petitions are related to mineral resources? How do you treat them?
  (有多少信访与矿产资源有关？一般如何处理？)
- Are there any stability-threatening issues arising from the consolidation of mineral resources? How do you treat these problems?
  (资源整合过程中有维稳问题吗？如何处理？)

6. Questions for Bureau of Civil Affairs

- Could you please tell us about the general conditions of social welfare in your region?
  (社会福利事业发展现状如何？)

- How about the low-income allowances in urban and rural areas?
  (城乡低保情况如何？)
- Are there any residents who become low-income allowance receivers
  due to the exploration of mineral resources?
  (有因自然资源开采产生的低保户的情况吗？)
- Are there any special policies for residents in mining areas?
  (对矿区居民有什么特别政策？)
- How do you evaluate the impacts of mineral resources on poverty in
  your region?
  (如何看待矿产资源对地方贫困的影响？)

7. Questions for Township and Village Cadres in Mining Areas

- Could you please tell us about the basic economic, demographic,
  and geographic conditions of your town/village?
  (请介绍一下乡镇/村的基本情况)
- What are the main sources of financial income of your town/
  village?
  (乡镇/村主要财政收入来源是什么？)
- What are the main fiscal expenditures of your town/village?
  (乡镇/村主要的支出责任包括哪些？)
- What measures do you adopt to maintain social stability in your
  town/village?
  (乡镇/村维稳的主要做法、措施有哪些？)
- When did mineral exploration start in your locality? How has it
  been progressing?
  (本地矿产开发什么时候开始的？发展过程如何？)
- What kind of mining enterprises does your locality host? Are they
  private or state-owned? Which level of government does the state-
  owned company belong to?
  (本地有哪些矿企？私营还是国有？国有是什么级别的？)
- How is the relationship between the mining enterprise(s) and the
  village?
  (矿企和村里的关系怎么样？)
- Have the mineral resources in your town/village been consolidated?
  How much progress has been made? Are there any difficulties in the
  consolidation process?
  (本地有无资源整合？情况如何？)

8. Questions for State-Owned/Private Mining Enterprises

- Could you tell us about the basic statistics of your company, such as your size, administrative rank (for state-owned companies) and profit, the number of employees, employees' geographical origins, their education levels, and your training programs for them?
  (请介绍一下企业规模、级别（中央、省、市等）、效益、职工人数、来源、教育水平、员工培训)
- How do you make use of your profits?
  (企业收益如何投资？)
- Could you please tell us about the tax burdens on your company, including types of taxes, tax rates, and payees of the taxes?
  (税费负担：税种、税率，交税到哪?)
- What downstream companies do you have connections with? How do you sell and transport your products?
  (与下游企业的联系：销售、运输如何进行)
- How do you describe your relationship with neighboring residents? Have you encountered any disputes with them?
  (与周边居民的关系如何，有无矛盾或纠纷？)
- How do you describe your relationship with administrative departments? Which departments do you deal with on regular basis?
  (与管理部门的关系如何?)
- Have you participated in the consolidation of mineral resources? How was the process?
  (有无经历资源整合？资源整合的过程怎样？)
- Have you encountered any difficulties or disputes during the consolidation process? How did you solve the problems?
  (整合过程中有无纠纷？如何解决的？)
- Has your operation generated any impacts on the environment in the neighborhood? How do you deal with them?
  (对周边环境的影响？如何处理？)

9. Questions for Local Residents in Mining Areas

- How do you describe your relations with the mining enterprise(s) in your area?
  (与矿企的关系如何？)
- Where do you and your fellow villagers work? Are there any employment opportunities in the mine(s)?

(村民就业情况如何？)

- Do you know the compensation policies for appropriated lands? How well are the policies actually implemented?
  (你们对征地补偿政策和实际政策执行情况了解吗？)
- Is there any environmental problem such as pollution in the mining area?
  (矿区污染问题严重吗？)
- Have you run into any disputes with the mining enterprise(s)? How would you find solutions for the disputes?
  (和矿企有无纠纷？出现纠纷如何解决？)
- Have the local mines been consolidated? How does the consolidation affect local residents?
  (本地有资源整合吗？资源整合对老百姓有什么影响吗？)

2 | Minerals, Capital, and Local Economic Development

Mineral Production in China: An Overview

China possesses a large variety of mineral resources, including fuels, such as coal, oil, and natural gas, nonfuel metals, and nonmetal minerals. Currently, more than 200 types of mineral are actively explored and extracted, covering almost all major types of mineral discovered on earth, thus making China one of the few countries that produce such high diversity of minerals. By the end of the 1990s, China had become the second-largest producer of solid minerals and the largest producer of coal, iron, and some other types of mineral in the world.

China's diverse and voluminous mineral reserves are widely but unevenly distributed across its vast territory. Across a land spanning more than 9.6 million square kilometers, tens of thousands of large and small mining sites lie scattered, producing a vast amount of mineral. In 2013, the State Council officially recognized 262 resource-rich cities (including 126 prefecture-level cities, 62 county-level cities, 16 urban districts, and 58 counties),[1] making up about one-third of all cities in China.[2] Following the Ricardian notion of comparative advantage (Ricardo, 1817), the Chinese government has designed specific industrial structures and set up major mineral production sites based on the resource endowments of different regions. As the most widely distributed mineral, coal exists in almost all provinces, although major production sites are often found in central and especially

---

[1] State Council, 2013. "Quanguo Ziyuanxing Chengshi Kechixu Fazhan Guihua (2013–2020 Nian) (Plans for Sustainable Development of Resource-Rich Cities in China (2013–2020))," www.gov.cn/zwgk/2013-12/03/content_2540070.htm, accessed on February 18, 2021.

[2] As of June 2020, there are 685 cities in China (excluding Taiwan, Hong Kong, and Macao), including 4 municipalities directly under the central government, 293 prefectural-level cities, and 388 county-level cities. See https://en.wikipedia.org/wiki/List_of_cities_in_China#cite_note-2, accessed on February 18, 2021.

northern China, such as Datong and Pingshuo in Shanxi Province,
Fushun in Liaoning Province, and Pingdingshan in Henan Province.
Oil is mostly concentrated in the northern part of China. Large oil
fields include Daqing in Heilongjiang Province, Shengli in Shandong
Province, Liaohe astride Liaoning Province and Inner Mongolia
Autonomous Region, Karamay in Xinjiang Uygur Autonomous
Region, and Dagang in Tianjin. Among the major nonfuel minerals,
iron and steel bases include Anshan in Liaoning Province, Wuhan in
Hubei Province, and Panzhihua in Sichuan Province, stretching from
the northeast to the southwest of China. In addition, there are many
nonferrous metal mines, such as Baiyin silver mine and Jinchuan nickel
and cobalt mine in Ganshu Province in the northwest, Tongling copper
mine in Anhui Province and Dexing copper mine in Jiangxi Province in
eastern China, and Dachang tin mine in Guangxi Province in the
southwest. Besides these mega mining sites, there are thousands of
large- and medium-sized mines, and tens of thousands of small mines.
Overall, mineral resources are mostly distributed across inland areas
and remote regions but sparingly dispersed in coastal regions, especially in the southeast.

Mining industries in China have undergone a gradual process of
liberalization and marketization since the 1980s. During the Maoist
era and under the planned economy, mineral resources used to be
tightly controlled by the state. Mineral exploration and production
were restricted to state-owned and collectively owned enterprises,
while private exploration was largely prohibited. Into the mid-1980s,
as part of the initiative of the post-Mao economic reforms, the Chinese
central government announced the policy of "speeding up the water
flow" to encourage non-state-owned enterprises and individuals to
explore and utilize mineral resources. In 1986, the Chinese People's
Congress passed China's first Mineral Resources Law, legally confirm-
ing the state ownership of all mineral resources within the Chinese
territory and allowing mineral exploration by different kinds of public
and private entities. While state-owned enterprises (SOEs) continued to
control the larger, richer mines and those of strategic importance, the
smaller and strategically less significant ones were opened up to collective and private investors. However, as mineral prices were still
suppressed by the government's economic planning and were volatile
in an underdeveloped market, the profitability of most mining industries remained low. Government institutions regulating the mining

industries were also seriously underdeveloped, with a major problem being the lack of protection of mining rights and private properties. Moreover, with rudimentary technology and inadequate awareness of environmental protection and work safety issues, Chinese mines commonly had dismal working conditions and high rates of accidents and casualties throughout the 1980s. Thus, mining was a highly risky and dangerous business largely dominated by SOEs or other types of government-sponsored agency, and only a few adventurous and entrepreneurial private investors set foot in it.

Into the 1990s, especially after Deng Xiaoping's southern tour in 1992 that officially set China onto the route toward a socialist market economy, the mining industries underwent considerable marketization, with the government gradually loosening its tight control over production quotas, prices, transportation services, administrative charges for mineral products, etc. When the Mineral Resources Law was revised and refined in 1996, it more clearly defined the procedures for mineral prospecting and exploration and the duties of relevant government bodies that regulate extractive activities. More importantly, the law, for the first time, guaranteed legal protection for the legitimate rights and interests of all mining enterprises, including non-state-owned ones. With improved market conditions and legal protection of property rights, mining companies mushroomed all over China under increasingly diversified ownership structures. In particular, along with the tide of the Chinese government's large-scale SOE reform that sought to bankrupt or privatize many loss-making SOEs in the late 1990s, a large number of formerly state-owned mining companies were acquired by private investors. By now, although the state still had a firm grip on oil and natural gas as strategic energy resources, which are explored by large SOEs, joint state-owned enterprises, and shareholding companies with the strong backing of state ownership, the mining of solid minerals, such as coal, and other nonmetal minerals and metals has been opened up to companies of all ownership types, including SOEs, collective-owned enterprises, cooperative stock enterprises, joint-ownership enterprises, limited liability corporations, shareholding companies, private enterprises, and foreign-invested companies.[3]

It is worth noting that around the mid-2000s, partly driven by concerns about environmental degradation, inefficient utilization of

---

[3] *China Land and Resources Statistical Yearbook 2016*, p. 62.

mineral deposits, and frequent workplace accidents, the Chinese government started to encourage the consolidation of mining industries through the merger and acquisition of smaller, especially privately owned mines by larger, often state-owned mining companies. The central and local governments also gradually raised the benchmarks on production capacity, technological equipment, environmental protection, etc., for newly established mining companies. In consequence, a growing number of small-scale mines were closed down or merged into larger mines, and mineral exploration and production were gradually concentrated in the hands of large companies. According to the *China Land and Resources Statistical Yearbooks*, the total number of solid mineral mines decreased from 148,556 in 2002 to 67,672 in 2017, while the number of large- and medium-sized mines increased from 1,514 in 2002 to 10,819 in 2017.[4] Take the coal industry for instance, there were a total of 6,794 coal mines in 2017, out of which more than 1,200 were large mines with an annual production capacity above 1.2 million tons. These large mines accounted for more than 75 percent of the total amount of coal in China, and the four largest coal mines alone produced 26.5 percent of the national total volume.[5]

After around four decades of economic reform, China's mineral market has grown tremendously. Especially after the turn of the millennium, both demand and price of all kinds of mineral product have risen remarkably, leading to what many insiders of the mining sector regard as a "golden decade." The golden decade spanned from the early 2000s until around 2012, as the effects of the Chinese government's massive stimulus package after the 2008 financial tsunami gradually subsided. And when the central government launched new economic restructuring reforms to reduce excess production capacity

---

[4] According to Ordinance No. 208 issued by the Ministry of Land and Resources in 2004, all Chinese mines are classified into four categories: large, medium, small, and small-scale. The classification standards are based on the annual production capacity of the mines depending on the type of minerals. For instance, large coal mines have annual production capacity at or above 1.2 million tons (underground)/4 million tons (open-cast), and medium mines are between 0.45 and 1.2 million tons (underground)/1–4 million tons (open-cast).

[5] China National Coal Association, 2018. *2017 Meitan Hangye Niandu Baogao (2017 Report of the Coal Industry)*, March 27, www.cbmf.org/cbmf/xgxy/mt72/6765780/index.html, accessed on March 20, 2020.

in coal, iron and steel, and other industries in 2016, it further contributed to the graduate decline of mineral production. Nevertheless, as of
2016, the total volume of mineral production was still massive when
compared to the mid-1980s, when the market was first opened up.
Among the five major categories of extractive industries in China,
namely coal, oil and gas, ferrous metals, nonferrous metals, and
nonmetallic mining industries, the coal mining and washing industry
has expanded tremendously and become the dominant component of
China's mining sector. According to the statistics reported in *China
Industry Statistical Yearbook*, the gross industrial output value of all
minerals in China totaled 4.62 trillion yuan in 2016, while that of coal
alone accounted for 1.98 trillion yuan (see Figure 2.1).

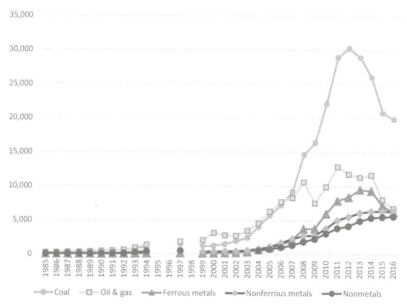

Figure 2.1 Industrial outputs of major mining industries (1985–2016)
(unit: 100 million yuan)

Source: Figure compiled based on statistics from *China Industry Statistical Yearbook
2013–2017* and *China Industry Economy Statistical Yearbook 1986–2012*

Notes: Because *China Industry Economy Statistical Yearbook* was not published in
1996, 1997, and 1999, the statistics of 1995, 1996, and 1998 are missing. As *China
Industry Statistical Yearbook* stopped publishing statistics on industrial output values
since 2013 and only released industrial sales output values, the data from 2012 to 2016
are industrial sales output values, which are only slightly different from the gross industrial output values based on the statistics of previous years.

Mineral Resources and the Chinese Economy: Is There a Curse?

The resource sector, with its expanding magnitude, has generated far-reaching impacts on the Chinese economy. Although China overall is not heavily resource dependent, mineral resources nevertheless have played indispensable roles in the process of industrialization and modernization, such as providing raw materials for agricultural and industrial production and meeting China's insatiable needs for energy. For example, according to the World Bank, coal, oil, and natural gas have contributed to more than 80 percent of China's energy consumption in the past three decades. Coal alone has sustained above 70 percent of China's electricity production since 1990.[6] For resource-rich regions in particular, mining industries exert various direct and indirect impacts on the local economy. They not only serve as important engines for growth but also provide fiscal income for the central and local governments. Therefore, the Chinese government, from the central level down to the grassroots level, enthusiastically encouraged the development of mining industries, at least up until 2016, when the Chinese central government started to rein in the expansion of certain industries with excess production capacity, including the iron and steel, coal, and cement industries.

The officially acclaimed contributions of mineral resources to the Chinese economy and local governments' zealous enhancement of the mining sector appear to be at odds with the thesis of resource curse, which argues that the abundance of natural resources poses a curse on the economy of the host country/region (Auty, 1993, 2001; Corden & Neary, 1982). As discussed in Chapter 1, comparative studies have found rather mixed evidence on whether resource endowment hampers economic development (Alexeev & Conrad, 2009; Andersen & Ross, 2014; Brunnschweiler & Bulte, 2008; Gerelmaaa & Kotani, 2016; Lederman & Maloney, 2008; Sachs & Warner, 1995). Within China, although some statistical analyses have revealed a negative correlation between resource endowment and economic growth at provincial and prefecture levels (Fu & Wang, 2010; Shao & Qi, 2008; Xu & Wang, 2006), there have not been conclusive findings

---

[6] World Bank, https://data.worldbank.org.cn/indicator/EG.ELC.COAL.ZS?locations=CN, accessed on February 18, 2021.

on how exactly the resource boom affects local economic development (Zhang & Brouwer, 2020).

To assess the impacts of mineral resources on the Chinese economy, we can start with a simple bivariate analysis on resource abundance and economic growth. To measure the level of resource abundance, existing studies have suggested mainly two approaches: One way is to look at the amount of resource stocks (Arezki & van der Ploeg, 2011; Brunnschweiler, 2008; Brunnschweiler & Bulte, 2008; Norman, 2009; Stijns, 2005); the other is to look at the amount of resource flows such as production and exports or their weight in the economy (Arezki & Bruckner, 2011; Leite & Weidmann, 1999; Norman, 2009; Sachs & Warner, 1995; Stijns, 2005). This research follows the second approach based on the following justifications. First of all, during the period of this study, the overall stocks of minerals in China did not change very much. Despite the sizable amounts of investments in geological exploration and search for new mines, the total amounts of discovered reserves do not change significantly over time. Second, unlike comparative studies that focus on a few selected minerals such as oil and gas, studying the stocks of more than 200 types of widely distributed mineral reserve, the value of which vary considerably, is technically unviable and theoretically fuzzy.[7] Third, it is the actual utilization rather than the stock of mineral resources that impacts local economy and governance. The change in resource flows is what gives rise to a series of significant socioeconomic and political consequences. And the variations in the volume and value of mineral products make cross-regional and longitudinal comparison more meaningful. Therefore, this research focuses on the amount of resource flows rather than stocks to measure resource endowment.

Throughout this book, I adopt two indicators to measure the absolute and relative levels of resource endowment, respectively: real per capita sales income from mineral products to measure the absolute size of resource rents (referred to as "size of resource production"

---

[7] There is great technical difficulty in measuring resource stocks in China at subnational levels. First, given the large variety of minerals in China, systematic statistics are not publicly available on all the mineral reserves at or below the provincial level. Meanwhile, the variation of resource types and fluctuation of mineral prices make it extremely difficult to assess and compare the overall value of the mineral stocks in different Chinese localities.

hereafter);[8] and the percentage of gross mineral industrial output value in total GDP to measure the relative level of resource dependence in a region (referred to as "rate of resource dependence" hereafter). Although both indicators measure resource flows, as Basedau and Lay (2009) note, the absolute size of resource production and relative level of dependence may have different effects, and both need to be considered. While the absolute size of resource abundance may affect the economic incentives of relevant stakeholders, the relative level of resource dependence weighs the resource sector against alternative sources of economic income and affects its perceived importance in the eyes of beholders. Thus, the two indicators can give us comprehensive information about the effects of resources on socioeconomic outcomes and serve different purposes in data analysis throughout this research. Based on statistics about mineral industrial production and sales as reported in *China Land and Resource Statistical Yearbook*, I calculate the size of resource production and rate of resource dependence for each Chinese province between 1999 and 2017.[9] The two indicators are highly positively correlated (see Figure 2.2), with a Pearson's correlation coefficient of 0.81 (p-value = 0.000), suggesting that resource-rich regions tend to be resource dependent as well. Both indicators vary considerably not only spatially due to geographical distribution of mineral resources but also temporally owing to the changes in the resource market.

How does resource endowment affect the economy of the host regions? I use real per capita GDP and annual GDP growth rate as the basic measures of the overall economic performance in a region. A simple bivariate regression between the size of resource production[10] and real per capita GDP and GDP growth rate, respectively, shows

---

[8] To offset the effects of inflation and make the statistics in monetary terms comparable across years, I calculate the real values of all monetary figures throughout this book by dividing the nominal values with the regional deflator, which is determined by the annual inflation rates of each province (with 1998 as the base year).

[9] As both variables are highly skewed, I normalize them by taking natural log and use the logged values in the data analysis below.

[10] Because the level of resource dependence as measured by the share of gross mineral industrial output value in GDP has GDP as the denominator, it is negatively correlated with per capita GDP with a Pearson's correlation coefficient of −0.106 (p-value = 0.015). The Pearson's correlation coefficient between resource dependence and GDP growth rate is 0.013 (p-value = 0.769).

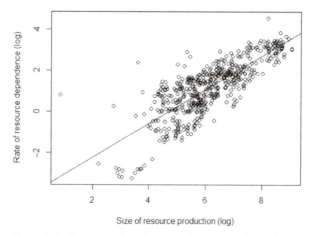

Figure 2.2 Resource abundance and resource dependence (1999–2017)
Note: As both the size of resource production and the rate of resource dependence are highly skewed, they are normalized by taking natural log when drawing the graph.

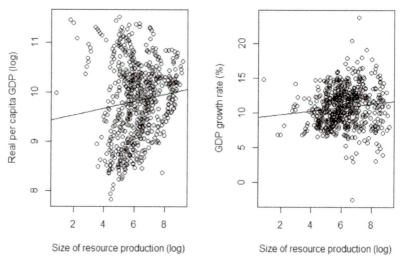

Figure 2.3 Resource abundance and economic development (1999–2017)
Note: As both the size of resource production and real per capita GDP are highly skewed, they are normalized by taking natural log when drawing the graph.

that, against the prediction of the resource curse thesis, the size of resource production is positively correlated with both per capita GDP and GDP growth rate (see Figure 2.3), with a Pearson's correlation coefficient of 0.12 (*p*-value = 0.004) for per capita GDP and 0.12

(*p*-value = 0.003) for GDP growth rate. Apparently, there is little evidence for a negative impact of resource abundance on local economic development.

The success story of Inner Mongolia Autonomous Region vividly demonstrates the benevolent effect of resource endowment on economic development. As an underdeveloped inland area bordering Mongolia, Inner Mongolia stayed in poverty and obscurity throughout much of the twentieth century, and its economic performance lagged far behind the other Chinese provinces, especially the coastal areas, after economic reforms started in the late 1970s. From 1978 to 2000, it was consistently ranked at the bottom of the 31 provinces in terms of GDP and GDP growth rate. However, after Inner Mongolia discovered huge deposits of coal, rare earth, and other mineral reserves in the early 2000s, such as in Dongsheng Coalfield near Ordos, its economy started to take off. In 2008, its GDP jumped to 776.1 billion yuan, a sixfold increase from 1998. Its GDP ranked the 16th among all the provinces, and GDP growth rate ranked on top of all the provinces. In particular, Ordos, the city that found its fortune in the mines, surpassed Hong Kong and became the richest city in China in terms of per capita GDP in 2011. Among its population of 1.5 million, there were more than 7,000 people whose assets exceeded 100 million yuan and more than 100,000 people whose assets exceeded 10 million yuan.[11] Nevertheless, as the mineral market went down, the economic growth of Inner Mongolia also slowed down. Though the total GDP of Inner Mongolia still more than doubled from 776.1 billion yuan in 2008 to 1,610.3 in 2017, the growth rate was much lower than in the last decade, ranking Inner Mongolia the 29th in terms of average GDP growth rate and the 22nd in terms of total GDP among all 31 provinces.[12] Besides Inner Mongolia, some other coal-rich provinces, such as Shaanxi and Shanxi, also rode on the resource boom and experienced accelerated economic growth during the same period.

[11] China Broadcast Net, 2011. "Erdos Renjun GDP Quanguo Diyi, Baiwan Zichan Zhineng Suanshi Qiongren (Per Capita GDP of Ordos Ranked Number 1 Nationwide, Millionaires Regarded as Poor)," June 11, http://finance.people .com.cn/GB/153179/153180/14834737.html, accessed on January 20, 2020.
[12] Gelonghui, 2018. "Gaige Kaifang 40 Nian, Geshengqu GDP Paiwei Yanbian Jianshi (Forty Years of Reform and Opening Up: A Brief History of Evolving Provincial GDP Ranking)," April 20, http://cj.sina.com.cn/articles/view/ 5115326071/130e5ae770200005l25?cre=tianyi&mod=pcpager_news&loc= 14&r=9&doct=0&rfunc=100&tj=none&tr=9, accessed on January 20, 2020.

Moreover, if we look further back in history, the establishment of various mining bases, such as Daqing Oil Field in the northeast of China, has significantly generated local economic development. But as the oil reserves were gradually depleted, the local economy also went into stagnation or recession.

Against the prediction of the resource curse thesis, the bivariate analysis does not find any negative impact of mineral resources on economic development as measured by GDP and GDP growth rate. Rather, the rise and decline of Inner Mongolia and other resource-rich regions seem to highlight the contributions of mineral resources and the extractive industries to the development of local and even national economy. If we take the findings at face value, rich mineral resources are hardly a curse, at least in economic terms. However, if we go beyond this naive analysis and further investigate how exactly resource boom affects the economic structure of the host regions and, more importantly, the interests of different stakeholders, more nuanced and intriguing stories come to the surface.

Who Benefits from the Resource Boom?

If it is true that resource boom propels overall economic growth of the host region, then how exactly do resources contribute to economic development? And who benefits from the resource boom? Based on my field research in multiple mining areas across China, resource-abundant regions commonly witness the dominance of mining-related industries in the local economic structure. In a developing country such as China, the discovery of mineral reserves or the boom of the mineral market inevitably creates substantial, albeit often unstable, inflow of revenue that neither the business sector nor the local government can afford to ignore. After all, it is a top priority to promote economic development in reform-era China. Therefore, when the resource market is on the rise, mineral resources, except those of limited economic value or those technically difficult to explore, usually attract an inflow of investments, either public or private, to set up mining companies and related businesses such as the processing and transportation of mineral products.

With the overall economic growth in the reform-era, mining-related businesses have witnessed extraordinarily high returns, especially after the turn of the millennium. First of all, the high returns result from the

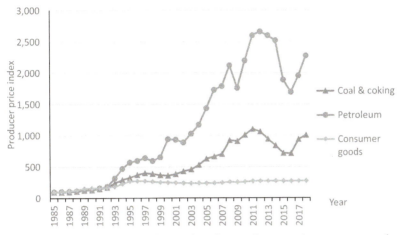

Figure 2.4 Producer price indices of coal, petroleum, and consumer goods (1985–2018)
Source: China Price Statistical Yearbook 2019 and 2020
Note: price of 1985 = 100.

rising prices of and demands for mineral products, which make mining industries highly profitable. Take for example the coal and petroleum industries, the largest two components of China's mineral resources, coal and petroleum prices have kept rising since the 1980s. As Figure 2.4 shows, the producer price indexes of coal and especially petroleum rose continuously from 1985 onward. Despite a sharp drop between 2013 and 2016, as of 2018, the coal price witnessed a nine-fold increase from 1985, while the oil price increased by 21.7 times. In comparison, the overall price of consumer goods increased by only 1.75 times during the same period. Similarly, other industrial products experienced moderate price increases. For example, the producer price of machineries increased by merely 1.77 times, building materials increased by 3.3 times, and electricity increased by 4.6 times from 1985 to 2018.[13] Given that the production costs did not rise significantly, the mining industries enjoyed remarkably widening margins in the past three decades and were much more profitable than many other industries.

[13] Calculated based on statistics from *China Price Statistical Yearbook 2019*.

The high returns for mining industries are also attributable to the peculiar taxation system in China. All enterprises in China pay largely the same taxes, such as value-added tax (VAT), income taxes, and business tax, at the same rates regardless of the industry. For exploiting the state-owned mineral resources, mining enterprises only need to pay resource taxes at very low rates.[14] For example, the resource tax rate remained 5% for oil and natural gas, around 3 yuan per ton for coal, and between 10 and 25 yuan per ton for iron ore until 2011, which were almost negligible compared with the unit prices of these minerals. For instance, in the oil-rich Xinjiang Uygur Autonomous Region, the VAT contributed to 42.48% of its tax revenue, while the resource tax contributed to only 4.56% between 2001 and 2007 (Zhang et al., 2011). Although a resource tax reform in 2010 increased resource taxes to certain degrees,[15] the total volume of resource taxes is non-comparable with the other major taxes. For instance, in a coal-rich Y City in Shanxi Province, the VAT and enterprise income tax took up 53.5% and 17% of the tax revenue respectively in 2011, while resource tax accounted for a staggering 3.7%.[16] In addition to taxes, mining enterprises need to pay a nontax fee named Mineral Resource Compensation Fee (*kuangchan ziyuan buchang fei* 矿产资源补偿费) since 1994 for utilizing the mineral resources, but the fee is chargeable on the sales values of mineral products at quite low rates between 0.5% and 4%, depending on the type of minerals and the method of extraction.[17] In comparison, the rates of similar charges in other

[14] Resource tax was first established in 1984 and exerted on coal, oil, and natural gas only. In 1994, with the overhaul of the taxation system in general, the scope of resource tax was expanded to cover coal, oil, natural gas, ferrous metals, nonferrous metals, nonmetallic minerals, and salt. Tax rates vary widely depending on the type and grade of minerals.

[15] Before the resource tax reform in 2010, resource taxes were calculated based on the volume of mineral products. After 2011, resource taxes are based on the sales value of mineral products. For example, the resource tax was only 30 yuan per ton for oil and 9 yuan per km^3 for natural gas. From 2011 onward, the resource tax rate of 5% translates into 200 yuan per ton for oil (assuming an oil price of 4,000 yuan per ton) and 57.75 yuan per km^3 (assuming an oil price of 1,155 yuan/per ton).

[16] Statistics are obtained from the author's interview with an official in the fiscal department of Y City in Shanxi Province, May 2012.

[17] Ministry of Land and Resources, "Kuangchan Ziyuan Buchang Fei Zhengshou Guanli Guiding (Regulations on the Collection and Management of Mineral Resource Compensation Fee)," www.mlr.gov.cn/zwgk/flfg/kczyflfg/200406/t20040625_587417.htm, accessed on May 17, 2018.

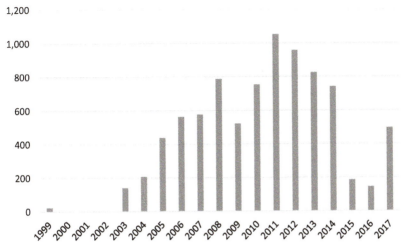

Figure 2.5 Total profit of mining industries in China (1999–2017)
(Unit: Billion Yuan)
Source: Figure compiled based on statistics from *China Land and Resources Statistical Yearbook 2000–2018*
Note: No data were reported from 2000 to 2002. From 2005 on, the total profit is the sum of the profits of solid minerals and profits and taxes of oil and gas.

countries on the use of mineral resources range between 2% and 8%.[18] Moreover, the Chinese central or local governments often make downward adjustments or even waive the fee on certain mining industries under various conditions. Therefore, the low resource tax rates make mineral resources almost costless for mining enterprises and grant them considerable competitive edge over other industries.

Under the booming resource market as well as China's taxation system on mineral exploration and production, the resource sector reaped huge profits during the golden decade from the turn of the millennium to the early 2010s. As Figure 2.5 shows, the total profits of the mining industries (including both solid minerals and gas and oil) skyrocketed between 1999 and 2011. Although the profit declined continuously in the following years, especially in 2015 and 2016, it

[18] Xui Huifeng, 2007. "Kexu Zhiding Kuangchan Ziyuan Youchang Shiyong Fei Biaozhun (Scientific Design of the Rates of Mineral Resource Compensation Fee)," www.npc.gov.cn/zgrdw/npc/bmzz/huanjing/2007-01/12/content_1384001.htm, accessed on March 16, 2020.

rebounded quickly in 2017. The resource capital, represented by the mining and related businesses, became the biggest winners in the resource boom. Take Xinjiang as an example, the income from its rich mineral resources including oil and natural gas rose sharply from 51.5 billion yuan in 2005 to 108.2 billion yuan in 2008, 73.03% of which went into the pockets of mining enterprises, while the central and local governments took up only 19.31% and 7.65%, respectively (Zhang et al., 2011).

The Spillover Effects of Resource Capital

The resource boom bred a large number of nouveau riches in the mining industries, who are popularly referred to as *kuang laoban* (矿老板 mine owners) in Chinese. They became an increasingly powerful and eye-catching social group in resource-rich areas such as Shanxi Province, Shaanxi Province, and Inner Mongolia Autonomous Region. The rapidly enriched *kuang laoban* have frequently made nationwide news headlines and drawn public attention to their eccentric behaviors and extravagant lifestyles. For example, many *kuang laoban* reportedly squandered on luxury vehicles and high-end consumer products. At the peak of the resource boom, numerous luxury SUVs such as Land Rover were roaming on the streets of resource-rich areas, with Ordos in Inner Mongolia as perhaps the best-known example.[19] A Shanxi-based entrepreneur who earned his fortune from coal mining famously spent RMB 70 million (about US$11 million) on the wedding ceremony of his daughter in 2012.[20] Keeping mistresses and engaging in high-stake gambling are also common ways for *kuang laoban* to spend their easily earned fortune. For a while, *mei laoban* (煤老板 coal mine owners) were the most sought-after customers in casinos in Macau and other Southeast Asian cities that legalized gambling. One *mei laoban* from Shanxi Province once legendarily won 90 million yuan in a casino in Macau, though he soon

---

[19] Author's interviews in Inner Mongolia, August 2012. Also see "Eerduosi Daliang Haoche Zao Shuaimai, Cengshi Quanguo Luhuche Zuiduo Difang (Ordos used to own the most Land Rovers in China)," *Yangzi Wanbao*, November 26, 2012, http://finance.sina.com.cn/china/dfjj/20121126/014013790957.shtml, accessed on August 5, 2017.

[20] "Xing Libin de Qifu Rensheng (The Ups and Downs of Xing Libin)," August 2, 2013, http://finance.ifeng.com/business/special/zhenxiang45/, accessed on September 9, 2017.

lost his good luck and ended up in deep debts to the casino totaling nearly one billion yuan (Laowu & Jingfei, 2011, pp. 51–52).

Despite these sensational stories, the super-rich mine owners and investors are businesspeople after all. They constantly seek lucrative opportunities to build up their business empires. Especially for those billionaires with strong ambitions, they often live in more frugal and low-profile lifestyles and choose to invest their resource windfalls to further expand their mining businesses and/or diversify their portfolios into other profitable businesses. Besides the downstream industries of the extractive industry such as mineral processing, energy production, and chemical engineering that appear as natural choices, mining entrepreneurs are also interested in exploring other business opportunities outside the resource sector, such as real estate, hoteling, tourism, logistics, and agricultural product processing.[21] While sometimes the diversification strategies of mining companies may be out of random decisions, more often than not there are logical reasons for mining businesspeople to set foot in other businesses. For instance, as the transportation of mineral products requires secure and stable shipping routes and warehouses along the routes, some mining companies made massive investment in the logistics industry. According to the author's observations and interviews in Shanxi Province, when the mineral market went down and the shipping facilities of mineral products became underutilized after 2012, such investment turned out to become highly profitable along with the rise of e-commerce and the soaring demand for logistics services in China. Alternatively, as mining companies are usually based in rural areas, the processing of agricultural products with local characteristics also appears as an appealing choice. For example, as Shanxi Province is traditionally famous for producing vinegar, some *mei laoban* in Shanxi diversified into the vinegar business. Another example is eco-tourism. Because mining normally causes various environmental damages to the surrounding areas, the Chinese government requires mining companies to restore the environment by refilling the excavated mine pits and planting trees or crops in the mined-out area. Sniffing out the business opportunities under the increasingly tightened environmental regulations, some mining companies innovatively make use of the recovered mines by

---

[21] See Laowu and Jingfei (2011); author's interviews in Shanxi Province also confirm this.

turning them into ecological parks that can not only grow agricultural products and raise poultries and livestock but also attract tourists from nearby cities for leisure and recreation.[22]

Besides the commercial drive of the mining businesspeople, local governments in some resource-rich areas also encouraged mining companies to diversify their portfolios and invest in other non-resource businesses. While it is commonly believed that Chinese local officials are driven by the cadre evaluation system and compete for political promotion by investing only in short-term projects with quick and visible deliverables, some farsighted local officials do plan for the long-term development of their localities and make economic policies accordingly. Some local governments try to promote the transition from a resource-based economy to a more diversified industrial structure and encourage the mining companies to invest in other businesses. For example, starting in 2004, some local governments in the coal-rich Shanxi Province required coal mining companies to set aside funds to invest in noncoal businesses such as agriculture and produce processing. Drawing on the experiences and lessons of the local experiments, the Shanxi provincial government decided in 2006 to make it a province-wide policy to use resource revenue to promote noncoal industries (Chen, 2016, p. 49).

Driven by both commercial motives and official policies, the resource capital has spilled over into other industries. The windfall revenues of mining industries can well facilitate capital formation and accumulation in multiple industrial sectors. However, the diversification strategies of mining companies seem to largely fall into low-tech sectors such as agriculture, manufacturing, and construction. The mine owners and investors, at least the first generation who grew up in the 1960s and 1970s and started the mining business in the 1980s and 1990s,

---

[22] Hao Yahong, 2016. "Meikuang gongren bian 'lvse weishi', shengtaiyuan li jianzheng 'hei' zhuan 'lv' (Mining Workers Turned into 'Green Guardians': Ecological Parks Testify Environmental Recoveries)," September 26, http://sx .xinhuanet.com/2016sxx/jj/20160926/3459767_c.html; Chen Hao & Li Junyi, 2017. "Weiguan 'Lvse Kaicai': Yuanlai Ni Shi Zheyang de Meikuang (Observing 'Green Mining': Unexpected Coal Mines)," September 11, www .xinhuanet.com/fortune/2017-09/11/c_1121645298.htm; Zhang Yi & Xu Haitao, 2012. "Taxianqu Jian Shengtaiyuan, Bainian Meicheng Zoushang Kechixu Fazhan Daolu (Ecological Park Built on Collapsed Land: A Hundred-Year-old Coal City Embarking on Sustainable Development)," February 6, www.nea.gov.cn/2012-02/06/c_131393562.htm, accessed on May 17, 2018.

commonly received very limited or disrupted education due to the Cultural Revolution that lasted from 1966 to 1976. Their low level of education imposes tangible barriers on their business strategies and discourages them from entering high-tech industries such as information technology (IT) and finance, which require high level of education and sophisticated technologies and operate under vastly different rules of the game from mining businesses. The low level of education also makes the mining entrepreneurs quite conservative investors. Many *kuang laoban* tend to be skeptical about the newly emerged business models and technologies that are beyond their scope of knowledge and ability to comprehend, but are more willing to put their money into businesses with physically visible assets or products. Moreover, as Chapter 5 will elaborate on, there commonly lacks sufficient investment in human capital in resource-rich areas. The lack of a well-educated labor force required by high-tech industries also prevents mining entrepreneurs from diversifying into these high-tech sectors.

One particular industry that the resource capital tends to favor is real estate. During the peak of the resource boom, mining areas commonly experienced burgeoning investment in the real estate market. Compared to other industries, the real estate industry appears a particularly attractive investment option for the resource capital. From the macroeconomic perspective, the rapid development of the resource sector since the early 2000s more or less coincided with the boom in China's real estate market. Housing prices all over China rose rapidly from the mid-2000s on, making real estate a highly lucrative business. Many mining entrepreneurs chose to stock up commercial properties, which notably drove up the housing prices on local markets. The coal-rich L county in Shanxi Province provides a vivid example. Although a small, underdeveloped county, its average price of commercial residential buildings rose along with the soaring coal price, and in 2012 it was almost on par with the level of Taiyuan, the capital city of Shanxi, and way above the average housing price of Chinese counties with similar socioeconomic conditions. And the average rental price of apartments in L county was twice as high as in the neighboring county with no coal mines (Chen, 2016, pp. 73–74).

Besides speculative purposes, there are also practical reasons for mining companies to set foot in the housing market. Because mining often causes various environmental hazards such as land subsidence and water shortage, which will be discussed in more detail in

Figure 2.6 A new village in a mining town, Inner Mongolia
Source: photo taken by the author

Chapter 3, residents in the neighborhood surrounding the mines often have to be relocated to other areas. The relocation of local residents in large numbers, sometimes the whole village, gives rise to substantial need for the construction of new houses and even new villages. The relocation of affected citizens to new villages is generally encouraged under the Chinese government's campaign of New Socialist Countryside Construction (*shehuizhuyi xinnongcun jianshe* 社会主义新农村建设) that started around 2006, and it also goes hand in hand with the general trend of urbanization occurring in China (see Figure 2.6 for a new village constructed near a coal mine in Inner Mongolia Autonomous Region). The demand in the housing market in mining areas naturally attracts investment from the mining companies, who not only have the fund for such investment but also the obligation to help settle the relocated residents.[23]

---

[23] Laowu and Jingfei, 2011. Author's interviews in Inner Mongolia, Henan, and Shanxi also confirm this.

As a result, mining-related businesses became a major contributor to China's real estate market during the resource boom, with many mining companies investing in real estate projects or becoming real estate developers themselves. They heavily invested in the local markets where their mining businesses, economic ties, and social connections were located, and they also reached out to the provincial capital and other cities in their provinces where housing prices were on the rise. Interestingly, some *kuang laoban* also reportedly shopped around nationwide and bought properties in major cities including Beijing and Shanghai, and Sanya, a tourist city in Hainan Province with pleasant weather in winter.[24] Beijing appears to be the most favored destination for super-rich *mei laoban* to acquire properties. The preference for Beijing is partly driven by the need of mining enterprises to build connections with high-level officials of the Chinese government stationed in Beijing. As the mining sector operates under heavy state control and frequent surveillance of multiple government departments, mining businesspeople are strongly motivated to establish patronage network and seek political protection from not only local officials but also higher-ups in the central government. Culturally, Beijing is also appealing for its adjacency to the center of power which has been highly respected and valued throughout the Chinese history. For some *mei laoban* from Shanxi Province, where the traditional culture still exerts heavy influence on people's mindset, they just enjoy sitting by the foot of the emperor (*tianzi jiaoxia* 天子脚下).[25] That being said, for the less ambitious or outward-looking *kuang laoban*, local real estate markets are still the safer and more preferred investment choices.

[24] Caixin, 2013. "'Fangjie' Gong Aiai Zhongshen Huoxing Yi Zhounian (Gong Aiai Sentenced to One-year Imprisonment)," October 31, http://special.caixin.com/event_1031/; Sohu News, 2010. "Xi'an Chaofang Neimu: Mei Laoban Yimai Yidonglou Congbu Anjie (Behind Real Estate Speculation in Xi'an: Coal Mine Owners Buying up Whole Building of Apartments without Mortgage)," November 12, http://news.sohu.com/20101112/n277562473.shtml; Tencent Finance, 2010. "Hainan Chaofang Zijin Jiegou: Shanxi Mei Laoban Anzhan Zhejiang Chaofangtuan (Sources of Investment in Hainan Real Estate Market: The Secret Battle between Shanxi Coal Mine Owners and Zhejiang Investors)," January 30, http://finance.qq.com/a/20100130/000745.htm, accessed on March 7, 2020.

[25] Laowu and Jingfei (2011). Author's interviews in Shanxi and Henan also confirm this.

Resources and Capital: Statistical Evidence

The empirical observations from the author's field research and secondary information sources suggest that mineral resources can bring tangible benefits to the local economy. At the very least, the resource sector enjoys considerable capital formation and accumulation, making resource capital, embodied by the mining-related businesspeople, the biggest winners. But capital accumulation is not confined to the mining industries but can also spill over into other industries. The anecdotal empirical evidence posits three possible impacts of mineral resources on the local economy. First, resource boom enhances capital income, which in consequence drives up capital investment, not only in mining but also in other industries. Second, resource capital, when seeking investment opportunities, tends to spill into industries with low technological entry bar but avoid high-tech industries. Third, resource capital tends to flow into the real estate market.

This section statistically examines and generalizes these qualitative findings through longitudinal and cross-regional data analysis on Chinese provinces between 1999 and 2017 (see Appendix 2.A for the details of the statistical analysis). As discussed earlier, I use two indicators to measure resource endowment: (1) the size of resource production as measured by real per capita mineral sales income and (2) the rate of resource dependence as measured by the share of industrial output of mineral industries in GDP. These are the key predictors of interest for all dependent variables throughout this book.

To assess the impacts of mineral resources on local economy, I use real per capita investment in fixed assets to measure total capital formation in a region, and I also examine the per capita fixed-asset investment in the mining sector in particular. As China's economic growth has been strongly driven by fixed-asset investment (Zhang et al., 2011), this investment-driven growth makes the fixed-asset investment a good indicator to gauge the impacts of resources on both the economy and capital as an interest group. To examine the spillover effects of the resource capital on other industries, I look at the fixed-asset investments in four industries, including manufacturing, construction, finance, and IT. Manufacturing and construction are two important industries in the Chinese economy that hire the largest labor forces among all industrial sectors, but they typically do not require high level of technology. Meanwhile, I take IT and finance as two typical cases of high-tech industries. From 2002 to 2017,[26] China witnessed massive growths in fixed-asset investment in almost all industrial sectors, which have been behind China's investment-driven economic growth. The total investment in fixed assets increased dramatically from 2.90 trillion yuan in 1999 to 64.1 trillion yuan in 2017, a more than 20-fold increase. For the mining sector in particular, the fixed-asset investment in mining industries rose from 0.14 trillion yuan in 2002 to 0.92 trillion yuan in 2017, during which there were considerable fluctuations across the years. During the same period, the overall fixed-asset investment in the manufacturing sector increased from 0.934 trillion yuan to 19.4 trillion yuan; that in construction increased from 0.073 trillion yuan to 0.384 trillion yuan; that in the financial industry increased from 0.01 trillion yuan to 0.112 trillion yuan; and that in IT increased from 0.166 trillion yuan in 2003[27] to 0.700 trillion yuan in 2017.[28] Against the backdrop of a generally increasing trend, the fixed-asset investments nevertheless saw vast variations across regions, with some developed regions overshadowing many other regions.

To assess the effects of mineral resources on real estate, I adopt a few indicators. Since the Chinese government opened up the housing market and allowed commercial transactions of properties in 1998, the real estate industry has become an attractive destination for investment, especially after the housing boom started in the mid-2000s. I examine both long-term and short-term investments in the real estate sector. To measure long-term investment in real estate, I use per capita annual fixed-asset investment in this sector because the investment in fixed assets is likely to stay for longer periods than hot money does. From 2002 to 2017, nationwide fixed-asset investment in real estate expanded tremendously from 0.82 trillion yuan to 14.62 trillion yuan. In contrast, to measure the short-term investment in real estate, I look at the sold area of commercial properties divided by the population size

[26] I choose this time period because systematic by-sector statistics on fixed-asset investment first became available in 2002, and 2017 is the latest date when resource-related data are available.
[27] The IT industry (including information transmission, software, and information technology) first became an individual category in the reporting of fixed-asset investment in China in 2003.
[28] Statistics are from *Statistical Yearbook of the Chinese Investment in Fixed Assets 2000–2018*.

to measure the inflow of money into the real estate market.[29] Commercial properties in China mostly consist of residential buildings, office buildings, and business buildings, with residential buildings being by far the largest component. As China did not levy any property tax on real estate properties during the period under study, and commercial properties could be transacted on the market relatively easily, they were an attractive destination for hot money, thus making the real estate a typical speculative industry in China.

The data analyses suggest that the size of resource production and the rate of resource dependence, which are highly positively correlated, have largely the same effects on the economic outcomes. The regression results (see Tables 2.2–2.5 in Appendix 2.A) reveal an interesting, threefold story: When controlling for socioeconomic factors including per capita GDP, GDP growth rate, foreign direct investment (FDI), rural population, and ethnic minority ratio, mineral resources boost overall capital formation and total fixed-asset investment. However, there are divergent impacts on different industries: While resource boom enhances investment in mining as well as other low-tech industries including manufacturing and construction, it seriously undermines investment in high-tech industries such as IT and finance. Moreover, resource capital appears to turn into hot money and drive up speculative investment in the real estate market.

First, resource-rich regions enjoy significantly more total investment in fixed assets. Both resource abundance and resource dependence in the previous year are significantly positively correlated with real per capita total fixed-asset investment in the current year, and the coefficients are consistent across the models (see Table 2.2). Based on the estimation in Model 4 in Table 2.2, other things being equal, the most resource-dependent region would invest 123% more in fixed assets than the least resource-dependent region; based on the estimation in Model 2, other things being equal, when mineral production doubles,

---

[29] I choose the area of real estate properties rather than the total value of the properties so as to segregate the influence of fluctuating housing prices, which are affected by not only the demand and supply on the real estate market but also by other factors such as economic development level, citizens' purchasing power, and monetary policies. The changes in the sold areas of properties allow us to discern the impacts of resource revenue on the transactions in the real estate market more clearly.

the total investment in fixed assets would also increase by 5%.[30] Thus, the statistical result indicates that resource wealth has a notable positive effect on capital formation overall. The inflow of resource revenue means good news for capital formation and should boost local economic development in general. After all, the Chinese economy up till now has been strongly pushed forward by capital investment. If the resource sector can inject more revenue into fixed-asset investments, it helps keep the engine of growth running.

However, if we disaggregate the fixed-asset investments by sector and look more closely, the statistical analysis finds that resource capital has divergent impacts on different industrial sectors. The mining sector unsurprisingly benefits from a resource boom. Resource abundance and dependence in the last year are significantly positively correlated with the fixed-asset investment in the mining sector in the current year, and the coefficients are statistically significant in all the models (see Table 2.2). Based on the estimation in Model 6 in Table 2.2, other things being equal, when the size of mineral production doubles, the fixed-asset investment in the mining sector in the next year would also increase by 87%. The findings suggest that resource revenue can further boost the investment in and the expansion of the mining industries and lead to an upward spiral of capital accumulation in the resource sector. Comparing the estimated effects of resource production on total fixed-asset investment versus the fixed-asset investment in mining, we can see that the impact of resource revenue is much greater on the mining sector than on all sectors put together.

Meanwhile, mineral resources also tend to enhance fixed-asset investment in the manufacturing and construction sectors (see Table 2.3). Based on the estimation in Models 2 and 6 in Table 2.3, controlling for other factors, when the size of resource production doubles, the fixed-asset investment in manufacturing would increase by 13% and that in construction would increase by 27%. A comparison of the estimates shows that although resource abundance and dependence exert positive effects on the fixed-asset investment in mining, manufacturing, and construction sectors, the

---

[30] It is worth noting that the increase of resource production and increase in fixed-asset investment do not follow a linear relationship, because the estimation uses the natural log of both variables. The same applies to the estimated effects of the size of resource production on the other dependent variables discussed in this section.

magnitude of the effects is notably larger on the mining sector than on the other two sectors. Therefore, the profits spilling from the mining sector into other industries are unevenly distributed and are modest when compared to the mining sector.

Nevertheless, the beneficial spillover effects of resource revenue are likely to be limited to such industries as manufacturing and construction that have low entry bar in terms of technology and human capital. When it comes to the IT and financial industries, two typical high-tech industries, the presence of rich resources turns out to undercut the investment in these sectors. Both resource abundance and dependence are negatively correlated with real per capita fixed-asset investment in IT and finance, and the coefficients are statistically significant and robust in all the models (see Table 2.4). It means that the more resource revenue a region enjoys, the less investment it makes in fixed assets in the IT and financial sectors. Based on the estimations in Models 4 and 8 in Table 2.4, other things being equal, the most resource-dependent region would make only 53% of the fixed-asset investment in IT and only 28% of the fixed-asset investment in finance made by the least resource-dependent region. The statistical findings confirm the impression that resource-rich regions tend to be backward and lack modern industrial sectors that require advanced technology, and they echo some existing studies that warn against the harmful effects of the resource sector on technological innovation (Yang et al., 2014). As Chapter 5 will discuss in detail, this phenomenon may have to do with the negligence of human capital development by local governments and citizens in these regions. In the long run, resource-dependent regions may be stuck in low-level extensive economic growth that relies on the exhaustion of raw materials and input of capital rather than transitioning into intensive growth, which builds on technological innovations and sophisticated labor force.

When we turn to the real estate industry, resource revenue does not seem to boost long-term investment in the industry, but it rather pushes up transactions of commercial properties on the market. The effects of the size of resource production and the rate of resource dependence on real per capita fixed-asset investment in the real estate sector are negative in some models but switch sign across the statistical models, and the coefficients are statistically insignificant in all the models (see Table 2.5). Therefore, we do not detect a clear impact of resources on the long-term investment in real estate, as in the other abovementioned industries. By contrast, resources are positively correlated with per capita sold area of commercial properties, and the coefficients are statistically significant in most of the models. Based on the estimation in Model 8 in Table 2.5, controlling for the level of economic development and other socioeconomic variables, the most resource-dependent regions would see 122% more transactions of commercial properties than the least resource-dependent region. These findings suggest that instead of making relatively long-term investment in the fixed assets, resource-generated wealth is more likely to enter the real estate market as hot money.[31] Thus, resource capital may compose a non-negligible force that pumps up housing bubbles in China, the danger of which has been clearly and repeatedly demonstrated in past financial crises such as the Asian financial crisis in the late 1990s and the 2008 financial tsunami that swept the world. In addition to causing financial uncertainty and instability, the flood of resource revenue into the real estate market may also be detrimental to the Chinese economy because the rising housing prices impose higher costs of rents and land prices on economic entities, and consequently may lead to declined profitability and competitiveness of other productive sectors. Due to the limit of scope, this research cannot fully assess the impacts of resources on land prices and competitiveness of other industries. If future research can substantiate this causal link, it may be a domestic variant of the deindustrialization effect of the Dutch disease theorem (Corden & Neary, 1982).

Conclusion

This chapter tells a mixed story about what resource endowment means for the economic development of the host region. In terms of overall capital formation, the existence of rich mineral resources can be regarded as a blessing, in the sense that the resource revenue can turn into capital and be further invested to propel economic growth. Obviously, the resource capital, represented by mining-related enterprises and businesspeople, most directly and greatly benefits from the booming mineral market and the inflow of resource wealth. They not only get rich individually but have formed a new interest group who

---

[31] Admittedly, the displacement due to mining may increase the purchase of commercial properties. Unfortunately, no systematic provincial-level data are available on displaced populations. We have to wait until such data become available in order to rigorously examine this causal effect.

have strong incentives to fortify their business empires and further expand their wealth by searching for and investing in lucrative business opportunities. As the statistical evidence shows, resources not only lead to more investment in the fixed assets of the mining sector but also in other industries, including manufacturing and construction. This means that resource boom can lead to an upward spiral of capital accumulation and investment, and the effect can well spill over into non-resource sectors. Generally speaking, resource revenue has a positive effect on capital investment that can promote economic growth.

Nevertheless, resource revenue is not equally beneficial to all non-resource sectors. While it favors low-tech industries, the reliance on the resource sector tends to undermine such high-tech industries as IT and finance that require more than just a pump of money but also well-educated labor force, sophisticated management skills, and advanced technologies. As mining businesspeople, at least the first generation that emerged under the post-Mao reform and became rich in the past two or three decades, normally lack the capacity as well as interest to invest in these high-tech industries, the spillover effects of resource capital are largely constrained to low-tech industries. Meanwhile, the underdevelopment of human capital and shortage of high-quality labor force commonly seen in resource-rich regions also prevent these regions from successfully transitioning out of resource dependence and embarking on industrial upgrading based on technological innovations.

Another dangerous impact of resource windfall is that it is prone to turn into hot money and flow into the highly speculative industry of real estate, which may increase financial instability and economic risks. The resource-rich city of Ordos in Inner Mongolia provides a telling example of the real estate boom and bust. At the peak of the mining industry in the late 2000s, Ordos erected a whole new town in the desert and built more properties than its citizens could possibly fill up. However, the gala for real estate developers did not last long. As the coal prices plunged and the mineral market contracted after 2012, the housing bubble busted, capital chain ruptured, and the investors went bankrupted. In a matter of a few years, Ordos turned from China's "city of the future" to the world's largest "ghost town."[32]

---

[32] Melia Robinson, 2017. "Surreal photos of China's failed 'city of the future'," May, www.businessinsider.com/ordos-china-ghost-town-2017-5, accessed on June 4, 2018.

APPENDIX 2.A *Statistical Analysis on the Impacts of Resources on Local Economy*

Statistical Methods and Data

To statistically examine the effects of resource wealth on the local economy, particularly capital formation in different sectors, I run panel data analysis on the 31 provinces between 1999 and 2017. I have eight sets of dependent variables, namely per capita fixed-asset investment in all industrial sectors[33] and that in mining, manufacturing, construction, IT, finance, and real estate, respectively. I also use per capita sold area of commercial properties as an indicator of speculative investment in real estate.

Besides the size of resource production and the rate of resource dependence as the predictors of interest, I also control for some commonly used socioeconomic variables that may affect the dependent variables. First, I include per capita GDP to control for the level of economic development and GDP growth rate as a measure of economic opportunities that should affect investment incentives. Second, per capita FDI is included as a control variable, because the inflow of foreign capital can potentially influence fixed-asset investments. Third, due to the notorious urban-rural divide, which affects many economic conditions and decisions, I include the percentage of rural employed persons in total employed persons as a measure of the weight of rural economy and population.[34] Fourth, I control for the proportion of

---

[33] The sectors include mining, manufacturing, construction, finance, IT, real estate, agriculture, energy and water supply, wholesale and retail, logistics and post, hotels and catering services, leasing and business services, scientific research and technical services, water conservancy and environment management, resident services, education, health and social service, culture, sports and entertainment, and public management, social security and social organizations.

[34] Increasing numbers of provinces stopped publishing their numbers of rural employed persons since 2013 and especially after 2015. To compute the missing values in the percentage of rural laborers between 2013 and 2015, I extrapolate the numbers of urban and/or rural employed persons based on the reported

ethnic minorities in total population to compare the situations of Han-dominated regions and ethnic minority regions. In addition, population density, namely the size of population divided by the total territorial area of a region, is controlled for in the regressions on the real estate market, because population density may affect the demand in the housing market.[35]

It is important to note that there may be some time lag for resource-generated capital to turn into investment. There may also be endogeneity problem between resource revenue and some dependent variables. For example, the fixed-asset investment in the mining sector is likely to affect the industrial output as well as the sales income of mining industries in the current year. Therefore, I use the one-year lag of the key predictors to explain the fixed-asset investments in the current year. Similarly, there is potential endogeneity problem between economic development and fixed-asset investments as well: While per capita GDP and its growth rate may affect fixed-asset investment, the investment may affect GDP as well. Therefore, I use the one-year lag instead of the current-year value of per capita GDP and GDP growth rate in the regression.[36] Arguably the economic development of the previous year can affect investment decisions in the current year but should not be affected by the latter.

numbers in the past two years, with the assumption that the numbers of employed persons change at a stable pace across years. From 2016 onward, as there are too many missing values that make the extrapolation unreliable, I supplement the data with the percentage of rural population in total population reported by *Statistical Yearbook of China*. The percentage of rural employed persons and the percentage of rural population are not identical but highly correlated. In the province-years when both indicators are available, the Pearson's correlation is 0.91 (p-value = 0.000). Therefore, it is reasonable to use the percentage of rural population as a supplementary data.

[35] Admittedly, the abovementioned explanatory variables may not fully account for the dependent variables, as there may be other macroeconomic factors such as monetary policies and market conditions in various industrial sectors. However, assuming that these variables are unlikely to be correlated with mineral resource extraction, omitting them should not lead to biased estimation of the effects of the key predictors of interest. Therefore, for the purpose of this study, I only include the aforementioned control variables, although we may need more sophisticated econometric models and control for more variables in order to fully explain the dependent variables.

[36] To check the longer-term effect of economic development on fixed-asset investments, I have also tried the three-year lag of per capita GDP in the data analyses. The results are highly similar to those using the one-year lag of per capita GDP.

To offset the effects of inflation and make the statistics in monetary terms comparable across years, all monetary figures are transformed into real values by dividing the nominal values with regional deflator, which is determined by the annual inflation rates of each province (with 1998 as the base year). The summary statistics of the independent and dependent variables are presented in Table 2.1. The statistics are collected from *National Land and Resources Statistical Yearbook of China, Statistical Yearbook of China, China Population Statistics Yearbook, China Population and Employment Statistics Yearbook, Statistical Yearbook of the Chinese Investment in Fixed Assets, China Commerce Yearbook, China Real Estate Statistics Yearbook, China's Ethnic Statistical Yearbook,* and *China Data Online.*

Following existing studies with panel data analyses (Arezki & Bruckner, 2011), this study adopts the fixed effects model to control for region-specific effects, such as local geographical, policy, and other factors that may affect economic performance, and time-specific effects, such as nationwide economic and monetary policies which potentially affect investment decisions.[37] I use the following formula to conduct the panel data analysis: $Y_{it} = \alpha R_{it} + \beta' X_{it} + \mu_i + \nu_t + \varepsilon_{it}$, where the subscript $i = 1, 2 \ldots, 31$ for the 31 provinces, and $t = 1, 2, \ldots, 19$ for the 19 years from 1999 to 2017. Y is the dependent variable. R is the predictor of interest, the size of resource production, and the rate of resource dependence, which will be included in the models separately. X is the set of control variables discussed earlier. The variable μ is the time-invariant and province-specific effect; and ν is the province-invariant and time-specific effect. The error term ε captures the effects of other disturbances on the dependent variable.

To satisfy the normal distribution assumption of the variables, all the highly skewed variables are transformed by taking natural log. For each dependent variable, multiple statistical models are tried out. Following a common practice in many existing studies, I use a stepwise regression approach to progressively introduce the independent variables into the models (Zhang & Brouwer, 2020). The models with different compositions of the independent variables yield largely robust and consistent results regarding the key predictors. Due to the limit of

---

[37] A fixed effects model is adopted over a random effects model because the latter does not pass the Hausman test in all the regression models, which suggests that it may be inconsistent. To be prudent, I adopt the fixed effects model in all the panel data analyses throughout this book.

Table 2.1. *Summary statistics*

Variable	N	Mean	Std. Dev.	Min	Max
Predictor of interest					
Size of resource production (real per capita mineral sales income)	589	1,077.7	1,564.0	2.34	9,209.7
Rate of resource dependence (percentage of mineral industrial output in GDP)	589	6.46	8.48	0.01	94.62
Dependent variable					
Real per capita fixed-asset investment	589	15,330	12,418.3	858.7	61,528.4
Real per capita fixed-asset investment in mining	496	622.6	754.1	0.33	4,949.0
Real per capita fixed-asset investment in manufacturing	496	4,864.9	4,452.9	45.9	21,913.8
Real per capita fixed-asset investment in construction	494	192.5	329.0	1.33	3,051.4
Real per capita fixed-asset investment in IT	465	225.9	182.3	7.31	1,040.8
Real per capita fixed-asset investment in finance	494	40.4	65.4	0.53	1,013.7
Real per capita fixed-asset investment in real estate	496	4,422	3,768.5	107	17,270
Per capita sold area of commercial properties	589	0.62	0.42	0.004	2.48
Control variables					
Real per capita GDP (1-year lag)	589	22,540	17,884	2,318	93,845
GDP growth rate (1-year lag)	589	111.0	2.65	97.5	123.8
Real per capita FDI	585	709.3	982.3	0.064	6,533.4
Weight of rural population	589	63.93	17.08	11.33	88.51
Ethnic minority ratio	589	12.71	21.43	0	99.99
Population density	589	408.9	582.9	2.08	3,826.2

Source: Authors' calculation based on statistics from *National Land and Resources Statistical Yearbook of China*, *Statistical Yearbook of China*, *China Population Statistics Yearbook*, *China Population and Employment Statistics Yearbook*, *Statistical Yearbook of the Chinese Investment in Fixed Assets*, *China Commerce Yearbook*, *China Real Estate Statistics Yearbook*, *China's Ethnic Statistical Yearbook*, and *China Data Online*.

space, only the baseline model with the key predictor of interest and per capita GDP[38] and the comprehensive model that includes the key predictor of interest and all the control variables are presented for each set of dependent variables. To deal with possible heteroscedasticity problem, I conduct Breusch–Pagan test (Wooldridge, 2013) on all the models, and quite a few do not pass the test at 0.05 level. Therefore, I report heteroscedasticity-robust statistical results for all the models in the regression tables.[39]

Tables 2.2–2.4 show the impacts of the size of resource production and rate of resource dependence on the investment in fixed assets in all industries and in mining, manufacturing, construction, IT, and finance, respectively. Table 2.5 shows the impacts of the size of resource production and rate of resource dependence on the real estate market in terms of the fixed-asset investment and sold areas of commercial properties, respectively.

Statistical Findings on the Control Variables

Besides the key predictors of interest, the control variables also have some noteworthy impacts on the dependent variables.

Capital Investment

Economic development level, as measured by the one-year lag of real per capita GDP, is significantly positively correlated with real per capita fixed-asset investment in general and in the manufacturing, construction, IT, and financial industries. The estimated coefficients are more or less comparable across the different industrial sectors. It confirms that economic development level is a significant determinant for fixed-asset investment. On the other hand, the one-year lag of GDP growth rate does not have statistically significant impacts on fixed-

---

[38] Per capita GDP is significantly correlated with the key predictors of interest, and both should affect the dependent variables. To avoid wrongly attributing the effect of per capita GDP on the dependent variables to resource abundance and dependence and leading to biased estimation of their effects, I include per capita GDP in the baseline models.

[39] I use the generic coeftest function in R to conduct the heteroscedasticity-robust estimation with White's estimator. I have tried different estimators and found the results highly similar.

Table 2.2. *Impacts of mineral resources on fixed-asset investment (I)*

	Overall				Mining			
	(1)	(2)	(3)	(4)	(5)	(6)	(7)	(8)
Predictor of interest								
1-year lag of size of resource production (ln)	0.063***	0.075***			0.880***	0.900***		
	(0.012)	(0.011)			(0.064)	(0.063)		
1-year lag of rate of resource dependence (ln)			0.073***	0.084***			0.957***	0.977***
			(0.011)	(0.010)			(0.054)	(0.051)
Control variables								
1-year lag of real per capita GDP (ln)	0.733***	0.687***	0.810***	0.767***	−0.364***	−0.335**	0.617***	0.611***
	(0.032)	(0.049)	(0.026)	(0.043)	(0.120)	(0.125)	(0.133)	(0.135)
1-year lag of GDP growth rate		0.007		0.007		0.011		0.017
		(0.007)		(0.006)		(0.023)		(0.022)
Real per capita FDI (ln)		0.057***		0.060***		0.056.		0.072.
		(0.016)		(0.015)		(0.033)		(0.032)
Weight of rural population		0.001		0.001		0.010		0.009
		(0.003)		(0.003)		(0.007)		(0.007)
Ethnic minority ratio		0.005***		0.005***		0.009***		0.008***
		(0.000)		(0.000)		(0.002)		(0.002)
Region effect	Yes	Yes	Yes	Yes	Yes	Yes	Yes	Yes
Year effect	Yes	Yes	Yes	Yes	Yes	Yes	Yes	Yes
R^2 (within)	0.682	0.717	0.688	0.723	0.639	0.653	0.678	0.690
Degree of freedom	508	500	508	500	449	441	449	441

The numbers in the parentheses are heteroscedasticity-robust standard errors. Significance codes: $***p < 0.001$; $**p < 0.01$; $*p < 0.05$; $.p < 0.1$.

Table 2.3. *Impacts of mineral resources on fixed-asset investment (II)*

	Manufacturing				Construction			
	(1)	(2)	(3)	(4)	(5)	(6)	(7)	(8)
Predictor of interest								
1-year lag of size of resource production (ln)	0.171*** (0.019)	0.174*** (0.018)			0.342*** (0.056)	0.350*** (0.055)		
1-year lag of rate of resource dependence (ln)			0.179*** (0.018)	0.189*** (0.017)			0.386*** (0.043)	0.395*** (0.041)
Control variables								
1-year lag of real per capita GDP (ln)	0.928*** (0.064)	0.524*** (0.075)	1.106*** (0.068)	0.707*** (0.074)	0.452*** (0.112)	0.617* (0.240)	0.856*** (0.124)	1.000*** (0.244)
1-year lag of GDP growth rate		-0.011 (0.015)		-0.010 (0.015)		-0.003 (0.043)		-0.000 (0.042)
Real per capita FDI (ln)		0.106*** (0.028)		0.109*** (0.028)		-0.013 (0.109)		-0.002 (0.106)
Weight of rural population		0.008 (0.006)		0.008 (0.006)		-0.009 (0.010)		-0.010 (0.010)
Ethnic minority ratio		-0.009*** (0.001)		-0.009*** (0.001)		0.008** (0.003)		0.008** (0.003)
Region effect	Yes	Yes	Yes	Yes	Yes	Yes	Yes	Yes
Year effect	Yes	Yes	Yes	Yes	Yes	Yes	Yes	Yes
R^2 (within)	0.344	0.432	0.344	0.437	0.096	0.114	0.110	0.128
Degree of freedom	449	441	449	441	447	439	447	439

The numbers in the parentheses are heteroscedasticity-robust standard errors. Significance codes: *** $p < 0.001$; ** $p < 0.01$; * $p < 0.05$; · $p < 0.1$.

Table 2.4. *Impacts of mineral resources on fixed-asset investment (III)*

	IT				Finance			
	(1)	(2)	(3)	(4)	(5)	(6)	(7)	(8)
Predictor of interest								
1-year lag of size of resource production (ln)	-0.073** (0.023)	-0.064** (0.020)			-0.140*** (0.031)	-0.115*** (0.034)		
1-year lag of rate of resource dependence (ln)			-0.072*** (0.026)	-0.067*** (0.023)			-0.156*** (0.028)	-0.132*** (0.032)
Control variables								
1-year lag of real per capita GDP (ln)	0.781*** (0.055)	0.966*** (0.079)	0.711*** (0.070)	0.901*** (0.088)	0.666*** (0.105)	0.600*** (0.101)	0.504*** (0.107)	0.471*** (0.099)
1-year lag of GDP growth rate		0.015 (0.016)		0.015 (0.016)		0.032 (0.023)		0.031 (0.023)
Real per capita FDI (ln)		-0.020 (0.027)		-0.020 (0.027)		0.109** (0.057)		0.105* (0.041)
Weight of rural population		0.002 (0.006)		0.002 (0.006)		-0.013 (0.008)		-0.012 (0.008)
Ethnic minority ratio		0.008*** (0.001)		0.008*** (0.002)		0.010*** (0.002)		0.010*** (0.002)
Region effect	Yes	Yes	Yes	Yes	Yes	Yes	Yes	Yes
Year effect	Yes	Yes	Yes	Yes	Yes	Yes	Yes	Yes
R^2 (within)	0.379	0.432	0.377	0.432	0.208	0.246	0.212	0.251
Degree of freedom	420	412	420	412	447	439	447	439

The numbers in the parentheses are heteroscedasticity-robust standard errors. Significance codes: $***p < 0.001$; $**p < 0.01$; $*p < 0.05$; $p < 0.1$.

Table 2.5. Impacts of mineral resources on real estate market

	Fixed-Asset Investment				Sold Area of Commercial Properties			
	(1)	(2)	(3)	(4)	(5)	(6)	(7)	(8)
Predictor of interest								
1-year lag of size of resource production (ln)	−0.039**	0.025			0.028.	0.081***		
	(0.014)	(0.017)			(0.016)	(0.020)		
1-year lag of rate of resource dependence (ln)			−0.043**	0.029			0.024	0.087***
			(0.016)	(0.019)			(0.017)	(0.021)
Control variables								
1-year lag of real per capita GDP (ln)	1.010***	0.773***	0.966***	0.800***	0.842***	0.583***	0.863***	0.663***
	(0.058)	(0.069)	(0.056)	(0.079)	(0.064)	(0.091)	(0.062)	(0.087)
1-year lag of GDP growth rate		0.021		0.021		0.020*		0.020*
		(0.014)		(0.014)		(0.010)		(0.010)
Real per capita FDI (ln)		0.049**		0.050**		0.044.		0.045.
		(0.022)		(0.024)		(0.026)		(0.025)
Weight of rural population		0.004		0.004		0.008		0.008
		(0.007)		(0.006)		(0.005)		(0.005)
Ethnic minority ratio		0.005**		0.005***		0.002		0.002.
		(0.001)		(0.002)		(0.001)		(0.001)
Population density (ln)		0.160***		0.162***		0.138***		0.141***
		(0.021)		(0.023)		(0.022)		(0.023)
Region effect	Yes	Yes	Yes	Yes	Yes	Yes	Yes	Yes
Year effect	Yes	Yes	Yes	Yes	Yes	Yes	Yes	Yes
R^2 (within)	0.669	0.716	0.669	0.716	0.459	0.520	0.458	0.521
Degree of freedom	449	440	449	440	508	499	508	499

The numbers in the parentheses are heteroscedasticity-robust standard errors. Significance codes: $***p < 0.001$; $**p < 0.01$; $*p < 0.05$; $\cdot p < 0.1$.

73

asset investment overall and that in different industries, although it is positively correlated with the fixed-asset investment in mining, IT, financial, and real estate industries. The inflow of foreign capital, as measured by real per capita FDI, appears to be positively correlated with overall fixed-asset investment and that in such industries as mining, manufacturing, finance, and real estate. However, the coefficients are not statistically significant in all the models. This suggests that the inflow of foreign capital may help boost fixed-asset investment in China in general and in specific industries, particularly manufacturing as a highly outward oriented industry closely connected with the international market.

The weight of rural population does not have substantially or statistically significant impact on overall fixed-asset investment or in specific industries. Ethnic minority ratio is positively correlated with overall fixed-asset investment and that in mining, construction, IT, and financial sectors, but is negatively correlated with fixed-asset investment in manufacturing. The estimated coefficients are statistically significant and robust across models. The generally positive correlation between ethnic minority ratio and fixed-asset investment may be due to the fact that ethnic minority regions tend to be remote, backward inland areas with greater need for development through investment. The only exception is the manufacturing industry, which seems to be more developed in Han-dominated areas. This is an interesting phenomenon worth exploring in a separate project.

Real Estate Market

The economic factors play important roles in the real estate market as well. Unsurprisingly, economic development level as measured by real per capita GDP is significantly and positively correlated with long-term fixed-asset investment in the real estate industry. Meanwhile, wealthier regions sell more properties on annual basis. The estimated coefficient of real per capita GDP is statistically highly significant in all the models. On the other hand, economic growth does not appear to have any statistically significant impact on the fixed-asset investment in real estate. However, GDP growth rate is significantly positively correlated with real estate transactions. It suggests that when the economy is going up, investors are more willing to buy commercial properties.

The inflow of FDI appears to boost both long-term investment and real estate transactions. Real per capita FDI is positively correlated with both real per capita fixed-asset investment and per capita sold areas of properties, and the coefficients are statistically significant in all the models. The findings indicate that, in addition to indigenous capital, foreign capital may also flow into the real estate industry and push up the demand on the housing market. The Chinese real estate market, despite many official restrictions on purchasing, especially in major cities with skyrocketing housing prices, is not entirely isolated from the international market or immune from the threat of international monetary volatility.

For the demographic factors, the weight of rural population is positively correlated with per capita fixed-asset investment and per capita sold areas of properties, which suggests that rural areas may invest more in developing the real estate industry in the process of urbanization. However, the estimated coefficients are very small and statistically insignificant in all the models, and thus we cannot draw any definitive conclusion on this. Meanwhile, ethnic minority ratio is positively correlated with both fixed-asset investment and sold areas of properties, though the coefficient is statistically significant only for the former. Last but not least, population density is positively correlated with both fixed-asset investment in real estate and sold areas of properties, and the coefficients are statistically and substantively highly significant in all the models. It confirms that population density does matter for the real estate industry. More densely populated regions tend to experience both stronger urge to develop the real estate industry through fixed-asset investment and larger demand for real estate properties on the market.

3 | *Resource Extraction and Victimization of Labor*

From the perspective of capital, one can hardly regard resource abundance as a curse. However, for common citizens as labor, resource abundance is barely a blessing. Through case studies and statistical analysis, this chapter examines the economic, social, and environmental impacts that the resource sector generates on local citizens in mining areas. Owing to the limited economic dividends and the enormous negative externalities of the mining and related industries, labor suffers considerable financial and health losses and experiences depressed income under the resource boom. The unequal distribution of the benefits and costs makes the resource economy an unfair game between capital and labor. It not only exacerbates the income inequality that has already been widening in reform-era China but also becomes a major source of social instability in mining areas.

Mining Industry: An Unfair Game

While the resource boom generates huge inflow of revenue to the mining and related industries, it brings very limited benefits to their workers in these lucrative businesses. Mine workers in China receive only modest payments and share a small fraction of the massive returns to mining enterprises. Throughout the golden decade of China's resource sector, Chinese mine workers' annual salaries did rise remarkably, from on average 7,251 yuan in 1999 to 91,068 yuan in 2019.[1] However, compared with other industrial sectors (see Figure 3.1), the

---

[1] The average wages discussed in this section are the average wages of employed persons in urban non-private units. The statistics are from *China Statistical Yearbook 2004 and 2020*. *China Statistical Yearbook* also reports the average wages of employed persons in urban private units starting in 2009, which are consistently lower than and on average are around 60% of those in urban non-private units. For consistent comparison over a longer time span, I use the average wages in urban non-private units between 1999 and 2019 in the data analysis.

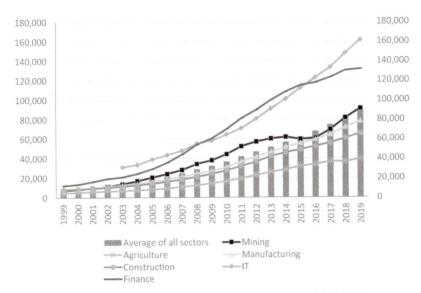

Figure 3.1 Annual wages in mining and selected sectors (1999–2019)
(Unit: Yuan)

Source: Figure compiled based on statistics from *China Statistical Yearbook* 2004 and 2020

Note: The trendlines show the annual wages in the sectors of mining, agriculture, manufacturing, construction, IT, and finance, respectively; the bars are the average annual wage of all major industrial sectors in China, including the aforementioned six sectors. The statistics for the wage level of the IT industry are unavailable from 1999 to 2002 and thus not shown in the figure.

wage increase in the mining sector is not impressive at all, and remains just around the average level of all sectors nationwide. Although slightly higher than the average income in typical labor-intensive industries such as manufacturing and construction and much higher than agriculture, the wage level in mining is much lower than that in high-tech sectors such as IT and finance.

The moderate labor income in the mining sector is attributable to a few structural factors. First of all, in the highly capital-intensive mining industries, labor has rather weak bargaining power in protecting their rights and advancing their interests. Given the limited demand for and reliance on the labor force, mine workers find themselves in a vulnerable position to negotiate with mining companies for salary increase. Their bargaining power is further undermined by the low requirement of labor skills, which make mine workers highly replaceable. Given the abundant supply of low-skilled labor in a populated country such as China, mining companies can easily recruit workers on the market and fire those who are deemed noncooperative or inefficient. Moreover, under the Communist Party rule that allows limited channels of political participation and is extremely wary about civic association, Chinese labor has rather weak organizational capacity and bargaining power in the face of capital. Thus, there is inadequate protection of labor rights in the mining sector. In large mines, the state-sponsored labor unions may play some roles in protecting mine workers' interests, but in smaller and especially private mines, which compose the vast majority of Chinese mines, labor unions may be malfunctioning or even nonexistent.[2] Therefore, mine workers can hardly organize themselves to demand better pay.

Meanwhile, mining industries are vulnerable to market shocks, which make mining jobs highly unstable. While a booming resource market can increase job opportunities, when the economy goes downhill, the prices and demands for mineral resources would drop sharply. In response to declining profitability, the first action that mining companies normally take is to cut down production and payment to the workers. Wage arrears are a common practice in the mining sector. For instance, due to the downturn of the coal market, some coal companies in Shanxi Province only paid salaries to their employees for 6 months in 2015, and only 4 months in 2016. Moreover, when mining companies go bankrupt, mine workers are laid off in large numbers. However, with inadequately protected labor rights, the hasty dismissal means that the mine workers lose not only their jobs but also their medical benefits and retirement pensions. For instance, when one coal company in Jiangxi Province suddenly declared bankruptcy and shut down its mines due to the plummeting coal price in 2013, its 357 workers were dismissed all of a sudden without any compensation. After the laid-off workers angrily protested to the county government and threatened to escalate tension using more radical means, the coal company eventually was pressured to pay 5 million yuan to settle

[2] China Labor Bulletin, 2006. "Youxiao de Gongren Zuzhi: Baozhang Kuanggong Shengming de Biyou Zhilu (Effective Labor Organizations: Necessary Path to Safety Protection of Mine Workers)," March, https://clb.org.hk/sites/default/files/archive/schi/File/No.6%20bloodycoal%28S%29.pdf, accessed on March 9, 2020.

Figure 3.2 A small-scale coal mine in Jiangxi Province
Source: Author's photo
Note: The picture shows the entrance of the coal mine, which also serves as the exit. The carts shown transport the workers as well as coal in and out of the mine.

the dispute, which translates to just above 14,000 yuan per worker on average, much less than the annual wage of a typical mine worker in that year.[3]

Moreover, the salaries of mine workers are hardly commensurable to the harsh and dangerous work conditions and the long work hours in the mines. Although technological improvements and rising safety standards have notably improved the working conditions in Chinese mines, especially into the 2000s, the mine workers who work dozens and even hundreds of meters underground commonly suffer extremely unpleasant working conditions. Even in the relatively modernized mines that meet official safety standards, the mine pits are dark, humid, and full of dusts. The mine workers, all of whom are male, sometimes worked nakedly in order to survive the unbearable heat and humidity. According to my observations at several mining sites (including the one shown in Figure 3.2), when the workers came out of the mines at the end of their work shift, they appeared exhausted and covered by dust all over their body. One can clearly tell from their blackened faces and

[3] Authors' interviews and official documents obtained from Jiangxi Province, June 2014.

hands that the safety requirements to wear dust mask and gloves were ignored when they worked underground. Under such harsh working conditions, it is fairly easy for mine workers to develop respiratory diseases such as pneumoconiosis. Although in recent years the Chinese central government stepped up safety and health regulations in mining industries, back in the 1980s and 1990s, mining companies, especially smaller, privately owned ones, rarely provided relevant equipment to protect workers' health and safety. They also refused to provide regular body checks for their workers, not only to save costs, but also to evade potential allegations and demands for compensation, because without body checks, the workers could hardly identify work-related diseases.[4] Therefore, after years of working in the mines, many mine workers develop various kinds of occupational disease. Sadly, many workers, lacking medical knowledge and awareness, even do not realize the existence of their diseases until late stages.

Even worse, mining is a highly dangerous industry in China, with very high casualty rates when compared internationally. Taking the coal industry for example, according to the Director of the State Administration of Work Safety, the death rate in Chinese coal mines was 2.041 per million ton in 2007, while the death rate was only about 0.5 per million ton in other major coal-producing developing countries such as India, South Africa, and Poland, and the rate was only 0.03–0.05 per million ton in advanced industrial countries such as the United States and Australia.[5] Based on China's national coal mining safety accident reports released by the State Administration of Coal Mine Safety, a total of 23,418 deaths and 2,498 related injuries were recorded between 2001 and 2008. There were multiple likely causes for mining accidents, including mine collapse, machinery malfunctioning, gas outburst, gas explosion, water leakage, fire, etc., among which gas explosion and mine collapse accounted for the majority of deaths (Wang et al., 2011). Coal mining accidents are largely due to the adoption of backward mining technology and the negligence of safety regulations, especially in underground mines. In

[4] Laowu and Jingfei, p. 44.
[5] Guanchazhe, 2014. "Woguo Meikuang Baiwandun Siwanglv Shouci Jiangzhi 0.3 Yixia, Rengshi Meiguo 10 Bei (Coal-Mining Death Rate Dropped Below 0.3 per Million Ton for the First Time, Still Ten times of the Rate in the US)," January 9, www.guancha.cn/indexnews/2014_01_09_198626.shtml, accessed on June 7, 2018.

the early years and even recently in small mines, mining companies used very crude methods to extract coal from underground, and paid inadequate heed to safety issues. For example, to prevent gas explosion, underground tunnels should be equipped with gas detectors, which can send out alarms and shut down mine operation when the gas concentrate exceeds certain level. However, driven by economic interests, mining companies usually manipulated the detectors to minimize their disruption to mining, which put the mine workers in extremely dangerous situations (Laowu & Jingfei, 2011, pp. 135–136). Meanwhile, in order to make more money as well as out of ignorance, mine workers usually acquiesced in such practices. In 2002, the Chinese government passed the first Law on Work Safety and gradually stepped up safety regulations in the mining industry. As a result, the accident and death rates in coal mines started to decline gradually in the following years and reached 0.159 per million ton in 2015.[6] Even so, safety regulations cannot be perfectly enforced. In the words of a mine manager, "if all the safety rules were strictly followed, it would be impossible for our mines to operate at all."[7] Under such conditions and mentality, mining accidents still take place frequently and remain a normality in the mining sector in China.

Overall, the mining industry is an extremely unfair and cruel game. Resource capital, once controlling the mining rights and making the initial investment in the infrastructure and equipment, can make money almost effortlessly, while the labor force has to work for long hours under dismal and dangerous conditions, and their modest wages are hardly commensurate with the high risks of casualties associated with their work. The mine workers unfortunately have to endure such exploitation because they do not have better alternatives. Given the low education level of the mine workers, most of whom have only junior high school degree or below,[8] there is no way for them to land a white-collar job with decent working conditions, let alone well-paid

---

[6] China Baogao, 2017. "2017 Nian Woguo Meitan Hangye Baiwandun Siwanglv Zoushi ji Xiangguan Cuoshi Fenxi (2017 Analysis of the Trend of Death Rate per Million Ton in China's Coal Industry and Relevant Measures)," October 9, http://market.chinabaogao.com/huagong/1092a0362017.html, accessed on February 24, 2021.

[7] Author's interview, Shanxi Province, October 2013.

[8] Guanchazhe, 2014, "Coal-Mining Death Rate Dropped below 0.3 Per Million Ton"; authors' interviews, Shanxi Province, October 2013.

positions in high-tech industries such as IT and finance. However, compared to agricultural, manufacturing, and construction jobs, which are the only job opportunities for poorly educated labor force, mining jobs are perhaps the dream work for many rural residents in China. Nothing can better illustrate the desirability of the mining job than the chilling story recounted by a *mei laoban*: During the high time of the coal industry, a lot of migrant workers traveled from Sichuan Province to seek mining jobs in Shanxi Province, which led to the oversupply of labor. In order to land a job in the fierce competition, some agents represented the Sichuan migrant workers and negotiated with the *mei laoban* by offering a life-and-death contract (*shengsi Zhuang* 生死状), which dictates that after the migrant workers were hired, the mining company did not need to worry about mining-caused injuries. Only if someone died, the company needed to offer some compensation for the deceased worker according to the commonly accepted standard, which was much lower than the cost of medical treatment for a seriously wounded worker (Laowu & Jingfei, 2011, p. 137). There was minimal protection for the safety of migrant workers enduring the dangerous working conditions.

Given the extremely unbalanced distribution of the resource revenue between the resource capital and the labor force, the mining industry is especially prone to labor disputes. According to the CLB "Strike" dataset,[9] a total of 389 labor strikes in mining industries were reported across China between 2011 and 2020.[10] A look at the reported cases reveals that wage arrears, demand for pay increase, demand for compensation, layoff, social insurance and pensions, and work-related disease especially pneumoconiosis have all caused labor disputes in the mining sector, among which wage arrears is by far the most common cause (see Figure 3.3). When the aggrieved workers' demands cannot be met, they may escalate the tension and stage mass protests, which inevitably requires the local government to intervene and mediate the conflicts. For instance, when one coal company in Jiangxi

---

[9] China Labour Bulletin. https://maps.clb.org.hk/, accessed on January 11, 2021.
[10] Because China Labour Bulletin Strike dataset covers the period from 2011 onward, I collect the labor disputes between 2011 and 2020. It is worth noting that the reported labor disputes may be an undercount of actual incidents, because media reports as the primary source of information for China Labour Bulletin may not be able to cover all actual incidents, especially those in remote, rural areas and in earlier years when social media usage was low.

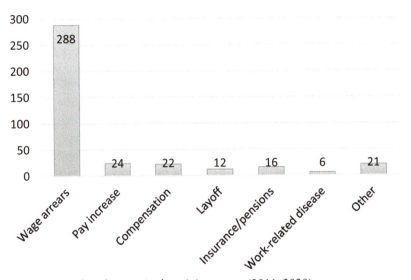

Figure 3.3 Labor disputes in the mining sector (2011–2020)
Source: Figure compiled based on the statistics collected from China Labour Bulletin Strike dataset, https://maps.clb.org.hk/
Note: The vertical axis is the number of incidents. The horizontal axis presents the causes of labor disputes. The number on each column is the number of incidents.

Province suddenly declared bankruptcy and shut down its mines due to the plummeting coal price in 2013, the workers angrily protested to the county government and threatened to use more radical measures if their demands were not satisfied. Eventually, the local government pressured the coal company to pay 5 million yuan to settle the disputes.[11] But not all displaced workers are lucky enough to receive compensation. When mining companies are bankrupted or the bosses run away to evade debts, the local governments have to take up the responsibility of settling the unpaid wages and/or other benefits to avoid the escalation of tension and breakout of mass protests. Therefore, the labor disputes between mine workers and mining companies have become a major source of social instability in mining areas.

---

[11] Authors' interview and official documents obtained from Jiangxi Province, June 2014.

Job Opportunities in the Mining Sector and Beyond

The mining sector as an employer offers very limited job opportunities. The capital-intensive mining industry requires limited labor force in the first place, and the increasing level of mechanization commonly seen in Chinese mines in the past three decades further decreases the demand for labor. Although under the resource boom the national mineral industrial output expanded dramatically from 357.3 billion yuan in 1999 to 2,428 billion yuan in 2017,[12] a nearly sixfold increase, the number of employees in urban mining units only increased slightly between 1999 and 2013, and then declined sharply in the following years (see Figure 3.4).[13] Compared with other industrial sectors, the mining industry accounted for only a small fraction of overall employment in urban units, and its share in total employment shrank continuously, from 4.45% in 2003 to only 2.14% in 2019.

T City in Shanxi Province provides a telling example. It has been a major coal production base since the Maoist era. Under China's resource boom since the beginning of the millennium, its coal, metal, and nonmetal mining industries contributed to increasing shares of the local economy. The share of these industries in total industrial added values of all industries rose from 16.9% in 2002 to 30.3% in 2011 during the golden decade of the mining sector. However, the mining industries created only around 15% of the job opportunities in the secondary sector, and the percentage remained largely stable over the years.[14] Compared to Shanxi, where most of the mines are buried

---

[12] The figures are nominal value. If adjusted by inflation rate (with 1999 as the base year), the constant-price value is 1,645 billion yuan in 2017. Statistics are based on *China Land and Resources Statistical Yearbook 2000–2018 and Statistical Yearbook of China 2018.*

[13] The statistics are based on *China Statistical Yearbook 2004–2020.* It is worth noting that the total and sectoral numbers of employed persons as reported in *China Statistical Yearbook* only include those working in urban units, and thus the numbers of employed persons in the mining sector are smaller than the statistics reported in *China Land and Resources Statistical Yearbooks,* which include employees in all the mining industry. According to the statistics from the *China Land and Resources Statistical Yearbooks,* the number of employees in the mining industries declined continuously, from 10.6 million in 1999 to 4.8 million in 2017. In order to compare the employment in the mining sector with other industrial sectors, I rely on the statistics from *China Statistical Yearbook.*

[14] Calculated according to statistics obtained from T City, Shanxi Province.

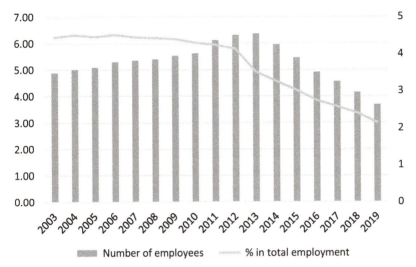

Figure 3.4 Employees in the mining sector (2003–2019)
(Unit: Million Persons/%)

Source: Figure compiled based on the statistics from *Statistical Yearbook of China* 2004–2020

Note: The vertical axis on the left and the columns are the year-end number of employees in the mining sector. The vertical axis on the right and the line are the percentage of the mining sector in total urban employment.

underground, mining in Inner Mongolia Autonomous Region is even more labor-efficient due to the prevalence of opencast mines and higher levels of mechanization. Between 1999 and 2015, the annual mineral industrial output value of Inner Mongolia was more than half the size of Shanxi Province, but the mines in Inner Mongolia employed only less than one-third of workers in Shanxi mines. The average mineral industrial output value per worker was around 194,000 yuan in Shanxi Province, while that in Inner Mongolia was more than 325,000 yuan during this period.[15] This means that mining companies in Inner Mongolia required much less labor force than those in Shanxi Province for the same amount of minerals produced.

In addition to the generally limited supply of job opportunities, the mining sector also tends to be biased against local labor force in its

---

[15] Calculated based on the statistics provided by *Statistical Yearbook of Land and Resource 2000–2016*.

employment. Based on my field observations, mining companies commonly prefer hiring migrant workers over local workers for a number of reasons. First of all, as the economic reforms greatly loosened the state control over cross-regional movement of the Chinese population, the national labor market has gradually developed, and a large number of migrant workers have been moving across China in search of better economic opportunities. Generally speaking, wherever there is an inflow of labor force, migrant workers tend to be cheaper than local workers. Thus, it makes economic sense for mining companies to favor migrant workers. More importantly, mining companies prefer migrant workers because they are more easily managed and disciplined than local residents are. Lacking social connections in the workplace, migrant workers can hardly organize themselves to protect their interests against the employers in time of conflict. By contrast, local residents, who enjoy extensive social connections and can easily mobilize support locally, are more likely to launch collective protests when they encounter labor disputes. For example, workplace injuries and fatalities, which are far from rare in the mining industry, especially in mines of medium and small scales with substandard safety conditions, are a routine cause of disputes and conflicts between the mining companies and their employees. If a nonlocal worker died, the mining company could deal with the worker's family members from far away with more ease, just offering some compensation and sending them off. By contrast, if a local worker died, the extended family members of the deceased worker would normally get involved and demand for compensation collectively. In my interview in Jiangxi Province, the manager of a mining company complained that according to the local custom, the mining company had to host funerals and banquets for three days for extended family members before the negotiation on compensation could start.[16] Therefore, mining companies usually have to offer higher compensations to local workers than to nonlocal ones, especially before the Chinese government stipulated official standards for work-related injuries and deaths (Laowu & Jingfei, 2011, p. 136). Because of these reasons, mining companies in resource-abundant provinces such as Shanxi, Inner Mongolia, and Xinjiang, tend to

---

[16] It is a social norm in many Chinese localities, especially in rural areas, for funerals to host banquets for extended family members, friends, and other guests to moan for the deceased for up to one week.

import workers from populated provinces such as Henan and Sichuan; even mines in less resource-rich provinces such as Jiangxi choose not to hire local residents from the villages and townships where the mines are located, but prefer laborers from other counties.

In view of the scant employment opportunities offered by the mining industry to local citizens, Chinese local governments indeed often encourage or require mining enterprises to create jobs for local communities, and local citizens also put forward such demands to the mining companies as well. Under pressure, mining companies sometimes offer mining-related positions such as property management, environmental recovery, security guard, and other marginal services. Local citizens may also provide catering and transportation services to the mining enterprises. However, these job opportunities are largely limited to the small number of local residents living in close adjacency to the mining sites, and they are often constrained by the lack of necessary skills and start-up funds.

Looking beyond the mining sector, resources can also affect job creation in other sectors. As the Dutch disease theorem argues, resource boom undermines the non-resource sector through the deindustrialization effect (Corden & Neary, 1982). Specifically, the Dutch disease takes effects through two channels: the direct deindustrialization, that is, the movement of labor from the non-resource manufacturing sector to the resource sector, and the indirect deindustrialization, that is, the appreciation of the national currency that further undermines the manufacturing sector (Corden & Neary, 1982). While the second effect necessitates a national setting for currency value change, the first, direct deindustrialization effect can operate on subnational levels. Moreover, because the mining sector lacks beneficial forward and backward linkages with the rest of the economy in terms of division of labor and demand for specialized labor skills (Sachs & Warner, 1995), the skills that mine workers acquire in the mining industry can hardly be applied to other economic sectors. Nor can the labor skills from other industries be transferred into the mining industry. Therefore, the mining sector in general works in isolation from other parts of the economy and does not generate sizable positive spillover effects on labor. Indeed, some Chinese scholars have provided evidence for such deindustrialization effects in selected resource-rich regions in China (Fu & Wang, 2010; Xu & Wang, 2006; Yang et al., 2014). For example, Fu and Wang (2010) find that the resource boom was accompanied by the decrease of personnel in science and technology in resource-rich regions such as Shanxi and Heilongjiang. Another study finds that from the late 1990s till 2008, more than 200,000 technological personnel moved out of Xinjiang, six times the number of technological personnel moving into Xinjiang during the same period. Among Xinjiang's lost talents, 96% held a bachelor's degree or above and 36% were senior researchers (Zhang et al., 2011). In a word, the existing studies pinpoint a direct impact of resource boom on job losses in other, especially high-tech, sectors.

Negative Externalities of Mining Industries

Besides the pure economic effects on labor in terms of job creation, the existence of rich mineral resources and mining industries also exerts far-reaching sociopolitical impacts on local citizens. Mining industries have been found to generate multifaceted negative externalities including social disorder, environmental hazards, and economic disputes, on local citizens in mining areas.

Violence and Social Disorder

One major negative externality is violence and disorder due to the contention for resource control rights. The ferocious fighting over mineral resources poses tangible threat to the social order in mining areas. Since the mid-1980s, the Chinese government's policy of "speeding up the water flow" to encourage private enterprises and individual citizens to explore and utilize the mineral resources has induced a swarm of investors into the mining sector. Many resource-rich regions have experienced enthusiastic and yet chaotic exploration of the mineral resources since the 1990s. In underdeveloped regions with weak rule of law, investors often compete for mining rights by force, which has frequently given rise to armed conflicts between the competitors.[17] For instance, in one major case in 1994, the competition between two investors for a gold mine in Sichuan Province escalated to a violent clash that involved more than 100 people and ended with

---

[17] Hu Jingguo and Tan Jian, 2011. "Heise de Caijue (The Dark Extraction)," *Liaowang*, February 27, http://news.sina.com.cn/c/sd/2011-02-27/ 144022022847.shtml, accessed on March 20, 2020.

dozens of casualties. The case shocked the Chinese government and eventually prompted the revision of the Mineral Resources Law in 1996, which established a relatively institutionalized system for the assignment and transaction of mining rights.[18] Nevertheless, mining companies, especially smaller and privately owned ones, tend to ignore the laws and regulations. For example, despite the legally demarcated boundaries of mining rights on the ground, mining companies can secretly invade into each other's properties underground. Such illegal behaviors continued to arouse conflicts after 1996. Moreover, contention was not limited to mining rights, but extended to the control over mining-related businesses. For instance, the transaction and transportation of mineral products are also lucrative businesses under good market conditions. The competition for the transportation contracts with mining companies or the dealership to sell mineral products often led to violent clashes between companies and social forces including criminal organizations (Liu, 2009).

Armed conflicts broke out not only between competing investors, but also between investors and local citizens on whose land the mineral resources were located. As land is collectively owned in rural China, mining companies have to first obtain the approval from the relevant villages in order to start mineral extraction. However, because of disagreements on land prices and compensation for relocation, environmental damages, etc. as well as other social and cultural reasons, villagers did not always welcome mining activities. When peaceful negotiations failed to resolve the problem, mine investors, driven by economic interests, often forcefully seized control of the mining sites from the villagers. According to the memoir of a coal mine owner, the growth of the mining industry starting in the 1980s was accompanied by incessant clashes between the mining companies and local residents. In a dramatic case, a *mei laoban* waged a bloody assault on a village in order to take over its coal mines, which ended with massive casualties including the village head. Although the *mei laoban* successfully seized the coal mine, constant battles and retaliations dragged on for decades between the two sides. Eventually, the *mei laoban* was fed up with all the painful memories and converted to Buddhism. He kowtowed to

---

[18] Tang Xiaojun and Liang Liang, 2014. "Xiese Huangjin (Bloody Gold)," *Chengdu Shangbao*, July 28, https://e.chengdu.cn/html/2014-07/28/content_481337.htm, accessed on March 20, 2020.

each household in the village and paid back his bloody debts by building schools, clinics, and a temple for the village in the 2000s (Laowu & Jingfei, 2011, p. 54).

The violent contention over mining-related business opportunities seriously undermined public security in mining areas, particularly in remote areas far away from administrative centers. In the absence of effective police force, professional criminal organizations tended to emerge to provide extralegal protection to mining companies. With the resource wealth, these organizations grew rapidly in terms of size and impacts.[19] As the power of the criminal organizations grew, they not only engaged in resource-related armed conflicts, but also threatened the security of the general public (Zhan, 2013).[20] Unfortunately, in many regions, instead of cracking down the organized crime, the local police force and legal apparatus often tolerated and even colluded with the gangsters for economic or other benefits (Zhan, 2017).[21]

Moreover, some Chinese local governments even actively employed extralegal forces to forcefully implement certain policies, especially unpopular ones facing strong resistance from the citizens (Chen, 2017; Ong, 2018). In mining areas, some local governments also hired criminal organizations to coerce local citizens into permitting certain mining companies to operate on the collectively owned village lands. It is worth noting that the criminal organizations did not always use outright violence to achieve their goals. For example, in order to take over the mines in some villages, a local government-hired gangster courteously invited the seniors of the villages to free banquets and chitchatted with them amicably. After days of fete and with the help of some cash, he talked the villagers into a deal. In a sense, the gangsters did all the dirty work for the local governments and mining companies, more effectively than the police force could. For this reason, the local governments sometimes turned a blind eye to the

---

[19] Hu and Tan, 2011, "The Dark Extraction"; Wei Yiping, 2008. "Weng'An Shijian Diaocha: Jingfang yu Heibang Guanxi Miqie cheng Gongkai de Mimi (Investigation of the Weng'An Incident: Close Ties between Police and Gangs are Open Secret)," *Sanlian Life Weekly*, July 10, http://news.sina.com.cn/c/2008-07-10/144915908486.shtml, accessed on March 20, 2020.
[20] Also see Hu and Tan, 2011. "The Dark Extraction."
[21] Also see Wei, 2008, "Investigation of the Weng'An Incident."

existence and operation of the underground forces, as they might come in handy someday.

As a result of the frequent conflicts and presence of mafia-like gangs, public security was a common issue in mining areas, especially those in remote regions and before the Chinese government started to fortify the police force and widely install surveillance systems in the late 2000s. The contention over resource control gives rise to violent conflicts between competing mine investors, local citizens, and sometimes organized criminals on behalf of the mining companies or local governments. The resource-aroused contentions generate tangible negative impacts on local citizens' security and properties, and breed widespread popular grievance, which may trigger popular protests and even riots. For instance, the infamous Weng'an Incident in 2008 as mentioned in the opening chapter, during which more than 20,000 citizens went onto the street and burnt down the CCP county headquarters and local police station, was partly triggered by local citizens' discontents with rampant criminal organizations and chaotic public security status in this phosphorus mining zone (Liu, 2009; Zhan, 2013).

Environmental Hazards

Besides violence and social disorder, another negative externality of the mining industry with more widespread impacts is the environmental hazards, including but not limited to pollution, water shortage, and land subsidence. These environmental hazards impose heavy costs on the health and livelihood of the citizens in surrounding areas, who usually cannot receive proper and timely treatment and compensation. As the tension between the victims and the mining industries accumulates, it easily erupts into popular protests and even riots that target not only the relevant mining companies but also the local governments.

As in other developing countries, extractive industries in China are highly polluting. The extraction of minerals, especially in opencast pits, usually generates dangerous amounts of industrial dust. For a long time in China's mining industry, raw mineral products were stored, processed, and transported in open air, which further exacerbated the dust problem. And the industrial and civilian consumption of minerals, especially coal, created even more far-reaching air pollution. Although in recent years the Chinese central government increasingly strengthened environmental regulation, such as prohibiting outdoor storage of mineral products, and shutting down highly polluting mines and factories, many mining companies continued to operate with substandard environmental protection measures. The coal industry, which is widely distributed across China, was responsible for the air pollution in many regions. The poor air quality of major coal-producing areas seriously threatens the health of citizens working in or living close to the mines and causes different forms and degrees of illness, with pneumoconiosis as the most common disease.

Meanwhile, the extraction and processing of minerals discharge various kinds of toxin. Among the 200 or so types of mineral actively explored in China, many require the use of toxic chemicals in the extraction process. The extraction of rare earth metals, for example, requires complicated procedures to inject hazardous chemicals into the soil in order to separate the minerals. The chemicals can remain in the soil for a long period of time and easily leak into rivers or groundwater nearby. As I observed in a deserted rare earth mining site in Jiangxi Province, the mining activities created patches of barren lands in the otherwise very green area (see Figure 3.5). Even years after the mining

Figure 3.5 Soil pollution due to rare earth mining in Jiangxi Province
Source: author's own photo
Note: The barren areas shown are former rare earth mining spots. As the soil is heavily polluted by the toxic chemicals used during the mining process, no plants or crops can grow on these areas.

activities were halted, these lands stayed desolate, reminding visitors of the unhealable wounds that human beings left on Mother Earth. For decades or even centuries to come, nothing can grow on the soil until the highly toxic chemicals finally clear up. Such soil and water pollution not only undercuts the productivity of agriculture, aquaculture, and animal husbandry around the mining zones, but also causes severe health problems to local residents. Unfortunately, due to the lack of environmental awareness in rural areas, many local residents often underestimate the danger of such invisible hazards and take no caution or action to treat the pollution.

Moreover, the extraction of minerals from underground often drains groundwater or surface water flows, which can lead to water shortage in surrounding areas. This is especially detrimental in the northern parts of China, which suffer severe water shortage chronically. Thus, water shortage is a commonly seen environmental damage to agriculture and water safety in mining areas and has become an unneglectable source of conflicts between the mining industry and citizens in surrounding areas.[22]

Another geological hazard that the mining sector engenders is land subsidence, which is widely seen in mining areas across China and extensively reported by the media. Due to the extraction of large volumes of minerals from underground, the surface of the land may subside gradually or collapse suddenly, causing buildings on the ground to crack or break apart.[23] Land subsidence not only leads to the damages of residential buildings and sometimes causes casualties, but also decreases the arability of the farmland and undermines

---

[22] Yang Congming, 2013. "Qiantan Xibu Diqu Kuangqun Maodun de Chengyin ji Huajie (Analysis of Causes and Resolutions of the Conflicts between Mining Industries and Citizens in Western Areas)," *Newspaper of Guizhou People's Political Consultative Conference*, July 4, www.gzzxb.com/pages/Show.aspx? ID=A6BCBB6C-75A2-4A27-A4AD-5DA445DA7A5F, accessed on August 14, 2014. Zhao Feng, 2014. "Guanzhong Meidu Hancheng Neihong, Kuangqun Zhijian Shenxian Liyi Zhizheng (Hancheng Mired in Conflicts of Interests between Mines and Citizens)," *China Business Journal*, July 14, http://news.cb .com.cn/html/money_10_18921_1.html, accessed on August 14, 2014.

[23] For example, see Liu Yiman, 2009. "Guansu Baiyin Kuangqu Zaoyu Dixian Nanti (Mining Area in Baiyin, Guansu Suffered Land Collapses)," *Liaowang Deongfang Zhoukan*, July 20, http://news.sina.com.cn/c/sd/2009-07-20/ 141718258136.shtml, accessed on March 28, 2021.

agricultural production, which seriously affect the livelihood of the peasants in mining zones and often force them to relocate to other areas.[24]

Finally, road damage is also an environmental hazard that I have observed in different mining areas. As heavily loaded trucks constantly transport mineral products out of the mines, they not only generate enormous air and noise pollution along the way, but also damage the roads connecting mining areas to other regions. The broken roads cause great inconvenience to local residents, such as traffic jams and accidents, but the citizens can hardly receive any compensation from the mining or transportation companies. Some local citizens have thus complained to the local governments or petitioned to upper-level authorities. Unfortunately, the local governments can hardly control these mining or transport companies. Although in recent years the Chinese central government gradually strengthened road safety regulations, local enforcement of the regulations remains a big issue.

Economic Disputes

The damages to the public security, health, livelihood, and properties of the citizens in mining areas have imposed heavy financial and health costs on local residents. However, technically it is difficult to determine the liabilities of the damages, and the mining companies are usually unwilling to claim responsibility. It is therefore very difficult for the victims to receive proper and timely compensations for their losses.[25] In some cases, the mining companies may offer some compensation to placate the aggrieved citizens and avoid trouble. For example, one state-owned coal company in Jiangxi Province, which frequently encounters complaints about its environmental problems, set up a public relations office to specifically deal with the conflicts with local

[24] For example, see Su Xiaozhou, Liang Peng, Yan Guozheng, and Dai Jinsong, 2010. "Caikuang Chenxian Qu Shenyin Lu (Groans of Sinking Mining Areas)," *Liaowang Dongfang Zhoukan*, September 25, https://news.qq.com/a/20100925/001361_1.htm, accessed on March 28, 2021.

[25] Yang, 2013. "Analysis of Causes and Resolutions of the Conflicts between Mining Industries and Citizens in Western Areas"; Zhou Rui and Xiao Konghua, 2014. "Weixin Huajie Shekuang Jiufen Diaoyan Baogao (Report on Resource-related Conflict Resolution in Weixin)," *Yunnan Net*, January 4, http://zhaotong.yunnan.cn/html/2014-01/02/content_3020359.htm, accessed on August 14, 2014.

citizens in the neighboring areas and spent around 10 million yuan per year on compensations. But more often than not, many mining companies pay little heed and minimal compensation to the citizens' complaints, or simply deny any responsibility for the damages they cause. As a result, there are frequent disputes between mining companies and local citizens. For example, one Shanxi village suffered chronic land subsidence and declined agricultural productivity due to coal mining, but the mining company "paid nothing (*sha ye bugei* 啥也不给)" to the villagers despite their repeated attempts to negotiate for compensation. "It did not help even when we played tough (*nao ye meiyou yong* 闹也没有用)," the helpless villagers lamented.[26]

The most common source of economic disputes is land expropriation and compensation. Due to the construction of infrastructure and mining facilities, the operation of mining industry inevitably involves land acquisitions from local communities. Moreover, because the abovementioned environmental damages, including land subsidence, water shortage, and pollution, seriously affect the habitability and arability of the lands in surrounding areas, local citizens often have to be relocated to other areas. For instance, since the discovery and exploration of rich coal mines, one town in Inner Mongolia lost a large part of its farmland and grassland to the coal industry. By 2012, around 50% of its farmers and herdsmen had to be relocated. However, land acquisition is a very thorny issue due to the conflicting interests between the mining companies and the land-losing rural citizens, who are not only losing their living space but also their essential means of production. Therefore, the two parties often get into disputes over the amounts of compensation. However, the conflicting parties can hardly settle their disputes through legal procedures, and more often resort to private negotiations or extralegal means. In case of irresolvable disagreements, forceful demolitions and violent clashes may ensue and sometimes even escalate into large-scale riots. According to some estimates, land- and resources-related social conflicts accounted for above 65% of the eruptive collective incidents in rural China in the 2000s.[27]

Meanwhile, disputes may also arise regarding the financial losses that local residents suffer due to declined agricultural productivity or

[26] Author's interview in Shanxi, June 2016.
[27] Hu and Tan, 2011. "The Dark Exctraction."

job loss. The aforementioned environmental damages such as land subsidence, water shortage, and pollution often lead to the deterioration of the quality of farmland in mining areas, which in consequence reduces agricultural production and the income of the farmers. Even worse, due to the risk of land collapse some farmlands may become too dangerous for farming. Although the affected residents can relocate to a safer zone, they may not be allocated new farmlands due to the collective land ownership by villages and limited land supply in densely populated areas. For these land-losing and job-losing farmers, they can hardly receive sufficient compensation from the mining companies for their unemployment. When they try to apply for jobs in the mines, which appear as the most sensible alternative job opportunity, for reasons discussed earlier, they cannot easily land a job.

Besides conflicts over land and economic income, disputes also frequently erupt between local citizens and the mining industry over property and road damages, health problems due to air, water, or soil pollution, and casualties due to mining accidents, traffic accidents, etc. Local citizens have to constantly bargain with mining companies in order to be compensated for the losses they suffer. Owing to the lack of a well-functioning and trustworthy judicial system in China, it is very difficult, if not impossible, for the citizens to resolve their disputes with the mining companies through legal procedures. Moreover, even if the citizens win the lawsuits, the courts are deemed ineffective in enforcing the court rulings and helping the citizens receive the compensation in a timely fashion. Therefore, the legal channels are often blocked for local citizens as the victims of the resource economy to redress the negative externalities that mining industries impose on them. In addition to the financial costs, the various disputes consume a lot of time and energy for the citizens involved, which are likely to translate into decreased labor income from productive activities.

Impacts of Resources on Labor: Statistical Evidence

The mining sector, through the extraction, processing, and transportation of minerals, has far-reaching economic, social, and environmental impacts on local citizens as the labor force. In spite of the massive inflow of resource revenue, the resource sector creates only limited job opportunities among all industrial sectors. The resource boom may also negatively affect the employment opportunities in other sectors.

Moreover, the mining sector generates various negative externalities on local citizens in the mining areas. The socioeconomic and health costs imposed on local citizens, translated in monetary terms, may outweigh the economic benefits from employment opportunities and make local citizens net losers of the resource economy. To systematically evaluate the overall impacts of the mining industry on labor, this section conducts a series of statistical analysis on Chinese provinces between 1999 and 2017 with two sets of dependent variables: job opportunities and labor income.

Job Opportunities

To examine the effects of resource abundance and dependence on job opportunities for local citizens, I look at the employment statistics in different industrial sectors. Same as in Chapter 2, I include manufacturing and construction, by far the largest two providers of job opportunities among all Chinese industries. I also include IT and finance as two representative high-tech industries.[28] According to the average wage levels reported by the *China Statistical Yearbook*, these two industries also provide the highest-paid jobs in China. As Chapter 2 finds out, resource abundance increases the fixed-asset investment in manufacturing and construction but hurts the fixed-asset investment in IT and finance. Thus, it is worthwhile to investigate what spillover effects resources generate on labor in these industries.

From 1999 to 2017, the total employment in the four industries grew rapidly and continuously in China. Manufacturing remained the largest employer among all the industrial sectors, whose employment rose from 41.6 million to 75.7 million. It is followed by the construction sector, whose employment increased sharply from 8.8 million 42.1 million in 2017. For the high-tech industries, the number of employees

---

[28] I have also examined the industrial sector of scientific research and technological services as a case of the high-tech industry. It exhibits similar patterns as the IT and financial sectors on various dimensions including the impacts of the resource sector. To save space, I do not report on this sector in the data analysis part, but the statistical findings are highly consistent with those regarding the IT and financial sectors and support the general conclusion regarding the impacts of resources on high-tech industries.

in IT increased from 1.17 million in 2003 to 3.95 million in 2017.[29] Employment in finance increased from 3.28 million in 1999 to 8.26 million in 2017. Although growing rapidly, IT and finance still contributed to only 2.2% and 3.9% of total employment in urban units in 2017, respectively. I use the number of employed persons in manufacturing, construction, IT, and finance divided by the total number of population in each province to measure the size of employment in these four industries, respectively.[30] The size of employment in all four industries vary widely across regions.

Same as in Chapter 2, I use the size of resource production and the rate of resource dependence as the key predictors of interest. In addition, I also control for some commonly used socioeconomic variables that may affect the employment opportunities in industrial sectors. First, I include per capita GDP to control for economic development level, which should affect the availability of employment opportunities. As the employment of labor may also affect economic output in a given year, I use the one-year lag of per capita GDP to deal with the endogeneity issue.[31] Second, per capita FDI is included because the inflow of foreign capital may potentially increase the provision of jobs. Third, I include the per capita fixed-asset investment in respective sectors, because the fixed-asset investment is likely to increase job opportunities. Fourth, I control for some demographic variables: Population density, namely the size of population divided by the total territorial area of a region, may affect employment. Due to the notorious urban-rural divide in China, which affects many economic

---

[29] The statistics on the IT sector, including its number of employed persons, first became available in 2003.

[30] The number of employed persons in manufacturing and construction sectors include the total number of employed persons in urban units and employed persons in private enterprises and self-employed individuals in rural areas at year-end. For IT and finance, two mainly urban industries, the number of employed persons includes only employed persons in urban units including state-owned, collective, joint-operation, shareholding, foreign-invested, and Hong Kong, Taiwan, or Macau-invested units at year-end. The limitation of the IT and finance employment data is that they do not include employment in private enterprises and self-employed persons in urban areas or employment in rural areas. As far as I know, both indicators are not reported systematically. Therefore, the data analysis on IT and finance can only speak of the urban areas.

[31] As a robustness check, I also try the current-year per capita GDP and the three-year lag of per capita GDP. The regression results are highly similar with the reported results in all the models.

conditions and decisions, I include the weight of rural population as a control variable. I also control for the proportion of ethnic minorities in total population to compare the situations of Han-dominated regions and ethnic minority regions.

I conduct a series of multivariate panel data analysis on the employment opportunities in manufacturing, construction, IT, and financial sectors separately (see Appendix 3.A for the detailed data analysis). The statistical analysis reveals that mineral resources tend to decrease job opportunities in general. This is not only true for high-tech industries, especially IT, but also for labor-intensive industries. Starting with the labor-intensive industries, both the size of resource production and the rate of resource dependence are negatively correlated with the employment opportunities in manufacturing, and the effects are statistically significant in all but the baseline models. Based on the estimation in Model 4 in Table 3.2 in Appendix 3.A, other things being equal, the most resource-dependent region would create only 44% of the manufacturing jobs per capita in the least resource-dependent region. Resource abundance and dependence have even stronger negative impacts on the employment opportunities in the construction sector. The estimated coefficients are statistically significant and highly robust across models. Based on the estimation in Model 8 in Table 3.2, other things being equal, the most resource-dependent region would create only 25% of the construction jobs in the least resource-dependent region. These findings pose a sharp contrast to what Chapter 2 finds about the beneficial effects of mineral production on capital investment in the manufacturing and construction sectors. It suggests that while resources lead to more investment, it does not necessarily create more job opportunities for the labor force. One possible explanation for the sharp contrast may be that the capital investment in the manufacturing and construction sectors may go into machineries and technologies that serve to cut labor costs, and thus it lowers rather than increases the demand for labor. The contradictory effects of resources on capital versus labor has to be explained more carefully against more empirical data, which is beyond the scope of this research and deserves to be investigated separately.

Unsurprisingly, mineral resources undercut employment opportunities in high-tech industries, especially the IT sector. Both the size of resource production and the rate of resource dependence are negatively correlated with the number of employees in the IT sector, and the estimated coefficients are statistically highly significant and robust across all the models. Based on the estimation of Model 4 in Table 3.3 in Appendix 3.A, other things being equal, the most resource-dependent region would create only 41% of the employment opportunities per capita in the least resource-dependent region. Meanwhile, resource abundance and dependence negatively affect employment opportunities in the financial sector, although the effects are substantially small and statistically insignificant in all the models. Based on the estimation of Model 8 in Table 3.3, other things being equal, the most resource-dependent region would create only 94% of the financial jobs per capita in the least resource-dependent region. The regression results indicate that resources generate substantially more pronounced negative effects on IT than on the financial industry in terms of employment opportunities. But overall, these statistical findings go hand in hand with the discoveries in Chapter 2 and suggest that resource production hampers not only capital investment but also the demand for labor in the high-tech industries, which depicts a rather gloomy future for resource-rich regions because they are likely to be stuck in low-tech, if not entirely resource-related industries and have limited chance for industrial upgrading and transformation.

Labor Income

Because of the infamous urban-rural divide, there exists huge income gap between urban and rural citizens in China. To examine the effects of resource abundance and dependence on labor income more accurately, I look at the annual income levels of urban and rural residents separately. Indeed, income statistics in China are fuzzy. For urban residents, the income level as reflected in official statistics is commonly believed to be an underestimation of the true income level, because there are many types of gray income that cannot be accurately captured by the statistical departments and records, such as the fringe benefits of civil servants, hidden income of private entrepreneurs, and off-payroll income of professionals such as doctors and entertainers, to cite just a few examples. But this study focuses on the wage income of urban laborers, which is relatively reliably captured by the statistical records. Similar problems exist with rural income statistics. Due to the technical difficulties in determining the sources and amounts of income for rural residents, the statistics are at best an estimation, most likely an underestimation, of the true income level in rural areas.

Nevertheless, cross-regional and longitudinal comparison can still yield meaningful information regarding the changes of income levels and their causes. Between 1999 and 2017, the average urban and rural income levels in all Chinese provinces underwent remarkable and continuous growth, although cross-regional discrepancies and urban-rural divide persisted.

Similar to the data analysis in the last section, I include the size of resource production and the rate of resource dependence as the key predictors of interest. And I control for per capita GDP, and such demographic factors as the weight of rural population, the ratio of ethnic minorities, and population density, which are likely to affect urban and rural residents' incomes. I conduct multivariate panel data analysis on the urban and rural annual incomes separately (see detailed data analysis in Appendix 3.A). The statistical results provide clear evidence for the resource sector's negative impacts on urban and rural citizens' incomes. Both resource abundance level and dependence rate are negatively correlated with not only urban but also rural incomes, and the coefficients are statistically highly significant in all the models (see Table 3.4 in Appendix 3.A). The consistent negative correlations reveal that both urban and rural citizens in resource-rich regions suffer lower income levels than their counterparts in other regions without rich natural resources. Based on the estimates in Model 4 and 8 in Table 3.4, other things being equal, urban citizens in the most resource-dependent region would receive only 53% of the income of the urban citizens in the least resource-dependent region, while rural citizens in the most resource-dependent region would receive 55% of the income in the least resource-dependent region. As the estimated coefficients of resource abundance/dependence on urban and rural income levels are of similar magnitudes, meaning that as the size of resource production or resource dependence rate increases, the urban and rural income levels will decrease at more or less the same rate. Therefore, both urban and rural residents suffer from the negative externalities of the resource sector. Mineral resources are indeed a curse to common citizens as the labor force.

Conclusion

Based on qualitative evidence and statistical analysis, this chapter examines the multidimensional impacts of the resource sector on local citizens and reveals a rather disheartening picture about the livelihood of the labor force in resource-rich regions. The findings of Chapters 2 and 3 essentially tell a two-pronged story of the impacts of the resource sector on capital and labor. On the one hand, capital benefits hugely from the resource boom and the inflow of resource wealth. China's resource boom since the turn of the millennium not only breeds an emerging group of resource-based nouveau riches famously known as *kuang laoban* and leads to capital formation in the mining sector, but it also helps boost capital investment in other non-resource industries, especially low-tech ones, which points to a largely beneficial effect of resource wealth on capital. However, labor appears to be the losers in the resource economy. Inside the resource sector, although mining jobs are slightly better paid than some other industries, the wage level barely reflects the many hidden health and safety costs in the profession. Due to weak bargaining power against the resource capital, mine workers commonly suffer inadequate protection of labor rights and frequent labor disputes. Looking beyond the resource sector, local citizens as laborers in resource-rich regions not only face limited and shrinking job opportunities in the mining sector but also suffer the crowding out effects on employment opportunities in other non-resource sectors, including both labor-intensive and high-tech ones. Moreover, mining industries generate various negative externalities that impose heavy socioeconomic and health costs on citizens living in the surrounding areas. All these problems translate into suppressed labor income in resource-rich areas. Therefore, from the labor's point of view, resource abundance is indeed a curse. The sharply contrasting findings of Chapters 2 and 3 reveal a more nuanced picture about the bifurcated effects of natural resources on capital versus labor. A key point we can take away from the constrast is that in order to fully understand what resource endowment means for the soceity, we need to disentangle the divergent impacts on different stakeholders. While rich natural resources may be a blessing to capital, it poses a curse to labor.

The fact that the resource economy favors capital but hurts labor has profound political implications. For one thing, the problem of income inequality due to the capital-labor divide is commonly seen in market economies, of which China is just one case. With China's economic reforms and transition to a market economy, the income gap between different social classes has been widening at alarming rates. China's officially announced Gini index rose from under 0.3 at the beginning of the reform to nearly 0.4 in the late 1990s,[32] and then to 0.49 in 2008.[33] Although the official Gini index showed a declining trend since 2008, scholars widely question the official statistics and believe inequality continued to rise sharply in China (Xie & Zhou, 2014). In resource-abundant regions, the rapid inflow and uneven distribution of massive resource revenue has further exacerbated the situation. As capital is concentrated in the hands of a small group of mining businesspeople, the vast majority of the labor force can hardly benefit from the resource windfalls. The capital-labor divide is especially protruding in resource-rich regions because the polarization emerged and accelerated within a time period of only one to two decades. In some mining areas, the same group of villagers who grew up together and used to be equally poor before the 1990s suddenly went onto divergent paths in the 2000s. While a few became millionaires or even billionaires by investing in mining businesses, the others stayed in poverty, struggling to make their ends meet and begging the rich brothers for jobs. Inequality can hardly be felt more acutely than in these areas.

While some scholars argue that income inequality has been an inactive volcano and has not yet caused major social unrest in China (Whyte, 2010, 2016; Whyte & Im, 2014), in resource-abundant regions, the rising inequality has given rise to a strong sense of relative deprivation and led to the accumulation of popular grievance. The uneven and unfair distribution of resource wealth, which is derived from nominally state-owned mineral resources and extracted from underground the collectively-owned land in Chinese villages, and the negative externalities that mining industries impose on local citizens have triggered frequent and widespread conflicts between mining companies and local citizens (Chen, 2016; Dong, 2016; Zhang, 2008). In lack of an effective and trustworthy judicial system that can resolve the conflicts through legal procedures, the social conflicts often escalate into violent clashes between the two parties. Angry citizens sometimes take radical measures such as blockading and assaulting the mining companies and their staff in order to demand compensation or more

---

[32] National Bureau of Statistics, "Gini Index and the Income Gap in China," www.stats.gov.cn/tjzs/tjsj/tjcb/zggqgl/200210/t20021024_37364.html, accessed on March 10, 2020.

[33] National Bureau of Statistics, "National Average Disposable Income Gini Index 2003–2016," www.stats.gov.cn/ztjc/zdtjgz/yblh/zysj/201710/t20171010_1540710.html, accessed on March 10, 2020.

fair land acquisition deals. The conflicts also prompt aggrieved citizens to launch collective protests to the local governments and petition to upper-level governments, in hope that the higher authorities can pressure the local governments into responding to their requests and helping redress their grievances. As conflicts accumulate between the local citizens and the mining businesses, the local governments are inevitably involved and become an important stakeholder in the power interplay in resource-rich regions.

It is worth noting that there seems not to be a strong class awareness in the contention between labor and capital in resource-rich areas. The citizens advance mostly individual-based instead of class-based claims and demands. Although they often take collective actions and protest in large numbers, the protests center on personal or group interests rather than showing the solidarity of the working class, and they are mainly about economic interests rather than political demands. The lack of class awareness thus makes individualized negotiation and settlement of resource conflicts possible – and even desirable for the involved parties. As the popular saying goes, "people's internal problems should be resolved by the people's money, namely the Chinese currency (*renmin neibu wenti renminbi jiejue* 人民內部问题人民币解决)." The lack of politicized demands such as collective labor rights or legal reforms makes the state more willing to step in, who can employ soft strategies such as payment and redistribution to facilitate the resolution of resource-aroused conflicts but does not have to deal with the daunting challenges of class struggle or regime change.

APPENDIX 3.A Statistical Analysis on the Impacts of Resources on Labor

Statistical Methods and Data

To examine the impacts of mineral resource production on labor, I use two sets of dependent variables: size of employment in four industrial sectors including manufacturing, construction, IT, and finance, and labor income as measured by the urban and rural annual wages. The key explanatory variable includes two indicators: the size of resource production measured by real per capita mineral sales income and the rate of resource dependence measured by the share of industrial output of mineral industries in GDP. Besides, I control for some commonly used socioeconomic variables that may affect the dependent variables, including per capita GDP (for employment opportunities, I use the one-year lag of per capita GDP), per capita FDI, per capita fixed-asset investment in respective sectors, population density, percentage of rural population, and proportion of ethnic minorities in total population.[34] The statistics are collected from *National Land and Resources Statistical Yearbook of China, Statistical Yearbook of China, China Population Statistics Yearbook, China Population and Employment Statistics Yearbook, China's Ethnic Statistical Yearbook,* and *China Data Online.*

To offset the effects of inflation and make the statistics in monetary terms comparable across years, all monetary figures are transformed

---

[34] Admittedly, the abovementioned independent variables may not fully account for the dependent variables. For example, employment opportunities could be affected by other socioeconomic factors such as the characteristics of specific industries, and citizens' incomes may be affected by the education level of local population and economic policies such as taxation, etc. However, the purpose of this research is to assess the impacts of mineral resources on the dependent variables. Assuming that these other variables are unlikely to be correlated with mineral resource extraction, omitting them should not lead to biased estimation of the effects of the key predictors of interest. Therefore, I acknowledge the limitation of this research method and leave it to future research to explain the dependent variables more rigorously.

into real values by dividing the nominal values with regional deflator, which is determined by the annual inflation rates of each province (with 1998 as the base year). The summary statistics of the independent and dependent variables are listed in Table 3.1:

I conduct multivariate panel data analysis on each set of independent variables. To satisfy the normal distribution assumption of the variables, all the highly skewed variables are transformed by taking natural logs in the estimation. Following existing studies with panel data analyses (Arezki & Bruckner, 2011), this study adopts the fixed effects model to control for region-specific effects, such as local geographical, policy, and other factors that may affect economic outcomes, and time-specific effects, such as nationwide economic and monetary policies which potentially affect employment opportunities and citizens' incomes. I use the following formula to conduct the panel data analysis: $Y_{it} = \alpha R_{it} + \beta' X_{it} + \mu_i + \nu_t + \varepsilon_{it}$, where the subscript $i = 1, 2 \ldots, 31$ for the 31 provinces, and $t = 1, 2, \ldots, 19$ for the 19 years from 1999 to 2017. For the data analysis on the spillover effects of resources on job opportunities, there are four different sets of dependent variables Y, namely per capita job opportunities in the industries of manufacturing, construction, IT, and finance, respectively. For the data analysis on the impacts of resources on labor income, there are two sets of dependent variables Y, including real per capita urban income and real per capita rural income. R is the predictor of interest, size of resource production and rate of resource dependence, and X is the set of control variables discussed earlier. The variable μ is the time-invariant and province-specific effect; and ν is the province-invariant and time-specific effect. The error term ε captures the effects of other disturbances on the dependent variable.

For each dependent variable, multiple statistical models are tried out. Following a common practice in existing studies, I use a stepwise regression approach to progressively introduce the independent variables into the models to avoid multicollinearity (Zhang & Brouwer, 2020). The models with different compositions of the independent variables yield largely robust and consistent results regarding the key predictors. Due to the limit of space, only the baseline model with the key predictor of interest and per capita GDP (or its lag)[35] and the

---

[35] Per capita GDP is significantly correlated with the key predictors of interest, and both should affect the dependent variables. To avoid wrongly attributing the effect of per capita GDP on the dependent variables to resource abundance and dependence and leading to biased estimation of their effects, I include per capita GDP in the baseline models.

Table 3.1. *Summary statistics*

Variable	N	Mean	Std. Dev.	Min	Max
Predictor of interest					
Size of resource production (real per capita mineral sales income)	589	1,077.7	1,564.0	2.34	9,209.7
Rate of resource dependence (percentage of mineral industrial output in GDP)	589	6.46	8.48	0.01	94.62
Dependent variable					
Percentage of population working in manufacturing	589	5.18	4.07	0.38	22.95
Percentage of population working in construction	589	1.68	1.37	0.34	8.89
Percentage of population working in IT	465	0.21	0.41	0.03	3.57
Percentage of population working in finance	589	0.38	0.28	0.13	2.51
Real annual urban income	589	14,178	7,453.9	4,486	48,626
Real annual rural income	589	5,263	3,429.9	1,325	20,934
Control variables					
Real per capita GDP	589	24,470	18,726.7	2,528	10,0510
Real per capita GDP (one-year lag)	589	22,540	17,884	2,318	93,845
Real per capita FDI	585	709.3	982.3	0.064	6,533.4
Real per capita fixed-asset investment in manufacturing	496	4,864.9	4,452.9	45.9	21,913.8
Real per capita fixed-asset investment in construction	494	192.5	329.0	1.33	3,051.4
Real per capita fixed-asset investment in IT	465	225.9	182.3	7.31	1,040.8
Real per capita fixed-asset investment in finance	494	40.4	65.4	0.53	1,013.7
Population density	589	408.9	582.9	2.08	3,826.2
Weight of rural population	589	63.93	17.08	11.33	88.51
Ethnic minority ratio	589	12.71	21.43	0	99.99

Source: Authors' calculation based on statistics from *National Land and Resources Statistical Yearbook of China, Statistical Yearbook of China, China Population Statistics Yearbook, China Population and Employment Statistics Yearbook, China's Ethnic Statistical Yearbook,* and *China Data Online.*

comprehensive model that includes the key predictor of interest and all the control variables are presented for each set of dependent variables. To deal with possible heteroscedasticity problem, I conduct Breusch–Pagan test (Wooldridge, 2013) on all the models. As some models do not pass the test at 0.05 level, I report heteroscedasticity-robust statistical results for all the models in Tables 3.2–3.4.[36] Tables 3.2 and 3.3 show the effects of resource production and dependence on employment opportunities in the four selected labor-intensive and high-tech industries, respectively; Table 3.4 shows the overall impacts of resource production and dependence on urban and rural citizens' income levels.

Statistical Findings on the Control Variables

Employment Opportunities

Among the control variables, economic development is the most important determinant for the availability of job opportunities in all the industries. Its estimated coefficients are statistically and substantially significant in all of the models. It is unsurprising that when the economy is going up, there are higher demands for labor force in different industries. The impacts of per capita GDP on employment in all four industrial sectors are of similar magnitudes, slightly larger in the high-tech industries than in the labor-intensive industries. Based on the estimates in Models 4 and 8 in both Tables 3.2 and 3.3, holding other variables constant, when per capita GDP doubles (between 1999 and 2017, real per capita GDP more than quadrupled across China), the job opportunities would increase by 63% in manufacturing, by 33% in construction, by 86% in IT, and 84% in finance. On the other hand, foreign direct investment does not appear to help with job creation. Real per capita FDI is negatively correlated with employment size in all four sectors, although the effects are substantively small and not statistically significant in all models. We may need more empirical data to draw definite conclusions on the effects of FDI on job creation.

As for the demographic factors, the weight of rural population is positively correlated with the employment in manufacturing and

---

[36] I use the generic coeftest function in R to conduct the heteroscedasticity-robust estimation with White's estimator.

Table 3.2. *Impacts of mineral resources on employment in labor-intensive industries*

	Manufacturing				Construction			
	(1)	(2)	(3)	(4)	(5)	(6)	(7)	(8)
Predictor of interest								
Size of resource production (ln)	-0.015	-0.074***			-0.083***	-0.1385***		
	(0.020)	(0.019)			(0.013)	(0.016)		
Rate of resource dependence (ln)			-0.024	-0.086***			-0.085***	-0.147***
			(0.021)	(0.018)			(0.020)	(0.016)
Control variables								
1-year lag of real per capita GDP (ln)	1.009***	0.789***	0.980***	0.706***	0.513***	0.549***	0.429***	0.407***
	(0.031)	(0.048)	(0.041)	(0.044)	(0.031)	(0.057)	(0.041)	(0.063)
Real per capita FDI (ln)		-0.078***		-0.079***		-0.006		-0.005
		(0.015)		(0.015)		(0.024)		(0.024)
Real per capita fixed-asset investment^		0.264***		0.270***		-0.010		-0.007
		(0.012)		(0.012)		(0.008)		(0.008)
Weight of rural population		0.000		0.000		0.002		0.002
		(0.004)		(0.004)		(0.004)		(0.005)
Ethnic minority ratio		-0.006***		-0.006***		-0.004***		-0.004***
		(0.001)		(0.001)		(0.001)		(0.001)
Population density (ln)		0.046***		0.038**		-0.090***		-0.093***
		(0.014)		(0.014)		(0.015)		(0.014)
Region effect	Yes	Yes	Yes	Yes	Yes	Yes	Yes	Yes
Year effect	Yes	Yes	Yes	Yes	Yes	Yes	Yes	Yes
R^2 (within)	0.641	0.794	0.642	0.797	0.429	0.477	0.427	0.477
Degree of freedom	538	440	538	440	538	438	538	438

^Real per capita fixed-asset investment is the investment in manufacturing for Models 1–4 and in construction for Models 5–8. The numbers in the parentheses are heteroscedasticity-robust standard errors. Significance codes: ***$p < 0.001$; **$p < 0.01$; *$p < 0.05$; ·$p < 0.1$.

Table 3.3. *Impacts of mineral resources on employment in high-tech industries*

	IT				Finance			
	(1)	(2)	(3)	(4)	(5)	(6)	(7)	(8)
Predictor of interest								
Size of resource production (ln)	−0.049** (0.015)	−0.081*** (0.020)			0.005 (0.008)	−0.011 (0.007)		
Rate of resource dependence (ln)			−0.054*** (0.015)	−0.093*** (0.019)			0.010 (0.008)	−0.007 (0.009)
Control variables								
1-year lag of real per capita GDP (ln)	0.945*** (0.053)	0.981*** (0.088)	0.890*** (0.055)	0.897*** (0.082)	0.691*** (0.026)	0.891*** (0.035)	0.704*** (0.026)	0.882*** (0.033)
Real per capita FDI (ln)		−0.051* (0.020)		−0.052* (0.021)		−0.060*** (0.011)		−0.006*** (0.001)
Real per capita fixed-asset investment^		0.186*** (0.046)		0.184*** (0.045)		−0.001 (0.015)		−0.000 (0.002)
Weight of rural population		−0.003 (0.004)		−0.003 (0.004)		−0.005. (0.003)		−0.005. (0.003)
Ethnic minority ratio		−0.004*** (0.001)		−0.005*** (0.001)		−0.001 (0.001)		−0.000 (0.001)
Population density (ln)		−0.106*** (0.018)		−0.114*** (0.020)		−0.019 (0.011)		−0.015 (0.011)
Region effect	Yes	Yes	Yes	Yes	Yes	Yes	Yes	Yes
Year effect	Yes	Yes	Yes	Yes	Yes	Yes	Yes	Yes
R^2 (within)	0.542	0.590	0.543	0.593	0.683	0.721	0.684	0.721
Degree of freedom	420	411	420	411	538	438	538	438

^Real per capita fixed-asset investment is the investment in IT for Models 1–4 and in finance for Models 5–8. The numbers in the parentheses are heteroscedasticity-robust standard errors. Significance codes: $*** p < 0.001$; $** p < 0.01$; $* p < 0.05$; $. p < 0.1$.

Table 3.4. *Impacts of mineral resources on labor income*

	Urban income				Rural income			
	(1)	(2)	(3)	(4)	(5)	(6)	(7)	(8)
Predictor of interest								
Resource abundance level (ln)	−0.073*** (0.004)	−0.061*** (0.004)			−0.065*** (0.005)	−0.053*** (0.004)		
Resource dependence rate (ln)			−0.080*** (0.004)	−0.067*** (0.004)			−0.075*** (0.004)	−0.063*** (0.004)
Control variables								
Real per capita GDP (ln)	0.395*** (0.011)	0.372*** (0.008)	0.313*** (0.013)	0.308*** (0.010)	0.649*** (0.013)	0.578*** (0.011)	0.569*** (0.013)	0.517*** (0.011)
Weight of rural population		−0.001 (0.001)		−0.002 (0.001)		0.001 (0.001)		0.000 (0.001)
Ethnic minority ratio		0.001*** (0.000)		0.001*** (0.000)		−0.001* (0.000)		−0.001*** (0.000)
Population density (ln)		0.034*** (0.005)		0.030*** (0.004)		0.039*** (0.0057)		0.033*** (0.005)
Region effect	Yes	Yes	Yes	Yes	Yes	Yes	Yes	Yes
Year effect	Yes	Yes	Yes	Yes	Yes	Yes	Yes	Yes
R^2 (within)	0.862	0.872	0.868	0.876	0.902	0.928	0.910	0.933
Degree of freedom	538	535	538	535	538	535	538	535

The numbers in the parentheses are heteroscedasticity-robust standard errors. Significance codes: ***$p < 0.001$; **$p < 0.01$; *$p < 0.05$; . $p < 0.1$.

111

construction, and negatively correlated with the employment in IT and finance. But the estimated coefficients are substantively small and statistically insignificant in most of the models except those regarding the financial sector. The findings indicate that the existence of larger rural population may facilitate employment in the labor-intensive industries by providing more cheap labor, but it does not help with the high-tech industries. But we need more empirical evidence to ascertain these effects. Meanwhile, ethnic minority ratio appears to be negatively correlated with the employment in all the four industrial sectors. The estimated coefficients are substantively small but statistically significant in all the models except those regarding the financial sector. The findings indicate that ethnic minority regions are slightly disadvantaged in terms of employment opportunities when compared to Han-dominated areas, and this is a common problem across industries. Thus underemployment of ethnic minority groups in modern industrial sectors may be a social issue that the Chinese government needs to address when designing its economic and ethnic policies. Finally, population density is significantly positively correlated with the employment in manufacturing, but negatively correlated with the employment in construction, IT, and finance, which means that employment in manufacturing may benefit from the economy of scale, but the other three industries may be negatively affected by overpopulation given the limited supply of jobs in these industries.

Labor Income

As for labor income, economic development level as measured by real per capita GDP is positively correlated with both urban and rural income levels, and the effect is substantively and statistically highly significant in all the statistical models. Based on the estimates in Models 4 and 8 in Table 3.4, other things being equal, when real per capita GDP doubles, real urban income increases by 24%, and real rural income increases by 43%. It suggests that economic development can boost rural citizens' incomes more notably than urban citizens' incomes.

The demographic factors affect urban and rural incomes in different ways. First, the weight of rural population is negatively correlated with urban income but positively correlated with rural income. But the estimated coefficients are substantially small and statistically insignificant in all the models, so we cannot draw definite conclusion on the effects of urbanization on citizens' income. Second, ethnic minority ratio is positively correlated with urban income but negatively correlated with rural income. The estimated coefficients are statistically significant and consistent across the models. One possible explanation for the opposite effects is that urban citizens in ethnic minority areas may benefit from the Chinese government's favorable policies for the minorities out of concern for national unity and social stability. But the favorable policies do not equally help the rural citizens in minority regions, who commonly suffer the lack of economic opportunities, marginal social status, and dismal geographical conditions in remote areas and as a result tend to receive lower incomes. Finally, population density is highly positively correlated with both urban and rural incomes, and the coefficients are statistically significant and robust in all the models. The findings confirm that the more densely populated regions can benefit from the economy of scale, and citizens in these regions are likely to enjoy more economic opportunities and better-paid jobs. This benefit is true for both urban and rural citizens. This result may have policy implications for poverty alleviation in China and lends support to the Chinese government's policies of relocating the poverty population scattered in remote and hard-to-reach regions to concentrated areas and creating job opportunities for them so as to lift them out of poverty. Such policies make a lot of economic sense, although there are also sociopolitical side effects and new problems, such as how to manage the new communities and resolve the social conflicts among the migrants, which warrant more attention from the policymakers.

4 | *Resources and Local State Capture*[1]

Besides capital and labor, the state is also a major stakeholder in the resource sector. Due to the state ownership of mineral resources in China and the technical features of the mining industries that necessitate regulations on a wide range of issues including environmental management and work safety, the resource sector operates under strong state monitoring and interference in China. Moreover, the various sociopolitical and environmental side effects of the mining industries, including the conflicting interests and contentions between the mining businesses and local citizens inevitably call the state, especially at the local levels, into play in the resource sector. How does the Chinese state interact with the resource capital and labor? This chapter and Chapter 5 bring the state onto the center stage as a key player in the state–capital–labor triad. Through qualitative case studies and statistical analysis, I examine in detail the behaviors of local governments in resource-rich regions and the interplay between the local state and the other two players, capital and labor, respectively.

The State: A Key Player

Comparative studies identify the existence of rentier state, which is defined as a government that receives dominant share of its revenue from resource rents instead of productive revenue, in many resource-rich countries (Mahdavy, 1970). Rentier states are believed to have loose connections with the society. As they rely on resource rents rather than taxation from the general public to finance the operation of the government, rentier states may have little compulsion to respond to the demands of their citizens (Brautigam et al., 2008; Humphreys, 2005),

---

[1] Part of this chapter is an updated revision of the article Zhan, Jing Vivian, "Do Natural Resources Breed Corruption? Evidence from China," *Environmental & Resource Economics* 66 (2017), pp. 237–259.

and they see less need to build socially intrusive and elaborate bureaucracies (Collier & Hoeffler, 2005; Fearon & Laitin, 2003; Ross, 2003).

Although Chinese local governments in resource-rich regions extract considerable fiscal revenues from the mining industries, they deeply penetrate the Chinese economy and society through extensive bureaucratic structure and grassroots organs, which make them fundamentally different from the rentier states in other resource-rich countries. Chinese local governments play significant roles in propelling economic development. Although China is constitutionally a unitary state with the central government dominating the political system, the Chinese economy has been highly decentralized along geographical lines. The decentralized economic structure had long existed under the command economy in the pre-reform era (Qian & Xu, 1993), and the post-Mao reform since the late 1970s further enhanced regional economic autonomy (Shirk, 1993). Chinese local governments enjoy considerable discretion in economic policymaking and benefit directly from local economic and fiscal growth. Meanwhile, under the cadre management system of the Chinese Communist Party-state, local governments and officials are strongly motivated to promote economic development, as it has been by far the most important yardstick for political promotion (Landry, 2008; Li & Zhou, 2005). Therefore, they have both the autonomy and the incentive to make growth-promoting policies in accordance with local conditions. Indeed, Chinese local governments are widely regarded as the locomotive of China's economic development, and their policy innovations have played indispensable roles in China's remarkable growth in the past four decades or so (Ang, 2016).

Besides propelling economic growth, Chinese local governments are major providers of a wide array of public goods. Since the 1994 tax reform that for the first time delineated and institutionalized the central versus local fiscal revenues and expenditures, the Chinese central government has claimed nearly half of the national fiscal revenue, while Chinese local governments have been responsible for more than 80% of the national budgetary expenditure. Except foreign affairs, which is almost entirely the responsibility of the national government, the local governments shoulder the expenditures of all other public services including even national defense, and they cover the vast majority of public services such as infrastructural construction, education, health care, social welfare, and public security. For instance, in 2017, a typical year during the period under this study, Chinese local governments, including provincial and subprovinical governments, shouldered 83.1% of the national expenditure on public security, 94.9% on education, 99.3% on medical care, and 95.9% on social security and employment.[2] Under such highly decentralized fiscal expenditure system in China, the local governments shoulder enormous responsibility of meeting citizens' needs for various public goods.

In sharp contrast to rentier states, which are believed to have weak connection with the citizenry, Chinese local governments are deeply entrenched in the society. Although China has notably moved away from a totalitarian state during the Maoist era that tightly controlled almost every aspect of the society, the Communist Party-state, especially at the grassroots level, still exerts considerable influence on the society, including the business sector and common citizens, in various ways. In the face of the business sector, which enjoys growing significance in the economy and increasing power during the reform era, the Chinese state not only maintains control over it but has forged strong partnership with the business players to push forward China's economic growth, which is generally referred to as local state corporatism (Oi, 1992; Unger & Chan, 1995). Local governments and their administrative departments maintain constant and close ties with big and small enterprises under the state ownership, collective ownership, private ownership, foreign investment, etc., through such channels as regulation and taxation. Especially since the early 2000s, the CCP has actively co-opted successful entrepreneurs into the party, such deliberative institutions as the National People's Congress (NPC) and the Chinese People's Political Consultative Conference (CPPCC), and grassroots public agencies (Dickson & Chen, 2010; Huang, 2014; Huang & Chen, 2020; Zhang, 2015). In addition, the CCP has paid special attention to setting up CCP branches in sizable companies, including private and foreign-invested ones, as an extra way to exert control over the business sector (Feng, 2004). The state can hand out favorable policy treatments as well as business opportunities to co-opted enterprises in exchange for the latter's cooperation on various issues (Breslin, 2012). At the same time, the state is also susceptible to business lobbying and influence on a wide variety of policy issues

---

[2] Calculated based on the statistics from *Finance Yearbook of China 2018*.

(Guthrie, 1998; Huang & Chen, 2020; Kennedy, 2005; Parris, 1995; Schubert & Heberer, 2017; Yu, 2006).

Meanwhile, partly as a legacy of the CCP's mass line (*qunzhong luxian* 群众路线), the party-state still strives to maintain close and frequent contact with the citizens. Although there lack formal channels of political participation such as elections and voting as in democracies, the petitioning system (*xinfang zhidu* 信访制度) that allows citizens to register their complaints about all kinds of socioeconomic problems to different government departments provides an alternative way for the Chinese state to collect political inputs from the citizens and prevent itself from losing touch with the society. Besides petitioning (*shangfang* 上访), the Chinese state has also devised a cadre-visiting system (*xiafang* 下访) that sends down CCP cadres, including county and township officials, to frequently visit local communities and citizens under their jurisdictions and/or to be stationed in rural households, during which the local officials are required to socialize with rural citizens and try to address the issues they may raise. Such visiting system allows grassroots officials to cultivate personal connections with local citizens and gain their trust, which may become useful tools for policy implementation and persuasion. In a society where social network and personal favors are highly valued (Yang, 1994), the personal ties are instrumental for extending the state reach into the society.

Symbiotic Relationship between Local State and Resource Capital

Under such circumstances, the Chinese state, especially local state, forges reciprocal patron–client ties with business elites and collaborate with them on multiple fronts, which some scholars refer to as socialist corporatism (Pearson, 1997) or symbiotic clientelism (Wank, 1999). This is especially true in resource-rich regions, where the local state and mining businesses are entangled in a symbiotic relationship with mutual benefits. On the one hand, the local governments heavily rely on mining industries for economic growth and fiscal income. In terms of fiscal revenue, natural resources contribute to both central and local treasuries through taxation and nontax exactions in China. In general, mining enterprises pay VAT and income tax, which are shared between the central and local governments at certain rates;[3] and they also pay business tax, resource tax,[4] and other local taxes that exclusively go to local treasuries. Besides tax revenues, local governments in resource-rich regions levy a large variety of nontax charges on the resource sector. For example, Shanxi Province collects from the coal industry various kinds of fee, such as Coal Sustainable Development Fund (*meitan kechixu fazhan jijin* 煤炭可持续发展基金), Enterprise Transformation Fund (*qiye zhuanchan jin* 企业转产金), and Environmental Protection Deposit Fund (*huanjing baohu baozheng jin* 环境保护保证金), which are all local revenues and not shared by the center. These resource-based tax and nontax revenues provide major income sources for resource-rich Chinese localities. For example, according to my interviews, around 60% of the fiscal revenue of Shanxi Province in 2012 came from the coal industry alone. As another example of coal-rich region, X City in Henan Province derived between 60% and 80% of its fiscal revenue from the coal industry in the good years. Although the Chinese central government does not rely on mineral resources for fiscal income as heavily as other resource-dependent MENA countries, resource rents do constitute significant sources of fiscal revenue for many resource-rich Chinese local governments.

Under the top-down cadre management system that heavily emphasizes on economic and fiscal growth as hard indicators to evaluate cadre performance (Landry, 2008; Li & Zhou, 2005), the local governments in resource-rich regions zealously promote the development of mining industries. For example, in order to facilitate the setup of mining sites, local governments would help mining companies acquire lands from local residents. Land acquisition is a tricky issue and often arouses conflicts between the residents and the acquiring companies due to disagreements on prices, compensation packages, and relocation plans. Some local governments actively played the role of middlemen and used their administrative and coercive power to take lands from the citizens, saving the mining companies a lot of hassle (Zhan &

---

[3] The VAT is shared between the central and local governments at a rate of 75:25. Income tax is shared between the central and local governments at a rate of 60:40. The locally shared taxes are further divided between the provincial, prefecture, county, and township governments according to locally determined formula.

[4] Most types of the resource tax go to local coffers, but the resource tax on offshore petroleum is collected by the central government.

Zeng, 2017). And local governments and officials also invested heavily in the operation of mining companies. Before the Chinese central government formally banned public officials from involving in mining businesses, many local officials and their family members used to be involved in mining companies as the owners or shareholders, reaping a lot of profits. Chinese local governments and officials have huge stakes and incentives, on both organizational and personal levels, to foster prosperous mining industries.

On the other hand, mining businesses are strongly motivated to establish friendly relationship with the local governments. First of all, the Chinese state monopolizes the ownership of resources and allocation of mining rights. The Mineral Resources Law stipulates that the state has ownership over all mineral resources in China, regardless of the ownership or user rights of the land to which the resources are attached, and that the exploration of mineral resources must be authorized by either the State Council or provincial-level governments. In practice, the authority to allocate the prospecting and mining rights (*tankuang caikuang quan* 探矿采矿权) is delegated to local departments of land and resources at county level and above, as the agents of the central and provincial governments. Meanwhile, mining industries in China are subject to extensive administrative surveillance on an array of issues, such as taxation, safety and environmental protection, and by a large number of government departments, including the Department of Land and Resources, the Department of Work Safety, Bureau of Coal (specifically for the coal industry), Department of Environmental Protection, Administration for Industry and Commerce, Bureaus of National Tax and Local Tax, etc. As a result, mining enterprises operate under extensive state control and intervention in China, and they have practical needs to cooperate with local governments and officials so as to minimize administrative disruption to their operation and to lobby for favorable policies that can enhance their profitability.

Collusion and Corruption in the Resource Sector

Under such symbiotic relationship and closely knitted interests between local governments and resource interests, there arises ample space for corruption by local officials in resource-rich regions. Noting the socially and culturally sensitive definitions of corruption, I follow the widely adopted definition of corruption as the behavior that deviates from the formal duties of a public role because of private-regarding gains (Nye, 1967), which is largely consistent with the legal definition of corruption by state employees (*zhiwu fanzui* 职务犯罪) in the Chinese Criminal Law (the 1997 version). Corruption in China consists of a series of offenses, among which the most common types include embezzlement (*tanwu* 贪污), bribery (*huilu* 贿赂), misappropriation (*nuoyong gongkuan* 挪用公款), collective embezzlement (*jiti sifen* 集体私分), holding huge property with unidentified sources (*ju'e caichan laiyuan buming* 巨额财产来源不明), misuse of authority (*lanyong zhiquan* 滥用职权), dereliction of duty (*wanhu zhishou* 玩忽职守), and fraud (*xunsi wubi* 徇私舞弊), with embezzlement and bribery as by far the largest two categories since 1998.[5]

Since its market reforms started in the late 1970s, China has experienced rampant corruption (Sun, 2004; Wedeman, 2012). Although China's political and economic institutions such as the one-party rule, the imperfect legal system, and the state-led market economy are believed to be the root of the widespread corruption in China, resource boom exacerbates the structural problems and makes resource-rich regions and the resource sector particularly prone to corruption. For instance, the mining sector is found to be one of the most corrupt sectors in China in terms of "tributes" paid to government officials (Zhu & Wu, 2014). The high-profile anti-corruption campaign under Xi Jinping further testifies the higher tendency of corruption in resource-rich regions. The coal-rich Shanxi Province stood out as a striking case. In 2014 alone, a total of 15,450 Shanxi officials were disciplined, including 5 out of the 13 provincial Communist Party standing committee members (the top provincial leaders), 45 prefecture-level officials, and 545 county-level officials. In addition, a large number of leading cadres in administrative departments such as land and resources, environmental protection, transportation, coal industry, and geological inspection were investigated for corruption.[6]

The high corruption rates in resource-rich regions in China echo what existing literature has found in other resource-rich countries.

[5] According to the statistics reported in the *Procuratorial Yearbook of China* 1998–2016.
[6] Zhou Qunfeng, 2015. "Shanxi Guanchang 'Zhenhou Chongjian' ('Post-quake Reconstruction' of Shanxi Officialdom)," *Zhongguo Xinwen Zhoukan (China Newsweek)*, August 4, www.banyuetan.org/chcontent/zx/mtzd/201587/145693 .shtml, accessed on March 11, 2021.

A burgeoning literature argues that resource abundance weakens political institutions and fosters corruption (Bulte et al., 2005; Kolstad & Søreide, 2009; Leite & Weidmann, 1999; Robinson et al., 2006). First of all, the presence of large resource windfalls creates enormous economic opportunities as well as temptations for corrupt behaviors by government officials (Caselli & Michaels, 2013; Franke et al., 2009; Karl, 1997; Leite & Weidmann, 1999). Additionally, due to the high volatility of resource markets (van der Ploeg & Poelhekke, 2010), resource revenues tend to overwhelm the normal budgeting process and lead to more corruption in the government (Ross, 2003). The abuse of resource rents by public officials is particularly facilitated by state ownership of resource sectors, as it simply puts more windfalls in the hands of government officials and creates more room for corruption (Luong & Weinthal, 2010; Ross, 1999). Politically, the competition for political positions and patronage in resource-rich regions provides added sources of corruption. As the bulk of resource rents are dispensed by bureaucrats, who mostly come from dominant political groups (Mbaku, 1992), resource discoveries or booms enhance the value of being in power, and thus there comes intense competition for access to powerful political positions. In the absence of good quality democratic institutions with open and fair elections, this fierce competition gives rise to political corruption in such forms as vote buying in elections and patronage networks, which can help political elites to come into office or stay in power (Caselli & Cunningham, 2009; Franke et al., 2009; Kolstad & Søreide, 2009; Vicente, 2010).

Drawing from my field research and collection of resource-related corruption cases exposed in the media, internal government reports, and scholarly works, I identify a variety of channels through which mineral resources induce corruption in China, among which the collusion between local state employees and resource capital appears to be a major driver for corruption in resource-rich regions. First of all, similar to many resource-rich developing countries with imperfect or missing markets for resource rents and ill-defined property rights over resources (Gylfason, 2001b), the Chinese state's monopoly on the ownership of resources and allocation of mining rights creates an avenue for corruption in the resource sector. As mentioned earlier, Chinese local governments are entrusted with enormous power to allocate the prospecting and mining rights. The prospecting and mining rights can be released through either approval of applications

or public bidding (*zhaobiao* 招标), auction (*paimai* 拍卖)and listing
(*guapai* 挂拍), which are all subject to manipulation behind closed
doors. Moreover, without an effective secondary market for the transaction of mining rights in China, local governments interfere in the
transaction of mines with a heavy hand. Local officials can illicitly issue
mining permits to favored companies or turn a blind eye to mines
operating without permit in exchange for bribes (Discipline
Inspection Commission of Jiangxi Province, 2010). For example, by
bribing local officials including the party secretary of Yunnan
Province, a private company paid merely 496 million yuan to obtain
60% of the shares of a lead and zinc mine with an estimated value of
over 100 billion yuan.[7] Moreover, some local officials offered favorable treatments or protection for mining companies. In return, they or
their relatives and associates were offered shares in these mining companies.[8] Although the Chinese central government prohibited state
employees from engaging in mining businesses starting in 2005, this
policy drove such practices underground, and many local officials
continued to hold shares of mining companies (Dong, 2016; Tan &
Hu, 2011). Furthermore, since the mid-2000s, some resource-rich
regions adopted a new policy to consolidate mineral exploration by
encouraging acquisition and merging of small mines by larger companies, which created added opportunities for corruption. As a major
corruption case in 2018 reveals, a former city mayor in Shanxi assisted
some companies in the acquisition process, and in return he received
bribes totaling 1.04 billion yuan.[9]

Second, under the extensive administrative surveillance over mining
industries, collusion abounds between administrative departments and
the mining companies they regulate. For example, as prerequisites for

[7] Xinhua Net, 2017. "Hongda Suochi Jinding Xinye 60% Guquan Beipan Wuxiao
(60% Share of Jinding Xinye Held by Hongda Invalidated)," October 10, www
.xinhuanet.com//fortune/2017-10/10/c_1121777475.htm, accessed on January
17, 2020.
[8] Wang Xin. 2014. "Meiye Xunzu Toushi (Rent Seeking in the Coal Industry),"
Time Weekly, May 22, www.time-weekly.com/html/20140522/24847_1.html,
accessed on March 20, 2020.
[9] Xinhua, 2018. "Zhang Zhongsheng Shouhui, Ju'e Caichan Laiyuan Buming An
Zai Linfen Zhongyuan Yishen Xuanpan (Linfen Intermediate Court Judged
Zhang Zhongsheng's Case of Bribery and Holding Huge Property with
Unidentified Sources)," March 28, www.xinhuanet.com/legal/2018-03/28/c_
1122602385.htm, accessed on January 18, 2020.

registration and operation, some localities required coal mining companies to apply for multiple permits from regulatory bodies including the Department of Land and Resources, Department of Coal Mine Safety, Bureau of Coal Industry, Administration for Industry and Commerce, etc. As the protracted application process could delay coal production by seven to eight months, the heavy costs strongly motivated mining companies to bribe the officials in charge to speed up the application process (Tan & Hu, 2011). Understanding the need to keep good relations with their regulators, some mining companies I interviewed in Shanxi Province would voluntarily pay tributes to the officials in various government departments simply to build up ties and secure protection from these officials to preempt trouble in the future. The work safety department, which enforces safety standards in mining industries, is particularly prone to corruption. In return for tributes, the officials may turn a blind eye to the dangerous working conditions and help underreport or even cover-up deadly accidents (Discipline Inspection Commission of Jiangxi Province, 2010; Jiang, 2016; Wang, 2007). According to an official in the Administration of Work Safety in Shanxi Province, "behind almost every fatal mining accident, there must be some officials who have taken bribes and neglected their official duties."[10]

Third, the Chinese state's interference in the mineral market creates added channels of rent seeking. The central economic planning agency, the National Development and Reform Commission (NDRC), macro manages the markets and prices of strategic mineral products such as oil and rare earth. Although NDRC allowed the market to set coal prices starting in 2001, it has frequently intervened in the market by imposing administrative hurdles such as permissions for transaction and transportation of coal products (Chen & Wang, 2006; Wang, 2014). For example, the prices of thermal coal supplied to power plants were artificially set below market rates, with substantial price gaps ranging from 100 to 400 yuan/ton between 2005 and 2012.[11]

---

[10] Author's interview in Shanxi Province, October 2013.
[11] Thermal coal prices fluctuated between 400 and 1,000 yuan/ton between 2005 and 2012, according to Sina Finance 2013, "Jinnianlai Woguo Donglimei Jiage Bianhua Qingkuang (Thermal Coal Price Changes in China in Recent Years)," September 23, http://finance.sina.com.cn/money/future/futuresroll/20130923/110216822551.shtml, accessed on March 20, 2020. The exchange rate of Chinese yuan to US dollar fluctuated around 6.2:1 during this period.

The price differentials greatly encouraged the profiteering of thermal coal. Such administrative meddling in the mineral market thus opened up substantial opportunities for corruption. In 2014 alone, 11 officials in NDRC were convicted of corruption, including a deputy director of the coal department, in whose apartment the prosecutors discovered more than 200 million yuan in cash.[12]

Fourth, corruption also arises in the fiscal and non-fiscal government departments managing resource revenues. China's decentralized taxation system diffuses considerable fiscal power into non-fiscal departments and seriously undermines local fiscal discipline (Zhan, 2009). In addition to paying taxes to national and local tax bureaus, mining enterprises in China must pay various nontax fees to local tax bureaus as well as other non-fiscal departments, who enjoy great autonomy in deciding the kinds and rates of the charges. For example, as China's taxation system only sets up rough ranges of resource tax rates for different types and grades of minerals, local authorities have substantial discretion in determining the rates of taxes and nontax charges case by case according to the type and quality of mines, quantity of resource reserves, mining conditions, and various other geographic, economic, and technical factors. Such a crude and decentralized taxation system greatly encouraged fiscal indiscipline and manipulation of tax collection by local officials (Jiang, 2016, pp. 36–38). In a detected case of tax evasion, a private coal company run by the head of a county coal bureau in Shanxi Province evaded taxes amounting to 18.71 million yuan between 2002 and 2008, which was equivalent to 82% of the total taxes it should have paid (Dong, 2016, pp. 222–223). Moreover, as in other resource-rich countries where the volume and volatility of resource revenues overwhelm the normal budgeting process and breed mismanagement (van der Ploeg & Poelhekke, 2010; Ross, 2003), the large amounts of resource-generated fiscal revenues, through dispersed collection and management by multiple government departments, fosters embezzlement, misappropriation, and squandering by officials individually or collectively (Liu, 2014; Tan & Hu, 2011).

---

[12] Supreme People's Procuratorate, 2014. "Meitansi Fusizhang Wei Pengyuan Jiazhong Souchu 2 Yi Yuan (200 Million Yuan Found in Home of Deputy Director of Coal Department Wei Pengyuan)," *Sina News*, October 31, http://news.sina.com.cn/c/2014-10-31/104831074959.shtml, accessed on March 20, 2020.

Fifth, resource rents not only foster corrupt transactions between mining companies and local government officials, but also intensify political corruption. Similar to some other resource-rich countries (Caselli & Cunningham, 2009; Vicente, 2010), the huge windfalls in resource-rich Chinese localities greatly enhance the value of official positions, and the fierce competition for these positions induces serious political corruption. Without open and fair elections or transparent appointment systems, the allocation of official positions is often controlled by the party secretaries in government branches, especially at the grassroots level (Ren & Du, 2008). Facing a swarm of subordinates eying the lucrative official positions, top officials are strongly tempted to make promotion decisions in exchange for bribes and/or sexual favors. For example, in one copper-rich city of Jiangxi Province, four city party secretaries in a row since the late 1990s have been convicted of corruption, with a common charge of public office selling. Even the Communist Party secretary of Jiangxi Province from 2007 to 2013 was accused of being involved in office selling in southern Jiangxi that hosts rich rare earth reserves (Cai, 2014). As the offices for sale usually carry hefty price tags that officials' salaries can hardly afford, *kuang laoban* often provide crucial financial support to selected officials, in hope that their sponsorship will be paid back in the form of more policy benefits or political protection once the sponsored official gets promoted. As President Xi Jinping's anti-corruption campaign uncovered in Shanxi Province, there existed extensive network and collusion between mining businesspeople and local officials, which heavily influenced cadre appointments in some localities since the resource boom started in the early 2000s (Jiang, 2016, pp. 135–136).[13] Similarly, after a thorough investigation of the coal mining industry throughout the period of 2000–2020, Inner Mongolia revealed more than 100 political corruption cases in which local officials utilized the tributes from the coal industry to build up ties with higher-level authorities (*da tianxian* 搭天线).[14] Therefore, resource

---

[13] Sina Finance, "Shanxi Heijin: Meilaoban Bang Guanyuan Maiguan, Guanyuan Bang Pingshi (Black Gold in Shanxi: Coal Mine Bosses Help Officials Buy Offices, Officials Help Settle Troubles in Return)," September 1, 2014, http://finance.sina.com.cn/china/20140901/023920173721.shtml, accessed on January 19, 2020.

[14] Guo Xing, 2021, "Neimonggu Tiewan Zhengzhi Shemei Fubai, Chuli Chufen 14000 Yu Ren (Inner Mongolia Cracks Down Coal-related Corruption with An Iron Hand, Disciplining over 1400 Officials)," Central Commission for

rents not only corrupt the administrative and fiscal departments, but also contaminate the personnel management system, which is core to the CCP's grip on the political regime.

Last but not least, mineral resources often attract organized crimes. Although mines of sizable magnitudes and controlled by central SOEs tend to be better safeguarded from criminal seizures, those dispersed, smaller reserves, especially in remote areas far from political centers, often invite violent contention over resource control as discussed in Chapter 3. In the absence of effective law enforcement, criminal organizations have emerged to forcefully seize mines and monopolize the processing and transportation of mineral products (Fan et al., 2013; Zhan, 2013). Ironically, criminal organizations often collude with local police force and judicial departments, who can provide political protection for them in return for direct or indirect sharing of the resource wealth (Zhan, 2013).[15] Thus, the capture of the law enforcement departments by resource interests composes an unneglectable form of corruption in resource-rich regions.

Resources and Corruption: Statistical Evidence

The empirical observations reveal the ample opportunities for resource-related corruption in the administrative, fiscal, personnel, and law enforcement apparatuses in the Chinese political system. Does it mean resource-rich regions are more likely to suffer corruption than other regions? This question still awaits a clear answer, given that cross-national statistical studies have so far yielded inconsistent findings on the relations between natural resources and corruption (Ades & Di Tella, 1999; Arezki & Bruckner, 2011; Bhattacharyya & Hodler, 2010; Bulte et al., 2005; Isham et al., 2005; Leite & Weidmann, 1999; Norman, 2009; Petermann et al., 2007; Treisman, 2000). This section statistically examines the effects of resource abundance on the occurrence of corruption in the Chinese context and aims to shed some new light on the important question.

Discipline Inspection, March 6, www.ccdi.gov.cn/yaowen/202103/t20210306_237234_m.html, accessed on March 7, 2021.

[15] Also see Wei, 2008, "Investigation of the Weng'An Incident"; Xi Zhigang, 2014, "Baiyun: Huoqi Yangquan (Yangquan the Source of Trouble for Baiyun)," *Zhongguo Xinwen Zhoukan (China Newsweek)*, September 11, 676, http://news.inewsweek.cn/detail-911.html, accessed on December 27, 2014.

Because of its secretive nature, corruption is notoriously difficult to measure and systematic statistics on corruption difficult to collect. Scholars and policy analysts have devised different strategies to circumvent these problems. One widely adopted measure of corruption, as seen in many cross-national statistical studies, is the perceived level of corruption based on opinion surveys, such as the International Country Risk Guide, Economist Intelligence Unit's corruption indices, and most famously, Transparency International's Corruption Perception Index. However, perceived level of corruption does not necessarily reflect the level of corruption that actually takes place. The measures of perceived rather than actual corruption may lead to inaccurate assessment of the impacts of resource dependence, because as Treisman (2007) points out, while perceived corruption correlates with fuel exports, statistical analysis has found little relationship between fuel and actual corruption experiences. In this research, I take an alternative approach and use the detected corruption cases to measure the degree of corruption in Chinese provinces. Despite the lack of transparency in the political system, the Chinese procuratorate, the primary state agency in charge of corruption investigation, prevention, and prosecution, reports the number of filed and investigated (*li'an zhencha* 立案侦查) corruption cases by state employees, which include not only government officials but also the employees of SOEs and state-sponsored social organizations, in most of the provinces for almost every year from 1998 till 2018.[16] The relatively complete and time-consistent statistics of corruption provide a rare and valuable opportunity for the study of corruption in China.[17]

---

[16] The numbers are reported in the annual work reports of provincial people's procuratorate. Data of filed and investigated corruption cases are available from as early as 1986. However, the revision of the Criminal Law in 1997 changed the definition of corruption, making the statistics before and after 1998 not comparable. In 2018, the procuratorial anti-corruption agencies were separated from the procuratorial system and merged with the CCP's Discipline Inspection Commission into a new Supervisory Commission. After that many of the provincial people's procuratorates stopped publicizing the number of filed and investigated corruption cases.

[17] Filed and investigated corruption cases reported by each provincial procuratorial work report are mostly local corruption cases within provincial jurisdiction. Some cases involving centrally managed cadres (*zhongguan ganbu* 中管干部), which include top central and provincial-level officials and top managerial personnel in central SOEs, are prosecuted in designated provinces (usually in provinces different from where the cases took place following the rule

Admittedly, the number of filed and investigated cases is an imperfect measure of actual corruption, because not all corruption cases can be captured by the procuratorial system, and for various, particularly political reasons, not all captured corruption cases are filed and investigated by the procuratorate.[18] The number of filed and investigated cases, as revealed corruption, is only a fraction of all corruption cases, and using it as the dependent variable can lead to an underestimation of the effects of the independent variables. Nevertheless, this measurement can still serve our purpose if the data analyses can substantiate the effects of resources on revealed corruption, on the premise that resources do not systematically increase the detection rate, an important condition that will be examined in detail later in this section. Therefore, I adopt the number of corrupt officials filed and investigated by the procuratorate divided by the total population in a province as a measure of corruption rate, expressed as a rate per million people.[19]

of avoidance), which may be counted toward the provincially reported number of cases. Such cases take up a very small fraction of all reported corruption cases. For example, according to the Supreme People's Procuratorial work report, the total number of investigated officials was 25,4419 between 2012 and 2017, while according to the official report of the Central Discipline Inspection Commission of the CCP, a total of 440 centrally managed cadres were investigated for the same period (www.xinhuanet.com/legal/2017-10/19/c_1121825888.htm), less than 0.2% of all corruption cases in China. Given the small percentage of such cases, their inclusion or omission in the provincial data should not seriously affect the validity of the findings.

[18] Under the Chinese legal system, when a suspected corruption case is reported, the procuratorate conducts an initial review and decides whether to accept it (*shou'an* 受案). Upon acceptance and after some preliminary investigation, the procuratorate files a formal charge and investigates the case (*li'an zhencha* 立案侦察). At the conclusion of the formal investigation, the accused may be referred to the court for prosecution (*tiqi gongsu* 提起公诉) or be exempted. Only some of the accepted cases are filed and investigated, and not all filed and investigated cases are recommended for prosecution, although the second ratio seems to be rising, according to some provincial procuratorial work reports.

[19] In some years (especially before 2003), some provinces did not report the number of corrupt officials filed and investigated, but only reported the number of filed and investigated corruption cases. For these province-years, I estimate the missing number of corrupt officials by first calculating national ratio of corrupt officials to corruption cases in that year and then multiplying it with the reported case number in the province. I also check the estimations with the reported official numbers of the same province in the years before and after and find that the estimated numbers are mostly of similar magnitude with adjacent years and fall around the trend line of the province concerned.

Resource abundance   **Resource dependence**

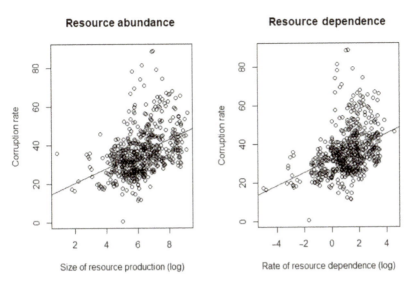

Figure 4.1 Mineral resources and corruption rate (1999–2017)

Note: Figures compiled based on statistics from *China Land and Resources Statistical Yearbook 2000–2018, Procuratorial Yearbook of China 2001–2017, provincial procuratorial work reports of 2017, Statistical Yearbook of China 2000–2018*, and China Data Online.

As in the earlier chapters, the key predictors of interest are the size of resource production measured by per capita sales income from mineral products and the rate of resource dependence measured by the share of the industrial output by mining industries in total GDP. While the size of resource production directly affects the economic incentives for corruption, the rate of resource dependence, taking into account alternative sources of income, may affect the opportunity costs and hence attractiveness of engaging in resource-related corruption. Thus, examining both indicators can give us more information about and confidence in the estimated effects of resources on corruption. A simple bivariate analysis reveals a striking positive correlation between corruption and resources. As Figure 4.1 demonstrates, the provinces witnessing more resource extraction and relying more on the resource economy tend to have higher rates of corruption.

Next, I conduct multivariate panel data analysis on resources and corruption in Chinese provinces between 1999 and 2017. Noting that the corruption rate as measured by the number of filed and investigated corrupt officials is determined not only by the intensity of actual corruption but also the willingness and capacity of the procuratorate to detect and pursue corrupt activities, we need to control for the strength of law enforcement, which may have significant impacts on the procuratorate's decision to investigate reported corruption cases. If a local government attaches greater attention to enforcing the law and cracking down on corruption as well as other crimes, the stronger efforts may uncover more crimes and thus enhance revealed corruption rates. However, stronger law enforcement may well deter corruption and decrease actual and consequently revealed corruption rates. In either case, it is necessary to control for law enforcement strength in the data analysis. I use the percentage of a province's fiscal expenditure that goes to the law enforcement organs, including the police, procuratorate, court of justice, armed police, etc., to measure the importance that the local government attaches to enforcing laws and cracking down crimes including corruption. It is worth noting that a local government's expenditure on law enforcement may be influenced by the intensity of corruption, so it may potentially generate the problem of endogeneity. To address this problem, I use the one-year lag of the percentage of fiscal expenditure on law enforcement organs[20] as a control variable in the data analysis, assuming that the expenditure on law enforcement in the past can affect the revealed corruption rate in the current year but should not be affected by the current corruption rate.

As the panel data analysis reveals (see Appendix 4.A for the detailed statistical method and regression results), both resource abundance and resource dependence have positive impacts on corruption rates, and the effects are statistically highly significant in all the models (see Table 4.2 in Appendix 4.A). The findings confirm that, even controlling for law enforcement strength and other pertinent factors, regions endowed with more mineral resources experience significantly higher rates of corruption. According to the estimates of Models 3 and 7 in Table 4.2, controlling for the other variables, the region producing the most mineral products per capita would detect about 39 more corrupt officials per million people than the region with the smallest resource

---

[20] To check the robustness of the lagged variable, I also use the three-year lag of the percentage of fiscal expenditure on law enforcement in the data analysis. The regression results are very similar in all the models.

production; and the most resource-dependent region would detect 51 more corrupt officials per million people than the least resource-dependent region. Considering that corruption rates range between 0.83 and 88.62 per million people and average 35.95 per million people each year, the impacts of resources on corruption rates are substantively significant. Resource-dependent regions are remarkably more prone to corruption by state employees.

Nevertheless, we should not forget that the corruption rate as measured by the number of filed and investigated officials is revealed corruption rate. The observed positive effects of resource abundance and dependence on revealed corruption rate do not necessarily lead to the conclusion that resources increase actual corruption rates. Because the revealed corruption rate is essentially the product of the actual corruption rate and the detection rate, we must rule out the possibility that resources increase detection rate of corruption in order to establish a positive association between resources and actual corruption rates. Then a crucial question needs to be answered: Is resource-related corruption more likely to be detected and investigated by the prosecutors than other types of corruption?

There are frequent media reports on resource-related corruption cases, and the extravagant lifestyles of some *kuang laoban* and their close ties with local officials as discussed earlier often make sensational news headlines and arouse suspicion of corruption. However, until the downfall of some high-level officials caused a series of corruption cases to be exposed in the oil sector and in the provinces of Shanxi and Yunnan in 2014 and afterward, there is little evidence that the Chinese government systematically targeted resource-related corruption in its anti-corruption efforts, which would arguably increase the detection rate of such cases.

To gauge the Chinese state's anti-corruption attention and the likelihood of detection for corruption cases in specific policy areas, I resort to the reports of the procuratorial departments. The procuratorial departments' annual work reports normally highlight the key anti-corruption areas every year, which receive special attention from the procuratorate and are likely to experience higher detection rates than the non-targeted areas. For example, when the Chinese government launched massive stimulus packages to boost infrastructural construction after the 2008 financial crisis, the procurators tightened their scrutiny on construction projects to prevent the abuse of the injected funds. As a result, they detected a surge of corruption cases in construction projects.[21] Similarly, when President Xi Jinping started the high-profile anti-poverty campaign in 2016, the procurators paid special attention to fighting corruption in the area of poverty alleviation, leading more corrupt officials to be investigated and disciplined.[22] To identify the key areas in the procuratorial departments' anti-corruption work, I manually analyze the contents of the work reports of the Provincial People's Procuratorates (PPPs) and record the mentioning of each anti-corruption area. The content analysis finds that between 1999 and 2017, the PPPs specifically targeted a large variety of policy areas for corruption investigation and prevention. According to the nature of corruption and the government departments involved, I classify these policy areas into 22 mutually exclusive categories (see Figure 4.2), including construction, state-owned enterprises, people's livelihood, agriculture, work safety, resources and environment, etc. Coding the mentioning of each policy area in the anti-corruption work as 1,[23] these anti-corruption areas are mentioned a total of 5,721 times. Figure 4.2 shows the distribution of the procuratorial anticorruption attention allocated to the 22 policy areas as measured by the total number that each area is mentioned by all the PPPs between 1998 and 2017. Among the 22 areas, only one area covers resource-related corruption, namely resources and environment (*ziyuan huanjing* 资源环境), which is mentioned a total of 417 times, accounting for about 7% of the total frequency of all key anti-corruption areas. Compared with some other key areas such as construction, market order and people's livelihood, resources and environment-related corruption does not appear to be a prioritized anti-corruption area or receive particularly strong attention from the procuratorial departments. Moreover, the area of resources and environment targets corrupt activities related to both the environment and

---

[21] BBC.com. 2010. "Zhongguo jinqi daliang fubaian she siwanyi ciji jihua (Many recent corruption cases in China are related to the four trillion stimulus package)," 20 May, www.bbc.com/zhongwen/trad/china/2010/05/100520_china_graft.shtml, accessed on March 3, 2021.

[22] Lu Junyu. 2017. "Jingzhun fanfu huhang jingzhun fupin: Weilai wunian jiang jiama (Safeguarding targeted poverty alleviation with targeted anticorruption measures: More to come in next five years)," Xinhuanet, November 4, www .xinhuanet.com/politics/2017-11/04/c_129732459.htm, accessed on March 3, 2021.

[23] No matter how many times a policy area is mentioned in the relevant section of one procuratorial report, I code the mentioning of that area as 1.

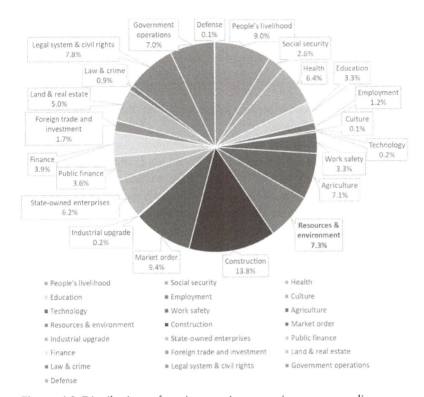

Figure 4.2 Distribution of anti-corruption attention across policy areas (1998–2017)

Source: Figure compiled based on the Provincial People's Procuratorate work reports from 1998 to 2017

Note: The percentage of each policy area is its weight in the procuratorial departments' overall anticorruption attention, as measured by the number of mentioning of each policy area divided by the total mentioning of all policy areas in the Provincial People's Procuratorates' annual work reports from 1998 to 2017.

natural resources, a large part of which concerns corruption that causes environmental degradation and is not related to mineral resources. Thus, only a small fraction of procuratorial anti-corruption attention has been paid to mineral resources. Assuming that the more attention an anti-corruption area receives in procuratorial investigation, the higher probability of detection the corruption cases in this area face, it is therefore unlikely that resource-related corruption faces particularly high rate of detection when compared to other types of corruption.

Besides the specific anti-corruption areas mentioned above, a top priority of the anti-corruption efforts in all Chinese provinces and throughout the years is major corruption cases that involve larger amounts of money (*da'an* 大案)[24] and higher-ranking officials (*yao'an* 要案).[25] The intensified anti-corruption attention and investigation presumably can lead to higher detection rates of major cases than of petty corruption. Could resource-related corruption cases face higher detection rates because of their larger economic magnitudes or higher level of officials involved?

To gauge the economic magnitude of corruption cases, I use the sum of the economic costs recovered from the investigated corruption cases (*wanhui jingji sunshi* 挽回经济损失), which is the financial loss to the state or relevant parties (such as SOEs) salvaged through the investigation of the cases. The recovered economic loss provides a valuable window for assessing the economic magnitude of corruption, although it is an imperfect measure, because it depends on the capability of the procuratorate to identify and retrieve the loss. Nevertheless, it can reflect the value of investigating and pursuing the cases in the eyes of the prosecutors. Dividing the sum of recovered economic cost by the number of cases, I derive the average economic cost per case, which varies widely from 14,683 yuan to 3,771,739 yuan across the provinces between 1999 and 2017.

Meanwhile, I use the number of officials at county (*xian* 县) or office (*chu* 处) level and above investigated for corruption to measure the political importance of the corruption cases. I divide the number of corrupt high-ranking officials investigated by the total population to calculate the major corruption rate in each province in a given year. Between 1999 and 2017, the rate of major corruption case ranges from 0.17 to 11.7 per million people. Compared to the total corruption rate, which ranges between 0.83 and 88.62 per million people and averages 35.95 per million people each year, the small proportion of major cases shows that the vast majority of revealed corruption involves low-level officials in China, while very few high-ranking officials are caught for corruption. This is hardly surprising, because only around 10% of the Chinese civil servants rank at the county/office level or above.[26]

---

[24] *Da'an* are corruption cases that involve at least 50,000 yuan for bribery and embezzlement cases and 100,000 yuan for misappropriation cases.

[25] *Yao'an* are corruption cases committed by officials with administrative rank at county (*xian* 县)/office (*chu* 处) level or above.

[26] Xinhua News Agency, 2016. "Renshebu: Xianchuji Fuzhi Yishang Zhiwu de Gongwuyuan Zhan Zhengge Gongwuyuan Duiwu 10% (Ministry of Human Resources and Social Security: Officials at County Level or Above Accounting for 10% of Total Civil Servants)," June 27, www.gov.cn/xinwen/2016-06/27/content_5086004.htm, accessed on January 16, 2020.

I next conduct panel data analysis to test the effects of resources on the economic magnitude and political importance of corruption cases, respectively. Considering that the strength of law enforcement may affect how much economic losses can be recovered from corruption investigation and how many higher-ranking officials can be put under investigation, I control for the one-year lag of law enforcement strength as before (for detailed statistical methods and data see Appendix 4.A).

The different estimation models demonstrate strong negative correlation between resources and the economic magnitude of corruption cases (see Table 4.3 in Appendix 4.A), which means that resource-related corruption cases tend to be of smaller economic scales. There may be two possible explanations. First, corruption cases in resource-rich regions are indeed of smaller economic scales. Second, it is more difficult for the prosecutors to identify and retrieve the economic losses of resource-related corruption cases. In either case, resource-related corruption cases appear less worthy of pursuing, because the prosecutors prefer investigating major cases through which they can recover greater financial losses.

Meanwhile, there is no evidence that mineral resources give rise to more major corruption cases that involve higher-ranking officials. As shown in Table 4.4 in Appendix 4.A, the size of resource production and the rate of resource dependence do not appear to have significant or stable effect on major corruption rate. Both predictors of interest are negatively correlated with major corruption rate, and the coefficients are statistically significant in some models. But when controlling for law enforcement strength and economic development level, the effects become unstable and statistically insignificant. Therefore, despite some high-profile corruption cases in the energy and resource sector revealed under Xi's anti-corruption campaign, there is little evidence that mineral resources systematically lead to more corruption by higher-ranking officials, who are under more intensive scrutiny and may face higher detection rates.

Given the findings on both the economic magnitude and political importance of corruption cases, we can safely assume that resource-related corruption cases are not likely to invite more attention and investigation from the prosecutors. Therefore, the additional evidence above confirms that resources do not increase the detection rate of corruption. Ruling out this causal effect, the positive correlation between resources and revealed corruption rate should be attributable to the positive effects of resources on actual corruption rate. Hence, we can conclude with confidence that resources indeed breed more corruption, although resource-related corruption may not incur greater economic costs than other types of corruption, and they may most likely involve lower-ranking officials.

Conclusion

This chapter reveals a symbiotic relationship between Chinese local governments and mining businesses in resource-rich regions. While the state-capital collaboration may help promote the development of mining industries and contribute to local economic and fiscal growth, it nevertheless breeds widespread corruption in the administrative, fiscal, personnel management, and law enforcement departments. In this sense, rich mineral resources do pose a curse by inducing local state capture by resource interests, as most of the corruption cases revealed in resource-rich regions take the form of collusion and exchange of favors between the resource capital and local government officials.

To begin with, the state's monopoly over mineral property rights and intervention in the resource market provide a most important and direct driving force for corruption. To correct the market distortion due to state intervention, mining-related businesses are strongly motivated to bribe officials in the administrative and economic management departments. Meanwhile, the Chinese central government's increasingly stringent regulations on environmental protection and work safety, etc. drive mining companies to build up political ties with local officials through corrupt exchanges, which may help the companies ward off or water down regulatory punishments. Similar to political corruption in other resource-rich countries, when resource rents increase the value of political positions, political corruption such as office selling and buying becomes a protruding issue in resource-rich areas, and the transactions are often backed by mining businesspeople who seek to build up patronage networks with the sponsored officials. In addition, in remote areas with weak rule of law, the ferocious contentions over resource control often drive the contenders, some of whom are linked with criminal organizations, to collude with local officials in the public security and judicial departments. With the notable exception of fiscal misappropriation and squandering of resource revenues, which are nontransactional corruption, most of the corruption cases are of transactional nature and involve the exchange of favors between the mining-related businesses as bribers and local officials as the provider of corrupt benefits such as favorable policy treatments and political protection. The widespread corruption in local governments and various functional departments contorts the state–business relations and undermines the long-term development of resource-rich regions in China.

It is worth noting that resources increase corruption in China not because they make the political regime less democratic or accountable, but rather because they exacerbate the institutional deficiencies that already exist in the Chinese political economic system. For instance, the heavy state control over mineral property rights and intervention in the resource sector are the legacies of a socialist planned economy. The collusion between local state and resource capital and the selling of political positions ultimately result from a nondemocratic regime that lacks open and transparent bureaucratic management system and fails to hold public officials accountable. And the protection of criminal organizations by law enforcement departments is a natural product of the weak rule of law. Although such institutional deficiencies widely exist all over China, the abundant resource rents exacerbate the situation by giving more people more incentives to exploit the loopholes in the system. The combination of economic incentives induced by resource rents and the structural opportunities provided by the institutional deficiencies lead to higher corruption rates in resource-rich regions.

Interestingly, resource-related corruption cases are generally of limited economic scale and tend to involve lower-level officials. As the statistical analysis suggests, the size of resource production and the rate of resource dependence are negatively correlated with the economic magnitude of corruption cases and do not drive up the rate of major corruption committed by higher-ranking officials. The findings suggest that local state capture by resource interests is somewhat contained to the lower echelons of the Chinese political hierarchy and cause less economic damages when compared to corruption cases in other non-resource areas. This is good news to some extent, as such low-level corruption can be relatively easily cracked down when the higher authorities have the political will and capacity to do so. For example, when the Chinese central government under the leadership of Xi Jinping launched the high-profile anti-corruption campaign, it led to the downfall and prosecution of thousands of local officials in the coal-rich Shanxi Province, the vast majority of whom are grassroots-level officials. Although it is unclear yet whether such top-down crackdown can eliminate all corruption or generate any long-lasting impacts, at least in the short run it can relatively effectively curb and deter low-level, petty corruption in resource-rich regions.

Appendix 4.A Statistical Analysis on the Impacts of Resources on Corruption

Statistical Methods and Data

To examine the effects of resources on corruption rate, I include the key predictors of interest, size of resource production, and rate of resource dependence. Besides law enforcement, the data analysis also includes other control variables. One major control variable that may affect corruption is the economic development level. Since many corruption cases, such as embezzlement, bribery, and misappropriation, are economic corruption in nature, they depend on the availability of economic resources. I use per capita GDP to measure the level of economic development. However, there may be an endogeneity problem between corruption and economic development, as corruption is believed to have negative impacts on economic growth (Mauro, 1995). I make two attempts to address the endogeneity problem. One way is to include lagged per capita GDP as a control variable. Arguably, economic development in the past provides the soil for corruption in the current year but should not be affected by the current corruption. I hence control for the one-year lag of per capita GDP.[27] The other way is to introduce an instrumental variable that is highly correlated with economic development but has no causal relationship with corruption. For this purpose, electricity consumption can be a good proxy, because it closely correlates with the economic activities that generate growth (Koech & Wang, 2012), but it should not affect corruption. Meanwhile, as electricity production and consumption are vertically regulated by the electricity management department under the leadership of the State Council, it should be subject to little influence from corruption at local levels. Thus, I use per capita electricity consumption as an instrumental variable in the data analysis. Between 1999 and

---

[27] I have also used the three-year lag of per capita GDP. The results are robust across the models.

2017, per capita electricity consumption (log) is highly correlated with real per capita GDP (log), with a Pearson correlation coefficient of 0.77 (p-value = 0.000), and it passes the weak instrument test.

I also control for some other factors that may affect the occurrence of corruption. The extensive government surveillance of the resource sector creates red tape and breeds corruption in multiple administrative departments. Because a larger state may create more bureaucratic hurdles and thus greater need for corruption to bypass them, I use the percentage of state employees, including those working in government departments and agencies, in total population to measure the bureaucratic size. Besides, corruption may be limited by the freedom of the market (Kaufmann & Siegelbaum, 1996). If a region sees a relatively free market economy with limited state interference, it may restrict the chance for government officials to engage in rent seeking. Based on the assumption that a better developed market economy is associated with a more important role of trade, I use the share of trade with foreign countries (including import and export) of a region in the regional GDP to measure the region's market freedom.

To offset the effects of inflation and make the statistics in monetary terms comparable across years, all monetary figures are transformed into real values by dividing the nominal values with regional deflator, which is determined by the annual inflation rates of each province (with 1998 as the base year).The summary statistics of the dependent and independent variables are reported in Table 4.1 In preparation for the additional check on the relationship between resources and corruption detection rate, I also include the two dependent variables for the additional check, real economic cost per corruption case and rate of major corruption per million people, in Table 4.1

Similar to earlier chapters, I adopt the fixed effects model to control for region-specific effects, such as local political culture and institutional quality (Ji et al., 2013), and time-specific effects, such as nationwide anti-corruption policies, which potentially affect corruption and detection rates. I use the following formula to conduct the panel data analysis: $Y_{it} = \alpha R_{it} + \beta' X_{it} + \mu_i + \nu_t + \varepsilon_{it}$, where the subscript $i = 1, 2 ..., 31$ for the 31 provinces, and $t = 1, 2, ..., 19$ for the 19 years from 1999 to 2017. The dependent variable is corruption rate; the key predictor of interest R takes one of two measurements, the size of resource production and the rate of resource dependence, and X is the set of control variables discussed earlier. The variable μ is the

Table 4.1. *Summary statistics*

Variable	N	Mean	Std. Dev.	Min	Max
Predictor of interest					
Size of resource production (real per capita mineral sales income)	589	1,077.7	1,564.0	2.34	9,209.7
Rate of resource dependence (percentage of mineral industrial output in GDP)	589	6.46	8.48	0.01	94.62
Dependent variables					
Corruption rate	589	35.95	11.70	0.83	88.62
Real economic cost per case	442	21,8819	28,873	16,037	2,615,993
Major corruption rate	558	2.58	1.60	0.17	11.73
Control variables					
Law enforcement strength (1-year lag)	589	6.25	1.25	3.48	10.79
Real per capita GDP (1-year lag)	589	22,540	17,884	2,318	93,845
Per capita electronic consumption	582	3,051	2,290	458.5	14,340
Bureaucratic size	589	1.18	0.49	0.58	4.38
Weight of foreign trade in GDP	589	27.80	37.76	0.17	180.6

Source: Authors' calculation based on statistics from *China Land and Resources Statistical Yearbook*, *Procuratorial Yearbook of China*, *Finance Yearbook of China*, *Statistical Yearbook of China*, *China Energy Statistical Yearbook*, and *China Data Online*.

time-invariant and province-specific effect; and v is the province-invariant and time-specific effect. The error term ε captures the effects of other disturbances on the dependent variable. To satisfy the normal distribution assumption of the variables, the highly skewed variables are transformed by taking natural logs in the estimation.

Following a common practice in existing studies, I use a stepwise regression approach to progressively introduce the independent variables into the models to avoid multicollinearity (Zhang & Brouwer, 2020). For each of the two key predictors of interest, four models are presented: Model 1 includes the parsimonious model with only the predictor of interest; Model 2 controls for the lagged strength of law enforcement; Model 3 introduces other control variables including the one-year lag of real per capita GDP, bureaucratic size, and weight of foreign trade; as another measure to address the endogeneity problem between corruption and economic development level, Model 4 replaces the one-year lag of real per capita GDP with per capita electricity consumption as an instrumental variable for economic development level.[28] The models yield highly consistent and robust results. To deal with possible heteroscedasticity problem, I conduct Breusch–Pagan test (Wooldridge, 2013) on all the models. As a few models do not pass the test at 0.05 level, I report heteroscedasticity-robust statistical results for all the models in Table 4.2.[29]

Mineral Resources and Corruption Detection Rate

To dissect the effect of resource abundance/dependence on corruption detection rate, I conduct another two sets of regression on the Chinese provinces between 1999 and 2017, with the economic magnitude and political importance of corruption cases as the dependent variable, respectively. The economic magnitude is measured by average economic cost per corruption case (deflated by annual regional inflation rates); the political importance is measured by the number of corrupt officials at county/office level or above per million people (the descriptive statistics are included in Table 4.1). Besides the key

[28] The instrumental variable passes the first stage F-test for weak instruments with p-value < 0.000. The estimation with the instrumental variable is done with Balestra and Varadharajan-Krishnakumar's method built in the R program.

[29] I use the generic coeftest function in R to conduct the heteroscedasticity-robust estimation with White's estimator.

Table 4.2. *Impacts of mineral resources on corruption rate*

	Dependent variable: number of corrupt officials per million people							
	(1)	(2)	(3)	(4)	(5)	(6)	(7)	(8)
Predictor of interest								
Size of resource production (ln)	4.871*** (0.354)	4.916*** (0.392)	4.702*** (0.448)	4.672*** (0.463)				
Rate of resource dependence (ln)					3.803*** (0.245)	3.930*** (0.253)	5.315*** (0.355)	5.284*** (0.365)
Control variables								
1-year lag of law enforcement strength		0.147 (0.304)	0.665* (0.324)	0.609. (0.324)		0.381 (0.312)	0.825** (0.304)	0.777* (0.306)
1-year lag of real per capita GDP (ln)			7.522*** (1.539)				12.067*** (1.517)	
Per capita electricity consumption (ln) (instrumental variable)				7.446*** (1.549)				11.982*** (1.545)
Bureaucratic size			-3.686*** (0.658)	-3.441*** (0.713)			-4.074*** (0.681)	-3.869** (0.760)
Weight of foreign trade in economy (ln)			-3.941*** (1.023)	-3.915*** (1.034)			-3.383** (0.901)	-3.368*** (0.908)
Region effect	Yes	Yes	Yes	Yes	Yes	Yes	Yes	Yes
Year effect	Yes	Yes	Yes	Yes	Yes	Yes	Yes	Yes
R^2 (within)	0.270	0.270	0.337	0.326	0.218	0.219	0.355	0.344
Degrees of Freedom	539	538	535	535	539	538	535	535

The numbers in the parentheses are heteroscedasticity-robust standard errors. Significance codes: ***$p < 0.001$; **$p < 0.01$; *$p < 0.05$; . $p < 0.1$.

predictors of interest, I also control for the strength of law enforcement as measured by the percentage of fiscal expenditure on law enforcement organs, including the police, procuratorate, court of justice, and armed police. And given that the economic development level may fundamentally determine the economic magnitude of corruption, which may also affect the level of officials involved (assuming that the larger economic magnitude of corrupt activities may attract higher-level officials to participate in them), I include the one-year lag of real per capita GDP as a control variable. To address the endogeneity issue between corruption and economic development level, I also use per capita electricity consumption as an instrumental variable for economic development level as in the original regression analysis on corruption rate.[30] Same as the original models, the additional panel data analyses also employ fixed-effects model. The statistical results are presented in Tables 4.3 and 4.4

Statistical Findings on the Control Variables

Besides the impacts of resources on corruption rate discussed in the main body of this chapter, there are also important findings regarding the other control variables. Law enforcement strength (one-year lag) is consistently positively correlated with corruption rate, and the effects are statistically significant in most of the models (see Table 4.2). It suggests that when a local government attaches greater attention to enforcing the laws, it can discover more corruption. In this sense, the revealing effect of law enforcement is stronger than its deterring effect on corruption, if there is any. Interestingly, lagged law enforcement is significantly negatively correlated with major corruption rate measured by the number of corrupt officials at county/office level or above per million people (see Table 4.4), which indicates some deterrence effect of law enforcement on high-level officials. In regions where law enforcement is strong, high-level officials are strongly discouraged from engaging in corruption. This contrast between general corruption cases and major corruption cases implies that law enforcement may have a stronger deterrence effect on high-ranking officials than on low-level cadres. It may be because that high-level officials are more aware

---

[30] The estimation with the instrumental variable is done with Balestra and Varadharajan-Krishnakumar's method built in the R program.

Table 4.3. *Mineral resources and economic magnitude of corruption cases*

	(1)	(2)	(3)	(4)	(5)	(6)
	Dependent variable: real economic cost per corruption case (ln)					
Predictor of interest						
Size of resource production (ln)	−0.180***	−0.145***	−0.125***			
	(0.034)	(0.035)	(0.033)			
Rate of resource dependence (ln)				−0.233***	−0.160***	−0.137***
				(0.033)	(0.038)	(0.035)
Control variables						
1-year lag of law enforcement strength		−0.025	0.002		−0.032	−0.003
		(0.025)	(0.022)		(0.025)	(0.023)
1-year lag of per capita GDP (ln)		0.532***			0.377***	
		(0.072)			(0.086)	
Per capita electricity consumption (ln)			0.540**			0.407***
			(0.073)			(0.085)
Region effect	Yes	Yes	Yes	Yes	Yes	Yes
Year effect	Yes	Yes	Yes	Yes	Yes	Yes
R^2 (within)	0.069	0.192	0.207	0.150	0.196	0.210
Degrees of Freedom	392	390	390	392	390	390

The numbers in the parentheses are heteroscedasticity-robust standard errors. Significance codes: ***$p < 0.001$; **$p < 0.01$; *$p < 0.05$; . $p < 0.1$.

Table 4.4. *Mineral resources and political importance of corruption cases*

	Dependent variable: number of corrupt officials at county/office-level or above per million people					
	(1)	(2)	(3)	(4)	(5)	(6)
Predictor of interest						
Size of resource production (ln)	−0.132*	−0.004	0.005			
	(0.056)	(0.080)	(0.087)			
Rate of resource dependence (ln)				−0.230***	0.060	0.074
				(0.054)	(0.076)	(0.113)
Control variables						
1-year lag of law enforcement strength		−0.128**	−0.138*		−0.106*	−0.105*
		(0.049)	(0.055)		(0.046)	(0.047)
1-year lag of per capita GDP (ln)		1.330***			1.417***	
		(0.192)			(0.229)	
Per capita electricity consumption (ln)			1.421***			1.477***
			(0.315)			(0.393)
Region effect	Yes	Yes	Yes	Yes	Yes	Yes
Year effect	Yes	Yes	Yes	Yes	Yes	Yes
R^2 (within)	0.010	0.173	0.173	0.041	0.174	0.175
Degrees of Freedom	508	506	506	508	506	506

The numbers in the parentheses are heteroscedasticity-robust standard errors. Significance codes: ***$p < 0.001$; **$p < 0.01$; *$p < 0.05$; . $p < 0.1$.

of the political settings and potential risks of corruption, and that they have a lot more to lose if caught than the rank-and-file cadres. So when perceiving tightened law enforcement, they may refrain from engaging in corrupt activities, or alternatively, they become more cautious and take smarter strategies to avoid being caught. In any case, law enforcement appears to curb high-level corruption more effectively than petty corruption. At the same time, law enforcement strength does not seem to affect the recovered economic costs of corruption cases. As Table 4.3 shows, the effects of lagged law enforcement strength are substantially small and statistically insignificant, and they change sign across the models. The findings suggest that law enforcement strength either does not affect the economic magnitude of corruption cases or does not help retrieve more economic losses from the investigated cases.

Counterintuitively, economic development appears to significantly increase corruption rates. Per capita GDP (one-year lag), and the instrumental variable per capita electricity consumption are all positively correlated with corruption rates in Table 4.2, and the estimated coefficients are all statistically significant. According to the estimates of Model 3 in Table 4.2, other things being equal, the richest region would experience 28 more corruption cases per million people than the poorest region, indicating substantial impacts of economic development on corruption rates. One possible explanation is that there exist greater economic incentives and/or opportunities for corruption in richer areas. An alternative explanation is that citizens in wealthier regions, who are better educated and more legally informed, may be more concerned and vocal about corruption, thus leading to higher detection rates of corruption. Moreover, economic development level appears to drive up both the economic magnitude and political importance of corruption cases. As the regression results in Table 4.3 show, both the lagged real per capita GDP and per capita electricity consumption as an instrumental variable are positively correlated with the economic magnitude of corruption cases, suggesting that the cases in wealthier regions tend to be economically more costly, and thus they may be more seriously handled and enthusiastically pursued by the prosecutors. The government's stronger incentive to punish the criminals and salvage the losses they generate may contribute to higher detection rates in wealthier regions. On the other hand, the higher economic stakes of corruption may also induce more high-level officials to engage in corruption by making the benefits of corruption overweigh the potential costs of being caught. This may explain why both lagged real per capita GDP and the instrumental variable per capita electricity consumption are significantly positively correlated with the major corruption rate (see Table 4.4). Therefore, wealthier regions not only tend to experience more corruption, but the corruption also tends to be of greater economic magnitude and involve more high-ranking officials.

Bureaucratic size appears to significantly negatively affect the rate of corruption. As manifested in Table 4.2, the ratio of state employees in total population is negatively correlated with corruption rate, and the effects are statistically significant in all the models. Based on the estimation in Model 3 in Table 4.2, when controlling for other factors, the region with the largest state employment would see 14 less corrupt officials per million people than the region with the smallest state employment. This evidence goes against the common impression that the oversized bureaucracy composes a source of corruption in China. It is an interesting finding that deserves more careful examination and explanation in a separate project.

Last but not least, market development and freedom appear to curb corruption. As shown in Table 4.2, the weight of foreign trade in the economy is negatively correlated with corruption rate, and the coefficients are both statistically and substantively significant in all the models. Based on the estimation in Model 3 in Table 4.2, holding other factors constant, when the weight of foreign trade in the economy increases from the minimum to the maximum, a region could cut its corruption rate by 28 corrupt officials per million people, a substantial drop. The findings confirm that the market openness can strongly drive down corruption. Therefore, the Chinese government should further open up its economy to international trade if it wants to fight against corruption.

5 | *Resources and Local Public Goods Provision*[1]

The existence of rich mineral resources not only shapes the state–capital relations, but also affects the local state's interaction with the citizens as the labor force. Based on mixed research methods that combine qualitative case studies and quantitative analyses, this chapter examines how mineral resources affect local governments' provision of different types of public goods that meet common citizens' diverse needs, namely education, health care, and social security. It tells a two-pronged story. While on the one hand the local governments in resource-rich regions tend to ignore public goods such as education and health care that enhance human capital development, on the other hand they generously hand out social security benefits to disadvantaged citizens to cope with the capital-labor conflicts. I first present the causal stories behind this intriguing contrast, and in the last section I test the qualitative findings against statistical evidence. In combination, Chapters 4 and 5 emphasize the local state as a key player in the state–capital–labor triad. Against the backdrop of China's political institutions and the top-down cadre management system in particular, the research findings show how the resource wealth and resource conflicts shape the incentives and behaviors of the local state.

Public Goods Provision in China: Incentives and Disincentives

One major responsibility of any state is to provide public goods for its citizens. The Chinese state is no exception. It provides a large variety of public goods to Chinese citizens, such as infrastructure, public security, education, medical care, social security, and environmental protection, which compose important sources of legitimacy for the Chinese

[1] Part of this chapter is revised and updated based on the article Jing Vivian Zhan, Haiyan Duan, and Ming Zeng, "Resource Dependence and Human Capital Investment in China," *The China Quarterly* 221 (2015), pp. 49–72.

Communist regime (Dickson et al., 2016; Lü, 2014). Under China's fiscal system, government expenditure and public goods provision are highly decentralized. Except for foreign affairs and some other items that necessitate national-level coordination, the responsibility of providing public goods primarily falls upon local governments, especially those at subprovincial levels. In this sense, Chinese local governments are the key providers of public services. Their incentives and capacities directly affect the types and levels of public goods that Chinese citizens receive.

Under China's nomenclatural system, local governments' incentives and behaviors are strongly shaped by the cadre management system, which is a powerful determinant of the political careers of Chinese government officials from the provincial level downward to the grassroots level (Edin, 2003). Guided by the evaluation standards of the cadre management system and facing intense competition for promotion with peers, local officials all strive to perform well on the indicators heavily emphasized in the evaluation standards, while ignoring the others that cannot notably advance their political career (O'Brien & Li, 1999). As rational beings, they distribute their efforts and resources among different tasks according to the yardsticks for promotion, and this incentive structure largely shapes their provision of public goods. Among the various tasks that Chinese local governments shoulder, it is generally agreed that the promotion of economic and fiscal growth is the foremost target (Landry, 2008; Li & Zhou, 2005). Thus local governments pay great attention to providing public goods that can promote growth, such as investment in infrastructure and all kinds of construction project, which can directly boost GDP growth. By contrast, public goods that cannot instantly and visibly contribute to economic growth, such as education, health care, and social security for local citizens, are often given lower priority and give way to economic construction and administrative expenses (Zeng & Zhan, 2013).

Despite the generally weak incentives for local governments to provide nonproductive public goods, different regional governments nevertheless demonstrate varying patterns of responsiveness to citizens' needs for basic public services. Among the different public goods, three types are particularly relevant to the welfare of common citizens, including education and health care that promotes human capital development and social security that provides a safety net for citizens to weather economic hardships and maintain subsistence. Although all of them benefit citizens as labor economically and socially, they carry different implications for local development and governance. Based on empirical evidence through field research and secondary information sources, the following sections tell a two-pronged story. On the one hand, education and health care are crucial for cultivating an educated and healthy labor force, which is essential for developing various industrial sectors including both labor-intensive industries and high-tech ones. However, as discussed earlier, because the mining industries do not have great need for labor, the local governments in resource-rich regions tend to lack incentives to spend on education and health care. On the other hand, wary of the popular grievance among local citizens about the negative externalities of mining industries and the threat to social stability, the local governments in resource-rich regions are strongly motivated to spend on social security, which can redistribute financial resources to disadvantaged social groups and partially address the unbalanced distribution of the benefits and costs of the mining industries.

Human Capital Development in Resource-Rich Regions

Human capital is crucial for long-term economic development. But comparative studies find that resource-rich countries and regions tend to lag behind in human capital development. For instance, a study by the Organization for Economic Cooperation and Development (OECD) compares countries' performances in the Program for International Student Assessment (PISA) exam, which tests math, science, and reading comprehension skills of 15-year-olds in 65 countries every 2 years, and finds a significant negative correlation between a country's total earnings on natural resources as a percentage of GDP and the knowledge and skills of its high school population (Friedman, 2012). Empirical observations in China also reveal similar patterns, with resource-rich regions apparently falling behind non-resource regions in terms of education. Taking higher education as an example, good universities are rarely located in resource-rich provinces. Of the 42 officially designated "first-tier universities (*yiliu daxue jianshe gaoxiao* 一流大学建设高校)" in China,[2] only 5 are found in the 6

[2] Ministry of Education of the People's Republic of China, 2017. "List of 'Double First-Tier' Universities ('Shangyiliu' Jianshe Gaoxiao Mingdan)," December 6, www.moe.gov.cn/s78/A22/A22_ztzl/ztzl_tjsylpt/sylpt_jsgx/201712/t20171206_320667.html, accessed on March 7, 2021.

resource-rich provinces including Qinghai, Shanxi, Shaanxi, Xinjiang, Heilongjiang, and Inner Mongolia, where mineral industrial outputs account for more than 10% of the provincial GDP,[3] and the other first-tier universities are mostly located in resource-poor regions, with Beijing and Shanghai taking the lead whose mineral industrial output-to-GDP ratios are well below 1%.

Going beyond the impressionistic evidence, my field research and case studies find that resource-rich Chinese localities generally witness weaker incentives to invest in human capital development, and there are systematic reasons behind that, including the local economic structure and diminished demand for labor, the myopia of local residents and officials, and the shift of responsibilities for public goods provision from the state to the mining sector. These structural factors all discourage government spending on human capital development in resource-rich areas.

Diminished Demand for Labor

Existing studies have advanced a few causal links between resource abundance and the investment in human capital. The Dutch disease theorem argues that the boom of natural resource sector diverts capital and labor force away from the non-resource sectors (Auty, 1993; Corden & Neary, 1982; Corden, 1984). Compared to the mining industries, which are capital intensive, the non-resource sectors, including manufacturing industries, require more advanced labor skills (Gylfason et al., 1999). However, the lack of attractiveness and competitiveness of these non-resource sectors, especially the high-tech and service industries that require high-level human capital, diminishes the demand for comprehensive education of the labor force beyond basic working skills. Moreover, compared to the manufacturing industries, the mining industries lack beneficial forward and backward linkages with the rest of the economy, which prohibits a more complex division of labor and the advancement of specialized labor skills (Sachs & Warner, 1995). Under such circumstances, the economic incentives to invest in the cultivation of human resources tend to be low.

[3] There are three first-tier universities in Shaanxi Province, whose average share of mineral industrial output in GDP was 22.15% between 1999 and 2017; one in Heilongjiang Province, whose share of mineral industrial output in GDP was 16.6%; and one in Xinjiang, whose share of mineral industrial output in GDP was 20.0% during the same period.

Although the reality in China does not square completely with these simple and elegant theories, resource-rich Chinese localities do appear to have diminished demand for labor, which consequently may weaken the local governments' incentive to invest in human capital. As discussed in Chapter 2, instead of generating a sweeping deindustrialization effect on all non-resource industries, resource wealth has mixed effects on other industrial sectors in China in terms of capital investment. While resource rents tend to crowd out high-tech industries represented by finance and IT, they help pump capital into low-tech industries including manufacturing and construction. Nevertheless, as revealed by the data analysis in Chapter 3, despite the spillover effects of resource capital, resource boom in general squeezes out job opportunities in other industrial sectors. This is not only true for high-tech industries including the IT and financial sectors, but also for the labor-intensive manufacturing and construction industries, which absorb the largest shares of the Chinese labor force.

Moreover, the crowding-out effects of natural resources are not limited to secondary industries. The resource boom in China also crowds out primary industries and related job opportunities in rural areas. E City in Inner Mongolia Autonomous Region provides a telling example regarding such crowding-out effects in mining areas. E City was traditionally an agricultural economy and famous for cashmere production. Local citizens have long relied on animal husbandry and cashmere production for income. However, since the discovery of rich coal, rare earth, and natural gas reserves around the turn of the millennium, mining and related energy and chemical industries rapidly became the staple industries of E City and dwarfed cashmere production and the cashmere-based textile industry (see Figure 5.1). Even the largest cashmere producer started to diversify its investment and entered coal-related business in 2003. Similarly, an A League[4] in Inner Mongolia also discovered large mineral reserves and turned from a traditional economy based on agriculture and husbandry to a mining-dominated industrial economy. By 2012, around 80% of A League' economy was contributed by the secondary sector, in which coal and coal chemical industries took up 80% and made by far the largest contribution to local fiscal revenue.[5]

[4] League is prefecture-level administrative unit in Inner Mongolia Autonomous Region.
[5] Data obtained in A League, Inner Mongolia Autonomous Region, August 2012.

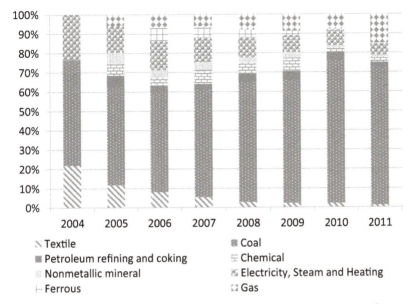

Figure 5.1 Composition of large-scale industries in E City, Inner Mongolia
Source: Figure compiled based on *E City Official Statistical Reports*

In addition, the mining industry also leads to diminished jobs in the primary sector by taking away lands, because mining activities and ensuing environmental damages such as land collapse and water shortage make agriculture and husbandry no longer viable in mining areas. In one town of E City for example, around 50% of its peasants and herdsmen lost their lands and hence their jobs due to the establishment of mining and processing facilities. Although the township government encouraged those citizens who lost their lands to engage in service industries such as transportation, sales, and catering (mainly serving the mining enterprises and their employees), many stayed jobless, partly due to the lack of necessary skills or start-up funds and partly due to the lack of incentives after receiving compensation packages and/or government subsidies for selling their lands. As a result of the decreased demand for labor in resource-rich regions, it is unsurprising that there are weak incentives for local citizens as well as local governments to spend on education and health care services to develop large supply of educated and healthy labor force.

While crowding out employment opportunities in other industries, the capital-intensive mining industries typically do not provide commensurate job opportunities due to increasing mechanization. As Chapter 3 reveals, during the decade of resource boom since the early 2000s, despite the huge increases of mineral production and sales, the number of employees in the mining sector as a share in total urban employment actually declined (see Figure 3.4). A coal-rich T City in Shanxi Province provides a concrete example. From 2005 to 2011, the industrial added value of coal industries in T City more than quadrupled from 4.9 billion yuan to 20.5 billion yuan, but the number of employees in the mining sector only increased slightly from 79,000 in 2005 to 87,000 in 2011.[6] Moreover, for the limited jobs in the mining industries, many do not require advanced education or labor skills. Except some managerial personnel and technicians, most of the workers in the mining companies are miners working underground and mechanical workers outside, who only need limited skills to fulfill their tasks. For a long time, neither mining companies nor the authorities set any education requirement for the mine workers. Only in recent years did the Chinese government start to set minimum education standards for jobs in the mining sector. According to the new regulations, mine workers must have attended junior high school, managerial and technical personnel must have associate college degrees or above, and high-level managers must have bachelor's degrees or above. However, according to my interviews in multiple mines in Shanxi Province, Jiangxi Province, and Xinjiang Autonomous Region, mining companies, especially private ones of smaller scales, commonly hire workers with inadequate education background to save cost.

Moreover, the reliance on migrant workers has further undermined the local governments' incentives to invest in human resources in resource-rich regions. Mining enterprises tend to prefer migrant workers to local laborers. Mining jobs mostly fall into two categories: For the small numbers of technician and managerial positions, they require technical expertise and higher education level, a requirement that local citizens mostly do not meet. Thus, mining companies tend to look beyond the local pool to hire qualified labor force from elsewhere. For example, one private coal mining company in T City of Shanxi Province hired the entire team of its managerial and technical personnel from Jiangsu Province for their rich expertise and work experiences. And for the vast majority of less technical but more dangerous

---

[6] Calculated according to statistics obtained from T City, Shanxi.

mining jobs that require purely hard labor, mining companies prefer hiring nonlocal workers, especially those from the populous provinces of Henan, Shaanxi, and Sichuan, who are attracted by the relatively high payments and low requirement for labor skills. As discussed in Chapter 3, one crucial reason is that nonlocal workers, lacking local connections and support by families and friends, are much easier to manage and discipline. Especially in the aftermath of mining accidents, it is much less costly for mining companies to compensate the wounded or deceased nonlocal workers and settle the disputes than dealing with local workers and their extended families.

As a result, instead of investing in the education and health of their labor force, the local governments of resource-rich regions would rather rely on labor-exporting regions to provide such public services. Under the highly localized public goods provision and the rigid household registration system in China during the period under this study, Chinese citizens could only receive education and health care mostly in the regions where they are registered, but the regions which they work for are free from such obligations. Therefore, the local governments in mining areas can just free ride on the efforts of the migrant workers' places of origin for the provision of education and medical services.

Myopia of Local Citizens and Officials

Besides decreased demand for labor force, resource boom also induces myopic behaviors among local citizens as well as officials and leads them to ignore the long-term development of human capital. In many resource-rich areas, a large number of local residents live on incomes derived from the resource wealth instead of actively using their labor force in agriculture or productive industries, as millions of farmers and workers do in other parts of China. As a result, they commonly lack incentive to increase their education level. In the words of a local resident in Shanxi Province, "elementary school education is enough for me to work in the mines. Why do I need more schooling? No other job can earn money faster than coal mining. Why should I look for those jobs (Zheng, 2011, p. 7)?"

There are a variety of ways for some local residents to derive cash flows, sometimes in large sums, from mineral resources, which undercut their willingness to take up real jobs. One way is by selling lands to mining companies. In E City of Inner Mongolia for instance, a typical rural household could receive as much as one million yuan (about US$150,000) in cash plus other housing and social welfare benefits from the local government and mining enterprises as a compensation for its loss of land, according to the local policy in 2012. Given that the national average annual income of rural citizens was only 8,389 yuan in 2012,[7] this compensation package was a huge income that would allow the household to live a very decent life for decades without working. In fact, quite some people chose not to work after winning the "resource lottery."[8] Among the winners, those with sufficient funds and strong political connections with local officials could invest in the mining businesses or become mine owners themselves. Many such private mine owners made a fortune in the past decade. And when the government started to shut down or consolidate small- and medium-sized mines around 2008, a lot of owners sold their mines for handsome prices. Moreover, some nouveau riche chose to put their resource wealth into speculative investments. As revealed in Chapter 2, resource-rich regions tend to experience more short-term speculation in the housing market, which generated huge returns when the Chinese housing market went up tremendously since the mid-2000s. Another speculative investment commonly seen in resource-rich regions is shadow banking. In some areas, many local citizens put their income and savings in usury. In some areas in Shanxi for example, shadow banking could yield annual interest rates as high as more than 30%. In the abovementioned ways, the relatively high and easy income from the direct or indirect involvement in the mining sector strongly discourages local residents from engaging in any jobs that require hard work or advanced labor skills. Under such circumstances, local residents tend to have lukewarm incentive to invest in their human capital by, for example, going for higher education. In some local residents' own words, the people in these mining areas are "lazy," "conservative," and "unambitious," and some "would rather live on social security checks than to work in the mines."[9]

Even worse, some local residents become psychologically parasitical on the resource wealth. Some local citizens living in adjacency to the mines often extort benefits from the mining companies, and they may

[7] Data according to National Bureau of Statistics of China, http://data.stats.gov.cn/easyquery.htm?cn=C01&zb=A0A05&sj=2019, accessed on July 2020.
[8] Interview with township-level officials, Inner Mongolia, August 2012.
[9] Interviews with local residents, Shanxi, May 2012 and Inner Mongolia, August 2012.

demand to share the profits of the mining companies even though they have no legal rights to do so. A complaint I often heard during my field research is the unreasonable requests put forward by local residents to coal mining companies. Some villagers, due to the sense of entitlement to the mineral resources located in their villages, would try every means to extort money from the mining enterprises. For example, when they have financial difficulties, they would block the roads to the mines (which go through their farmlands) and ask the mining companies for money or coal. And when some villagers' properties incur any damages, they would ask the mining companies for compensation, even when there is insufficient evidence to support the claims. To appease the villagers and avoid trouble, the companies often have to provide them with extra benefits such as food and coal during festive times. Meanwhile, the local governments, wary about social instability, also pressure the mining enterprises into succumbing to such unreasonable requests. As a result, some local residents quickly realize that blackmailing the mining companies is a most efficient way to make money (Zeng & Xia, 2013). To be fair, these fringe benefits that local residents demand sort of function as partial compensation to the environmental damages and heath and economic losses that local residents suffer, as discussed in Chapter 3. However, such parasitical psychology (*chidahu xinli* 吃大户心理) does discourage the local citizens from engaging in meaningful work that requires human capital. In consequence, they tend to lack the incentive to invest in their own personal development.

When the citizens pay less attention to the cultivation of human capital, the local governments are under less pressure to provide human capital-enhancing public goods. Moreover, similar psychological dependence on mineral resources also shows up among local officials in the mining areas. Because the hard indicators of their performance, economic growth and fiscal revenue, are largely determined by the resource market and macroeconomic environment, there is not much local officials can do to improve their performance. As a result, they are uninterested in making policies other than boosting the mining industries, such as spending more on education or health care.

Indeed, some scholars dispute such cognitive effects of resource abundance, arguing that policymakers should understand the unsustainability of resource booms in the long run and that people should be revenue maximizers instead of revenue satisficers (Ross, 1999). However, the empirical evidence from China confirms the existence of shortsighted behaviors. On the part of policymakers, local officials in China do not have long horizon due to the limited tenure of political positions, and hence they tend to pursue policies that can generate instant returns but ignore those that are beneficial only in the long run. On the other hand, the abovementioned citizens' behaviors should not necessarily be understood as revenue satisficing, because compared with farming and manufacturing jobs, riding on the mining sector is a most cost-efficient way to maximize their revenue, especially considering the low wage levels prevalent in agriculture and labor-intensive industries such as manufacturing in China.

Shedding Government Responsibilities onto Mining Companies

Besides weakened incentives to spend on education and health care, the existence of the resource sector also allows local governments to conveniently shift their burden of public goods provision to mining enterprises. State-owned mining companies, especially those established under the Maoist planned economy, normally form closely knitted communities that accommodate the employees and their families and take up many social tasks that should be assumed by the government (*qiye ban shehui* 企业办社会). They provide various public services for not only their employees but also the residents in the neighborhood, including childcare, elementary and secondary education, medical care, and even public security, and shoulder the financial costs of these services. In Y City of Shanxi Province, the coal sector had its own education bureau, which managed more than 10 elementary, junior high and high schools. In F City of Jiangxi Province, one mining company even had jurisdiction over the entire town where it is located. Besides sponsoring schools, it constructed roads and provided water and electricity at low prices for the neighboring villages. Before the agricultural taxes were abolished, the company even paid the agricultural taxes for the villagers. Although many work units in non-resource sectors have long been dismantled as a result of the market reform, the mining enterprises continue to carry on the multiple functions inherited from the Maoist era and shoulder considerable responsibilities of providing public services to the local residents. Only recently did the local governments start to take over the mining enterprise-run schools,[10] but the other services including medical services still remain

---

[10] In Y City, the local government took over the schools starting in 2005, but in other localities, such as those field sites in Shanxi, Inner Mongolia, and Jiangxi, the transfer of schools started in 2008.

on the shoulders of the mining companies.[11] For example, according to my interview with a state-owned coal enterprise in T City of Shanxi Province in 2013, it had to spend more than two million yuan per year on the elementary and secondary schools before they were transferred to the T City government. Even after the transfer, it still had to finance the salaries and welfare benefits of the school employees for two more years. And it continued to run the hospital, which cost around two million yuan per year. Under such circumstances, mining enterprises share a large part of the public service responsibilities and expenses that should have been borne by the local governments.

Not only state-owned companies, but private mining companies are also requested to provide various public goods such as public facilities and funding for schools. On the claim that mining companies make profits with state-owned resources, local governments often expect mining companies to pay back to local communities. Unlike the regularized school and medical care services that state-owned companies provide, private companies face contingent fundraisings by local governments. Whether due to strong social responsibility or out of business calculations such as to increase publicity and improve relations with local governments and citizens, private mining companies usually willingly or grudgingly accommodate these requests. For example, in L City of Shanxi Province, a private coal company generously contributed 20 million yuan to a local high school and 3 million yuan to a kindergarten. In return, the schools were renamed after the company. Such tributes by mining enterprises no doubt allow the local governments in mining areas to decrease their expenditures on education and other public services.

It is worth noting that although partly financing the public services that local governments should shoulder, the quality of the enterprise-provided services may not be comparable to government-provided services. Indeed, the education and medical services provided by mining enterprises suffer the risks of substandard quality and unstable supply because of the nature of mining enterprises. In pursuit of economic profits, mining enterprises do not necessarily prioritize expenditures on the public services or ensure that they hire the best staff for the schools or hospitals, and thus the quality of the services is hardly guaranteed. Moreover, when the mining enterprises suffer poor market conditions, they often cut back expenditures on the public

---

[11] Official regulations on production safety require all mining enterprises to operate at least one medical service unit.

services. For example, when the coal price went down shortly after the Asian financial crisis in the late 1990s, the mining companies in Y City of Shanxi Province paid their teachers in arrears, which greatly undercut the teaching quality and led to the loss of many good teachers in the schools.

Stability Maintenance and Relief Policies in Resource-Rich Regions

In addition to human capital-developing public goods, natural resources also influence the local governments' provision of relief policies. As discussed in Chapter 3, mining activities directly contribute to labor disputes in the mining sector and more broadly, contentions between the mining sector and local communities. However, due to the weak rule of law and the lack of effective and impartial judiciary system trusted by the citizens, the resource-aroused conflicts usually cannot be settled through judicial procedures. Local citizens commonly prefer lodging complaints to local and/or upper-level governments through the petitioning system and calling for direct intervention by the state. As a result, Chinese local governments in mining areas are frequently embroiled in the resolution and prevention of resource conflicts.

As the CCP attaches top priority to maintaining social stability and the top-down cadre management system exerts heavy pressure on local officials to prevent the outbreak of large-scale collective incidents, local governments in resource-rich areas devise a wide range of hard and soft strategies to cope with resource conflicts (Zeng & Zhan, 2015; Zhan & Zeng, 2017). In addition to forceful repression of mass protests and arrests of protestors, local governments widely utilize social welfare benefits to pacify aggrieved citizens and prevent them from escalating the contention. In the face of farmers who lose their lands and means of livelihood due to mining-caused land subsidence or decreased land productivity due to pollution, local governments hand out subsidies to help them relocate and build new houses for them. For instance, one coal-rich Y town in Inner Mongolia handed out a generous compensation package to farmers and herdsmen who lost their land, which contained a one-off subsidy of 250,000 yuan in 2009,[12] another subsidy of 4,000 yuan and

---

[12] Bureau of Land and Resources of Y Banner, Inner Mongolia, 2009, "Y Qi Zhengshou Tudi Buchang Anzhi Banfa (Compensation and Relocation Measures of Expropriated Lands in Y Banner)."

monthly subsidy of 500 yuan per person starting in 2011,[13] and a further extension of monthly pension insurance of 550 yuan per person in 2012.[14] According to *Statistical Yearbook of China*, the annual income of rural residents in Inner Mongolia was 4,938 yuan in 2009, which means these subsidies are sizable income for the recipients. For local citizens who were incapacitated due to mining accidents or chronic diseases such as pneumoconiosis due to mining-caused pollution, some local governments would arrange health check and offer compensation to them.[15] More generally, local governments can offer low-income subsidies, medical assistance, disability pensions, senior benefits, etc. to disadvantaged citizens to alleviate their hardship and sustain their subsistence. Such relief policies often work hand in hand with stability maintenance work in mining areas.

Essentially, when mining companies are unable or unwilling to compensate for the negative externalities they impose on neighboring communities and the unequal distribution of resource wealth breeds popular discontents, local governments, out of concern for regime stability, often choose to step in to redress the grievance and compensate the victims through redistributive means. The abovementioned relief policies are financed directly by local fiscal expenditures, but an important part of the fiscal revenue comes from the resource sector. Mining companies pay all kinds of taxes such as VAT, income tax, business tax, and resource tax. For example, the oil and gas industry contributed 6.44 billion yuan to the fiscal coffer of Xinjiang in 2009, accounting for 16.57% of Xinjiang's total budgetary income (Zhang, et al., 2011). In addition to taxes, local governments in resource-rich regions commonly collect various administrative fees from mining companies, such as environmental management fees, resource compensation fees, and land compensation fees, which greatly help finance the local governments' relief policies. For example, in reaction to the eruption of clashes between mining industries and local citizens, the coal-rich Shanxi Province since 2004 made it mandatory

---

[13] Y Banner Government, Inner Mongolia, 2011, "Y Qi Kuangqu Yimin Anzhi Buchang Zanxing Banfa (Interim Measures of Migrant Relocation and Compensation of Mining Areas in Y Banner)."

[14] Y Banner Government, Inner Mongolia, 2012, "Y Qi Kuangqu Yimin Anzhi Buchang Zanxing Banfa (Interim Measures of Migrant Relocation and Compensation of Mining Areas in Y Banner)."

[15] T Town Government, Jiangxi, 2013, "2013 Nian T Zhen Xinfang Gongzuo Zongjie (2013 Work Report on Petitions in T Town)."

for coal companies to contribute to public welfare projects (Chen, 2016). A pioneer county of this initiative required all coal mines within its territory to devote 15 yuan for each ton of coal produced to providing welfare benefits for local citizens.[16] With these financial incomes, local governments can afford to hand out social welfare benefits to appease the grieved citizens, relieve their difficulties, and prevent them from turning against the Communist regime. In the mining areas I visited, while the residents complained about all kinds of damage and inconvenience that the mining activities caused to their daily lives, their complaints mainly targeted the mining companies instead of the government. Instead, they showed a certain degree of appreciation to the government for helping them survive the hardship. Apparently, the government's relief policies are relatively effective in alleviating the popular grievance and preventing the resource conflicts from escalating into major threat to social stability.

Resources and Public Goods Provision: Statistical Evidence

The empirical observations presented in the previous sections pinpoint the distorting effects of resources on the preferences of local public goods provision. On the one hand, due to the diminished demand for labor, psychological dependence on natural resources, and the shifting of responsibilities for public goods provision onto mining companies, local governments in resource-rich regions have less need for an educated and healthy labor force and hence weaker incentives to invest in human capital development. On the other hand, under the heavy pressure to prevent the conflicts between the mining businesses and local communities from escalating into social unrest that threatens social stability, local governments in resource-rich regions are strongly motivated to deploy relief policies to appease disadvantaged citizens suffering the negative externalities of mining activities. In a word, local governments in resource-rich regions have divergent preferences for providing public goods of different kinds. In this section, I test these qualitative findings against statistical evidence on Chinese provinces between 1999 and 2017.

---

[16] X County Government, Shanxi, 2004, "Guanyu Kaizhan 'Yikuang Yiye Yishi' Huodong de Shishi Yijian (Opinions on the Implementation of the 'One Mine—One Business—One Project' Policy)."

To examine the bifurcated impacts of mineral resources on human capital-enhancing public goods and redistributive public goods, I focus on three types of public service, including education and health care, which are crucial for developing human capital, and social security, which provides a safety net for disadvantaged citizens. To measure the provision of education services, I use per capita budgetary expenditure on education of each province. The education expenditure includes government expenses on preschool education, elementary schools, junior high schools, high schools, vocational schools, universities, professional training, and distance education. For the provision of health care, I use per capita budgetary expenditure on health care, including government expenses on hospitals, community medical services in urban and rural areas, epidemic prevention, maternity and child care, and drug administration.[17] I measure local governments' redistributive efforts with per capita budgetary expenditure on social security, which is the most important tool that the Chinese government devises to provide a safety net for vulnerable social groups such as unemployed, disabled, and senior citizens. Social security expenditure in China includes subsidies to low-income citizens, retirement pension subsidies, social insurance subsidies, medical assistance, employment subsidies, pensions for disabled citizens and veterans, disaster reliefs, the operating expenses of departments of civil affairs which handle social security issues, and the operating expenses of other public service organs that provide reliefs to needy citizens such as the Red Cross. Per capita education, health care, and social security expenditures all saw notable rising trends between 1999 and 2017, reflecting the Chinese government's increasing attention to public goods provision, although cross-regional variations persisted in all three expenditures.

Same as in previous chapters, the key predictors of interest include the size of resource production, measured by real per capita sales income from mineral products, and the rate of resource dependence, measured by the share of mineral industrial output in total GDP. In addition, previous studies have suggested a few other factors that may influence local expenditure on public goods and need to be controlled

---

[17] The accounting methods of government expenditures remained largely stable between 1999 and 2006, but changes occurred between 2007 and 2009 regarding certain expenditures. I have checked the subcategories of the education and health care expenditures each year and made adjustments in calculation to ensure the time consistency of the expenditure data.

for in the data analysis. First of all, economic development level has been identified as an important determinant of public goods provision. With economic development, citizens tend to demand more public goods with higher quality (Martinez-Vazquez & McNab, 2003). Meanwhile, local economic development level determines the fiscal capacity of local governments and consequently affects their provision of public services (Du, 2000). Therefore, I include real per capita GDP to control for economic development level.

Second, Chinese local governments commonly have weak incentives to spend on public services that cannot instantly promote economic growth, such as education and health care (Zeng & Zhan, 2013). A previous study finds that localities less reliant on subsidies from above tend to spend a lower share of their annual expenditures on public education (Wang et al., 2012). To ensure that local governments do provide public goods to meet the citizens' needs, the Chinese central government has installed various central fiscal transfers to provide funds for such purposes. Therefore, we need to control for the effects of central fiscal transfers on local expenditures on the public goods. But there exists a potential endogeneity problem, because the central government may make fiscal transfers in response to the local needs of public goods provision. To address the endogeneity problem, I include the lagged (one year) real per capita central fiscal transfer as a control variable, which arguably influences the current public expenditures but should not suffer reverse causality.

Third, some demographic factors may also affect public goods provision. Population density may influence the demand for and supply of public services. With higher population density, the society may become more congested and the demand for public services may increase accordingly (Litvack & Oates, 1971). On the other hand, some argue that economies of scale may decrease the unit cost of public services as the population density grows (Wu & Wang, 2013). Therefore, I include population density, that is, total population divided by the geographical area of a province, as a control variable. Besides, public goods provision may also be influenced by the composition of local population, because different age groups may have varying needs for public goods. For example, the younger generation needs more education services, while the elderly may require more medical services and social security. Thus I include child ratio, defined as the percentage of the population under age 15, and senior ratio, defined as the percentage of the population at or above age 65, to control for the age structure of the population. Meanwhile, to examine the effects of the notorious urban-rural divide in China on the provision of public services to citizens, I control for the weight of rural population. Finally, for purposes of national unity, ethnic minorities generally receive more favorable policies from the Han Chinese-dominated government, and thus their presence in the population may increase local expenditure on public services. I use the share of ethnic minority population in total population to measure the ratio of ethnic minorities.

To evaluate the effects of mineral resources on local provision of different public goods, I conduct three sets of panel data analyses, with per capita fiscal expenditure on education, health care, and social security as the dependent variable, respectively (see Appendix 5.A for the detailed descriptive statistics and data analysis). I have tried different statistical models by progressively introducing the independent variables. The regression results are robust across the regression models, revealing statistically significant and yet divergent impacts of resource abundance and dependence on local provisions of the three types of public goods.

On the one hand, the findings as presented in Tables 5.2 and 5.3 in Appendix 5.A confirm that both resource abundance and resource dependence negatively affect local public expenditures on education and health care, and the effects are statistically significant in all the models. According to the estimation of Model 6 in Tables 5.2 and 5.3 respectively, holding other factors constant, the most resource-dependent region would spend 26% less on education than the least resource-dependent region, and 46% less on health care, an even sharper drop. Considering that the per capita fiscal expenditure on education on average was only 795 yuan (about US$120) per year and the per capita expenditure on health care was merely 327 yuan (about US$49) per year during the period of this study, mineral resources would lead to serious cut into the already meager health care expenditure that local citizens receive. Moreover, given the grave environmental pollution caused by mining activities and the various health problems that local citizens suffer, this finding depicts an ominous picture for public health in mining areas, which deserves serious attention from policymakers as well as the public. If the issues of environmental pollution and health care deficits are left unattended, resource-rich regions may run into public health crisis sooner or later.

On the other hand, as shown in Table 5.4 in Appendix 5.A, both the size of resource production and the rate of resource dependence are positively correlated with social security expenditure, and the estimated effects are statistically significant in most of the models. According to Model 6 in Table 5.4, controlling for other factors, the most resource-dependent region would spend 28% more on social security than the least resource-dependent region would. During the period of this study, the per capita fiscal expenditure on social security averaged 629 yuan (about US$94) per year. Although not a large sum, mineral resources can still generate tangible impacts on social security expenditure, especially for vulnerable social groups who live on low incomes and rely on the government's financial assistances. This finding poses sharp contrast to the negative effects of resources on education and health care expenditures. Therefore, the statistical analysis reinforces the qualitative observations that while local governments in resource-rich regions tend to ignore human capital-developing public goods, they do pay more attention to building a safety net for those disadvantaged and aggrieved citizens who are likely the victims of the negative externalities of the mining industries.

Conclusion

Based on empirical observations and quantitative data analysis, this chapter reveals that the resource economy deeply shapes the state–labor relations in resource-rich regions by changing the incentives of local governments to provide different types of public goods. On the one hand, as existing studies on the resource curse suggest, countries endowed with rich natural resources such as fuel and minerals often fall behind in human development. The empirical evidence from China lends strong support to this argument and discovers some important causal channels through which the endowment of rich mineral resources affects local governments' incentives to invest in human capital. First of all, the booming resource sector crowds out jobs in other non-resource sectors, including not only high-tech but also labor-intensive industries as well as primary industries. The diminished demand for labor is aggravated by the mining enterprises' reliance on migrant workers for both economic and political reasons. The decreasing need for labor together with the inflow of nonlocal labor force weakens the incentive of the local governments in mining areas to provide education and health care services in order to ensure the supply of skilled and healthy labor force. Meanwhile, resource abundance induces myopic sloth among local residents and officials. The easy and lucrative income from resource wealth has tangible impacts on people's mentalities and discourages them from seeking jobs that require hard labor and advanced labor skills. Last but not least, local governments in resource-rich regions in China shed their responsibilities of public goods provision onto mining companies, partly as a legacy of the Maoist planned economy and partly due to the symbiotic relationship between the state and the mining enterprises.

On the other hand, the resource economy does encourage the provision of social security as a safety net to vulnerable social groups. As the resource economy generates unfair distribution of benefits and costs between the resource capital and local citizens as labor, it frequently arouses social conflicts between the two social groups. Because the CCP attaches top priority to maintaining regime stability and exerts heavy pressure from top-down to prevent the eruption of social unrest, buying peace appears to be a rational choice. Chinese local governments in resource-rich regions are strongly motivated to hand out relief policies to appease the aggrieved citizens. The various social security benefits help relieve their difficulties and sustain their livelihood, which ultimately can decrease the likelihood for them to launch large-scale protests out of desperation.

Overall, the findings shed new light on how resources affect the welfare of labor, which is a rather mixed story. While for the labor force at large resources discourage public investment in their education and health, which are important for their long-term development and sustainability, for those disadvantaged groups struggling for subsistence, resources do prompt local governments to care more about them, both driven by the fear of resource-aroused conflicts and enabled by the financial support from the resource revenue. Meanwhile, this research reveals a more nuanced picture about public goods provision in China. The traditional wisdom believes that Chinese local governments tend to undersupply public goods that cannot generate instant economic or political returns because the cadre evaluation system overly emphasizes such hard indicators as GDP and fiscal revenue growth. However, this research finds that the resource economy can be an important explanatory variable and poses additional incentives and disincentives for local public goods provision that have been overlooked by existing studies.

Appendix 5.A Statistical Analysis on the Impacts of Resources on Public Goods Provision

Statistical Methods and Data

To statistically test the impacts of resources on the provision of different public goods, I devise three sets of dependent variables, including per capita budgetary expenditure on education, per capita budgetary expenditure on health care, and per capita budgetary expenditure on social security. I use the size of resource production and the rate of resource dependence as the key predictors of interest. I also control for per capita GDP, the one-year lag of per capita central fiscal transfer, population density, weight of rural population, ethnic minority ratio, child ratio, and senior ratio.

To offset the effects of inflation and make the statistics in monetary terms comparable across years, all monetary figures are transformed into real values by dividing the nominal values with regional deflator, which is determined by the annual inflation rates of each province (with 1998 as the base year). The summary statistics of the dependent and independent variables are presented in Table 5.1.

As in previous chapters, I use the fixed effects model to conduct the panel data analysis with the following formula: $Y_{it} = \alpha R_{it} + \beta' X_{it} + \mu_i + \nu_t + \varepsilon_{it}$, where the subscript $i = 1, 2 \ldots, 31$ for the 31 provinces, and $t = 1, 2, \ldots, 19$ for the 19 years from 1999 to 2017. I conduct three sets of regression analyses. In each set, the dependent variable Y represents the real per capita expenditure on education, health care, and social security, respectively. R is the predictor of interest, the size of resource production, and the rate of resource dependence. X is a vector of control variables, including real per capita GDP, lagged real per capita central transfer, population density, child ratio, senior ratio, percentage of rural population, and ethnic minority ratio. The variable μ is the time-invariant and province-specific effect; and ν is the province-invariant and time-specific effect. The error term ε captures the effects of other disturbances on the dependent variable.

Table 5.1. *Summary statistics*

Variable	N	Mean	Std. Dev.	Min	Max
Predictor of interest					
Size of resource production (real per capita mineral sales income)	589	1,077.7	1564.0	2.34	9,209.7
Rate of resource dependence (percentage of mineral industrial output in GDP)	589	6.46	8.48	0.01	94.62
Dependent variable					
Real per capita education expenditure	589	795.04	669.53	32.14	4,602.57
Real per capita health care expenditure	589	326.56	304.25	10.15	1,900.18
Real per capita social security expenditure	589	628.75	563.05	25.91	4,368.28
Control variables					
Real per capita GDP	589	24,470	18,726.7	2,528	100,510
1-year lag of real per capita central transfer	589	2,234.0	2,922.9	146.2	29,211.8
Population density	589	408.9	582.9	2.08	3,826.2
Child ratio	589	18.60	4.92	7.56	35.14
Senior ratio	589	8.86	2.10	4.08	16.38
Weight of rural population	589	63.93	17.08	11.33	88.51
Ethnic minority ratio	589	12.71	21.43	0	99.99

Source: Authors' calculation based on statistics from *National Land and Resources Statistical Yearbook of China*, *Finance Yearbook of China*, *Statistical Yearbook of China*, *China Population Statistics Yearbook*, *China Population and Employment Statistics Yearbook*, and *China Data Online*.

169

To satisfy the normal distribution assumption, the highly skewed variables are normalized by taking natural log. Following a common practice in many existing studies, I use a stepwise regression approach to progressively introduce the independent variables into the models (Zhang & Brouwer, 2020), starting with the key predictor of interest. The models with different compositions of the independent variables yield largely robust and consistent results. Due to the limit of space, I include three models for each set of data analysis: the baseline model with the key predictor of interest and real per capita GDP,[18] an enhanced model that further introduces the one-year lag of real per capita central fiscal transfer, and the comprehensive model that contains all the independent variables including the demographic factors. To deal with possible heteroscedasticity problem, I conduct Breusch–Pagan test (Wooldridge, 2013) on all the models. As some models do not pass the test at 0.05 level, I report heteroscedasticity-robust statistical results for all the models in the regression tables.[19] The regression results are presented in Tables 5.2–5.4.

Discussion of Findings on the Control Variables

Besides the key predictors of interest, economic development level and central subsidies appear to be significant determinants of local expenditures on education, health care, and social security. First, economic development as measured by real per capita GDP significantly enhances local governments' expenditures on education, health care, and social security (see Tables 5.2–5.4), because the governments in richer regions have more financial resources to provide such services. Meanwhile, the citizens in better developed regions may have higher demand for these public goods as well. Based on the estimates in Model 3 of Tables 5.2–5.4, holding other factors constant, when real per capita GDP doubles, the real per capita expenditure on education,

[18] Per capita GDP is significantly correlated with the key predictors of interest, and both should affect the dependent variables. To avoid wrongly attributing the effect of per capita GDP on the dependent variables to resource abundance and dependence and leading to biased estimation of their effects, I include per capita GDP in the baseline models.

[19] I use the generic coeftest function in R to conduct the heteroscedasticity-robust estimation with White's estimator. I also tried different estimators and the results are highly similar.

Table 5.2. *Impacts of mineral resources on education expenditure*

	Dependent variable: Real per capita budgetary expenditure on education (ln)					
	(1)	(2)	(3)	(4)	(5)	(6)
Predictor of Interest						
Size of resource production (ln)	−0.021*	−0.055***	−0.025***			
	(0.009)	(0.006)	(0.006)			
Rate of resource dependence (ln)				−0.017.	−0.062***	−0.031***
				(0.009)	(0.005)	(0.005)
Control Variables						
Real per capita GDP (ln)	0.541***	0.553***	0.592***	0.527***	0.489***	0.560***
	(0.035)	(0.014)	(0.015)	(0.039)	(0.017)	(0.016)
1-year lag of real per capita central transfer (ln)		0.419***	0.337***		0.425***	0.339***
		(0.013)	(0.015)		(0.013)	(0.015)
Population density (ln)			0.050***			0.047***
			(0.009)			(0.009)
Weight of rural population			−0.001			−0.001
			(0.001)			(0.001)
Ethnic minority ratio			0.006***			0.006***
			(0.001)			(0.000)
Child ratio			−0.009			−0.008
			(0.007)			(0.008)
Senior ratio			−0.004			0.004
			(0.008)			(0.00)
Region effect	Yes	Yes	Yes	Yes	Yes	Yes
Year effect	Yes	Yes	Yes	Yes	Yes	Yes
R^2 (within)	0.484	0.806	0.837	0.483	0.809	0.838
Degree of freedom	538	537	532	538	537	532

The numbers in the parentheses are heteroscedasticity-robust standard errors. Significance codes: $***p < 0.001$; $**p < 0.05$; . $p < 0.1$.

Table 5.3. *Impacts of mineral resources on health care expenditure*

	Dependent variable: Real per capita budgetary expenditure on health care (ln)					
	(1)	(2)	(3)	(4)	(5)	(6)
Predictor of Interest						
Size of resource production (ln)	−0.031**	−0.077***	−0.060***			
	(0.010)	(0.008)	(0.008)			
Rate of resource dependence (ln)				−0.023*	−0.082***	−0.065***
				(0.011)	(0.006)	(0.007)
Control Variables						
Real per capita GDP (ln)	0.515***	0.532***	0.563***	0.499***	0.449***	0.499***
	(0.052)	(0.018)	(0.024)	(0.055)	(0.022)	(0.024)
1-year lag of real per capita central transfer (ln)		0.552***	0.497***		0.559***	0.501***
		(0.021)	(0.019)		(0.021)	(0.021)
Population density (ln)			0.024*			0.022*
			(0.011)			(0.011)
Weight of rural population			−0.001			−0.002
			(0.003)			(0.003)
Ethnic minority ratio			0.004***			0.004***
			(0.001)			(0.001)
Child ratio			−0.010			−0.008
			(0.011)			(0.011)
Senior ratio			0.010			0.011
			(0.010)			(0.010)
Region effect	Yes	Yes	Yes	Yes	Yes	Yes
Year effect	Yes	Yes	Yes	Yes	Yes	Yes
R^2 (within)	0.350	0.779	0.788	0.347	0.780	0.789
Degree of freedom	538	537	532	538	537	532

The numbers in the parentheses are heteroscedasticity-robust standard errors. Significance codes: ***$p < 0.001$; **$p < 0.01$; *$p < 0.05$; .$p < 0.1$.

Dependent variable: Real per capita budgetary expenditure on social security (ln)

	(1)	(2)	(3)	(4)	(5)	(6)
Predictor of Interest						
Size of resource production (ln)	0.088***	0.046**	0.015			
	(0.016)	(0.016)	(0.015)			
Rate of resource dependence (ln)				0.109***	0.056**	0.026
				(0.016)	(0.017)	(0.016)
Control Variables						
Real per capita GDP (ln)	0.367***	0.382***	0.337***	0.488***	0.442***	0.364***
	(0.041)	(0.045)	(0.045)	(0.049)	(0.040)	(0.039)
1-year lag of real per capita central transfer (ln)		0.510***	0.615***		0.503***	0.612***
		(0.030)	(0.048)		(0.031)	(0.048)
Population density (ln)			-0.049*			-0.042**
			(0.020)			(0.020)
Weight of rural population			-0.002			-0.002
			(0.003)			(0.003)
Ethnic minority ratio			-0.007***			-0.007***
			(0.001)			(0.001)
Child ratio			0.011			0.010
			(0.011)			(0.011)
Senior ratio			0.046*			0.046*
			(0.018)			(0.018)
Region effect	Yes	Yes	Yes	Yes	Yes	Yes
Year effect	Yes	Yes	Yes	Yes	Yes	Yes
R^2 (within)	0.165	0.543	0.585	0.185	0.547	0.587
Degree of freedom	538	537	532	538	537	532

The numbers in the parentheses are heteroscedasticity-robust standard errors. Significance codes: ***$p < 0.001$; **$p < 0.01$; *$p < 0.05$; . $p < 0.1$.

173

health care, and social security would increase by 51%, 48%, and 26%, respectively. Second, the significant positive effects of central fiscal transfer on all three types of public goods indicate that the central subsidies to local governments are extremely important for financing local public services. Given the generally weak local incentives to prioritize public expenditures that do not directly and visibly boost local economic growth or the political careers of local officials, the Chinese central government's fiscal transfers are an important tool to correct such tendencies. Based on the estimates in Model 3 of Tables 5.2–5.4, other things being equal, when real per capita central fiscal transfer doubles, the real per capita expenditure on education, health care, and social security would increase by 26%, 41%, and 53%, respectively.

The demographical factors also matter, but to varying degrees. Population density appears to moderately increase per capita expenditure on education and health care. It is positively correlated with both education and health care expenditures, and the estimated effects are statistically significant in all models. But population density decreases expenditures on social security, although the effects are not very stable across models. The contrasting results suggest that the citizens in more densely populated areas can enjoy better education and health care services. This finding is in line with the general impression that good schools and universities as well as hospitals tend to concentrate in mega cities like Beijing and Shanghai or capital cities of individual provinces, while people living in less populated third- or fourth-tier cities can hardly enjoy such benefits. Interestingly, governments in more populated regions spend less on social security. One possible explanation is that citizens in more densely populated area may be able to solicit support from each other and resort to local communities for financial assistance, which may relieve the government part of its burden to provide safety net for the citizens. But the conjecture needs to be tested against more empirical evidence.

The weight of rural population is negatively correlated with all three expenditures, although the effects are statistically and substantively insignificant in all the models. This result thus lends some, but not strong support to the urban-rural divide in public services in China. On the other hand, ethnic minority ratio slightly increases education and health care expenditures, and the effects are statistically significant and robust. The favorable treatment of minority population is probably a deliberate tactic for the Han-dominated Chinese government to win the support of the ethnic minorities. However, this effect does not show up in social security expenditure. It suggests that the Chinese government may not provide as elaborate social security coverage to ethnic minority areas as to Han-dominated areas, or that the Chinese government may use other forms of redistributive policies to meet the needs of vulnerable minority groups.

In terms of the age composition of population, a perplexing result is that child ratio is negatively correlated with the expenditure on education and health care, but positively correlated with that on social security. However, the estimated coefficients are statistically insignificant in all the models, which prevents us from drawing definite conclusion on the effects of the younger generation on public goods provision in China. On the other hand, senior ratio has unstable and statistically insignificant effects on the expenditure on education. It increases the expenditure on health care, but the effects are substantively small and statistically insignificant. Nevertheless, it significantly increases the expenditures on social security, which makes sense, because senior people need more social security benefits such as retirement pensions. Overall, the Chinese government's public goods expenditures appear insensitive to the younger generation, but they respond to China's aging population to some degree.

6 | Coping with the Resource Curse

China's Contained Resource Curse

Since the 1990s, a growing number of scholars have heatedly debated the socioeconomic and political impacts of natural resources including oil, gas and minerals on human society. The existing studies have revealed a variety of channels through which resource abundance and dependence may undermine economic development, weaken political institutions, arouse social conflicts, etc., which in general are referred to as the curse of natural resources. Nevertheless, controversies persist regarding the existence and causal mechanisms of the resource curse. Focusing on different geographical regions and historical periods, and depending on the scope and sources of empirical data, scholars have come up with vastly divergent and sometimes contradictory findings. Thus the resource curse, similar to most social socience theories, is far from being established as a definite rule like the laws of physics that human beings cannot escape from. However, the inconclusiveness does not make the quest on the resource curse less scientifically valuable, but rather makes it intellectually more intriguing. It motivates researchers to collect more empirical evidence, dig deeper into the microfoundations, and pay more attention to the sociohistorical and political contexts so as to rigorously identify the causal effects and clearly dissect the conditions under which these effects take place. With the gradual accumulation of empirical findings and incremental advancement of theories, we may eventually get close to some general rules that regulate human behaviors and that cannot be easily altered by free-willed human beings, if they ever exist.

Driven by such motivations, this book investigates China, the largest developing country that hosts rich mineral resources in many of its localities. Although China does not appear as a typical resource-rich country that suffers nationwide adverse impacts of mineral resources, the experiences of its numerous mining areas bear resemblance to

176

many other resource-rich developing countries. This makes China an interesting case that can shed new light on the causal relationship between mineral resources and socioeconomic and political outcomes. Taking a subnational approach by examining resource-rich Chinese localities and conducting cross-regional and longitudinal comparisons, this research reveals a nuanced picture about how mineral resources affect local development and governance in China. Disaggregating the society into different social groups, this study discovers disparate effects of mineral resources on three key players, namely capital, labor, and the state, as well as on their interrelations.

Based on the empirical evidence presented in the earlier chapters, I argue that there has been a contained resource curse in China. Mineral resources have generated distinctive impacts on the economy, the society, and the state's interaction with the economic and societal forces, and these effects are contained to limited scales and geographical scopes. If we look at the aggregate effects of mineral resources on the Chinese economy, resource boom can hardly be regarded as a curse, at least in the short run. From around the turn of the millennium till the early 2010s, the resource sector experienced exponential growth as a result of both rising mineral prices and increased demands on the market. Most resource-rich regions benefited from the rapid, massive inflow of resource revenue and enjoyed remarkable economic and fiscal growth. As perhaps the best-known example, Inner Mongolia Autonomous Region rode on the resource boom. After discovering coal reserves in 11 of its 12 prefecture-level units, it quickly became one of the largest producers of coal in China, with raw coal production accounting for 27.6% of the national total in 2019. Between 2000 and 2010, Inner Mongolia's GDP growth rates averaged 18%, way above the national average.[1] As the poster boy of Inner Mongolia, the city of Ordos became prosperous owing to the discovery of not only coal but also rare earth and natural gas, which transformed Ordos from a traditionally agrarian economy based on animal husbandry and cashmere production to a rapidly industrializing economy. It experienced extraordinarily high GDP growth rate, and within the span of a few years, it rose to one of the richest cities in China. Its nominal per capita GDP even surpassed that of Hong Kong in 2011. Similar to Ordos,

---

[1] Guo Xing, 2021, "Inner Mongolia Cracks Down Coal-related Corruption."

many other mining areas in Shanxi Province, Shaanxi Province, etc. also underwent resource-driven growth throughout the 2000s.

However, if we disaggregate the effects of resources on different social groups, we detect divergent impacts on capital and labor, the two major stakeholders in the economy. Resource capital, embodied by mining businesses, came out as the biggest winner of the resource boom. The huge inflow of resource revenue greatly facilitated capital accumulation and investment in mining and related industries, leading to an upward spiral of the development of the resource sector. Moreover, the benefit of the resource boom was not limited to the resource sector but generated spillover effects and led to increased capital investment in other non-resource industries. Such spillover effects particularly favored low-tech industries such as construction and manufacturing, which is partly due to the investment preferences of first-generation Chinese mining entrepreneurs who became rich in the 1990s and 2000s. As most of them grew up in poverty and shortage during the Maoist years and received limited or disrupted education due to the Cultural Revolution, they had natural preferences for industries that produce concrete materials and have low technological entry bar. Meanwhile, the accumulation of resource capital also spurred speculative investments in real estate, which could generate quick and high returns under China's soaring housing market that overlapped with the resource boom. However, these investment strategies also generated considerable financial risks and could hamper long-term economic development, as resource-rich regions may be stuck in backward industrial structures and can hardly embrace emerging technologies that are pushing other non-resource regions onto newer and faster tracks of development.

On the other hand, mineral resources are largely a curse to labor. To begin with, compared with other industries, especially labor-intensive ones, the increasingly mechanized mining industries provide small and shrinking numbers of employment opportunities. Although mining jobs are slightly better paid than those in other low-tech industries such as construction and manufacturing, the salaries are hardly commensurate with the harsh working conditions and poor protection of workers' health, safety, and labor rights in Chinese mines. Considering the long-term financial costs of many mining-caused health problems such as pneumoconiosis and high casualty rates of mining accidents, mining jobs can hardly be regarded as a desirable vocation. Moreover, resources not only affect those working in mining industries, but have far-reaching implications for labor at large. First of all, by taking away farmlands and undermining agricultural productivity, mining activities cause displacement of rural residents and take away job opportunities in the primary sector. Resource boom also tends to squeeze out jobs in other industries, not only the high-tech ones such as IT but also labor-intensive ones including manufacturing and construction. Furthermore, extractive activities generate enormous negative externalities to surrounding areas, such as environmental hazards, economic disputes, and public insecurity. As these negative externalities can hardly be accounted for or compensated properly, local citizens suffer huge financial and health losses. All these impacts are ultimately translated into lowered incomes for local citizens in resource-rich regions. In short, whereas the resource sector is pro-capital, it can be said to be anti-labor.

The negligence of labor welfare also shows up in the provision of public goods in resource-rich regions. Under the highly decentralized provision of public goods in China, the local governments at and below the provincial level are the main providers of most public goods and shoulder the vast majority of the fiscal expenses. However, under the cadre evaluation system that heavily emphasizes economic growth above other government responsibilities, Chinese local governments are not strongly motivated to spend on public goods that cannot instantly or visibly boost GDP and/or fiscal growth. The resource-based local economic structure further exacerbates this problem. Due to the limited need for labor in the resource sector as well as psychological dependence on resources, there are much weaker incentives for resource-rich regions to invest in the cultivation of a healthy and well-educated labor force. Such mentality leads local governments in resource-rich regions to spend significantly less on education and medical services than non-resource regions do. The weakened public investment in education and health care further hurts the welfare of labor, and it impedes the accumulation of human capital, which is crucial for long-term economic development and industrial upgrading.

When resources facilitate capital accumulation but hurt the welfare of labor and suppress its income, the imbalance between capital and labor makes the resource sector an extremely unfair game. Since the market reform started in the late 1970s, China has gradually transformed from an egalitarian society under the Maoist rule into one with aggravating income inequality across both geographical lines and social groups (Xie & Zhou, 2014). Against this backdrop, the unequal and unfair distribution of resource wealth between capital and labor further exacerbates the social inequality in resource-rich regions. While some scholars argue that income inequality has been an inactive volcano and has not yet caused major social unrest in China (Whyte, 2010, 2016; Whyte & Im, 2014), many resource-rich regions have witnessed a growing sense of relative deprivation and widespread popular grievance, and have experienced frequent eruption of social conflicts and even violent clashes between mining businesses and local citizens (Chen, 2016; Dong, 2016; Zhang, 2008). In Zhan (2021), drawing from three databases on social conflicts across China including the CLB "Strike" dataset, the CASS "Collective Incidents" dataset, and the "China Strikes" dataset constructed by Elfstrom (2017), I find that resource-rich regions tend to suffer higher tendencies of resource-triggered social conflicts. The number of reported resource conflicts and the size of resource production of each province are highly positively correlated, with a Pearson correlation coefficient of 0.73 (p-value = 0.000). In this sense, the endowment of rich mineral resources has been a curse to social equality and stability in China.

Furthermore, resource wealth exacerbates the loopholes in the Chinese political and economic system. The resource sector and resource-rich regions appear to be particularly corrupt. The rapid, massive inflow of resource wealth creates irresistible temptations for state employees to abuse their power for private gains. Due to the state ownership of mineral resources and extensive regulation over a wide array of issues in the mining industries, such as environmental protection, work safety, taxation, transaction of mining rights, pricing of mineral products, quality control and transportation, the strong and often unchecked administrative power creates structural opportunities for collusion between local bureaucrats and resource interests. Resource revenues corrupt not only the regulatory agencies and fiscal departments but also the personnel management system, which is core to the CCP's grip to power. Given the enormous opportunities as well as incentives for corruption in the resource sector, resource-rich regions suffer significantly higher corruption rates than resource-poor ones.

Overall, the empirical evidence suggests that China does suffer the curse of natural resources in various forms at subnational levels.

Although resource boom contributed to economic growth in aggregate, it generated disparate impacts on different social groups, namely capital and labor, in extremely unequal and unfair ways. Moreover, there are far-reaching and potentially long-lasting political and social impacts: Resource abundance undermines the quality of local political institutions and gives rise to social conflicts. These adverse socioeconomic and political effects suggest that China is not immune to the curse of natural resources. Its symptoms to a large extent echo the local resource curse that comparative studies have identified in some other resource-rich developing countries (Aragón et al., 2015; Sexton, 2020).

What Contains the Resource Curse in China?

While acknowledging the existence of the resource curse in China, it is worth noting that the adverse impacts of natural resources are mostly contained at subnational levels and to limited scales in China. There have not been nationwide, full-blown symptoms of the resource curse as seen in other resource-rich countries. How do we explain the contained resource curse in China?

One direct answer is that China at the national level is not heavily dependent on mineral resources for its economy or exports. Resource dependence only exists at the provincial level or below and pertains to certain localities, which are mostly located in inland areas, whereas the more developed coastal regions rarely rely on the resource sector for their economic growth. The lack of resource dependence nationwide puts a natural cap on how much the Chinese central government can be swayed by resource interests. There is very limited representation of resource interests in the Chinese Communist Party-state's key decision-making bodies at the central level. Within the CCP, the Politburo and Politburo Standing Committee are entrusted with the ultimate power to make all the major decisions. A screening of all the members of the 15th to the 19th CCP Politburo and Politburo Standing Committee (1997–2022), which covers the period under this study, reveals that Xinjiang is the only resource-rich region whose party secretaries have been included in the Politburo. No local leaders from other resource-rich provinces such as Shanxi, Shaanxi, and Inner Mongolia have made it into the Politburo. And no official representative from the resource sector, such as the oil and coal industries, has served on the

Politburo.[2] Overall, the top leaders of resource-rich provinces and of the resource sector are rarely included in the Politburo, let alone the Politburo Standing Committee. Inside the government, among the dozens of central ministries and organs under the State Council, only the Ministry of Land and Resources (restructured and renamed as Ministry of Natural Resources in 2018), National Energy Administration, and State Administration of Coal Mine Safety specifically handle mineral resources, and they are far from the most powerful central departments.

Given the lesser status of resource players in the top layer of China's political power structure, it is very unlikely for the Chinese central government to be captured by resource interests, as what happens at the local levels. Without vested interest, the Chinese central government can easily rein in resource-rich localities when it becomes alert of local problems such as widespread corruption and resource conflicts that threaten regime legitimacy and stability. For example, the central government can launch anti-corruption campaigns from top-down to combat corruption in resource-rich regions such as Shanxi and Inner Mongolia, and it can emphasize stability maintenance to deter social conflicts from spiraling out of control. Therefore, the central intervention can relatively effectively contain local resource curse without much resistance at the central level.

In addition, some have noticed China's deliberate movement toward a "circular economy" to decrease the reliance on mining for its mineral supply. The "circular economy" can be defined as an economic system that minimizes resource input and waste, emission, and energy leakages by cycling, extending, intensifying, and dematerializing material and energy loops (Geissdoerfer et al., 2017). After the notion was introduced into China from industrialized countries, it has gradually shifted from the narrow focus on waste recycling to broad efficiency-oriented control during the closed-loop flows of materials at all stages of production, distribution, and consumption (Su et al., 2012). Since the early 2000s, the Chinese central government has promulgated a series of laws and regulations to support the development of a circular

---

[2] Zhou Yongkang was the only Politburo member who had substantial work experience in the resource sector. He worked in the oil industry from 1967 to 1998, but he served on the Politburo (2002–2007) and Politburo Standing Committee (2007–2012) as the Secretary of the Central Political and Legal Affairs Commission, not representing the oil sector.

economy, and various ministries and localities have formulated their own policies (Yuan et al., 2006). For example, efforts have been made to retrieve metals from anthropogenic minerals to improve the efficiency of mineral utilization (Zeng et al., 2020). According to the report of the National Statistical Bureau, in 2014, China made use of nearly 250 million tons of waste and recycled resources and saved nearly 200 million tons of coal in energy supply.[3] Therefore, the strategy of promoting a circular economy can be regarded as an added buffer to resource dependency and may help alleviate the adverse consequences of extractive industries.[4]

Moreover, the abovementioned negative socioeconomic and political impacts of resources are largely confined to specific resource-rich localities and rarely contagious to other non-resource regions. This can be partially explained by China's traditionally decentralized economic system. Since the Maoist years, China has followed an M-form rather than the Soviet-styled U-form economic organization across the country, which allowed regional economies to be highly self-sufficient and autonomous from each other (Qian & Xu, 1993). The industrial structures and other characteristics of regional economy are to a large extent confined within administrative units such as counties, prefectures, or provinces along geographical lines. Meanwhile, the Chinese government has followed the Ricardian notion of comparative advantage (Ricardo, 1817) in its economic planning of regional development since the Maoist era. It has developed specific industrial structures in different regions according to their resource endowments and geographical features. Into the reform era, the Chinese government continues the spatial economic planning and encourages the utilization of regional resource endowments, including not only natural resources but also human resources and other regional specialties.[5] Hence

---

[3] Wang Hanjuan and Xu Fuxian, 2015. "Woguo Fazhan Xunhuan Jingji Qude Shida Chengguo (Ten Achievements towards a Circular Economy in China)," Xinhua Net, November 19, www.xinhuanet.com/politics/2015-11/19/c_128444984.htm, accessed on March 9, 2021.

[4] I thank one anonymous reviewer for suggesting this very important point.

[5] For example, see Xi Jinping, 2019. "Tuidong Xingcheng Youshi Hubu Gaozhiliang Fazhan de Quyu Jingji Buju (Promoting Mutually Supplementing Regional Economic Layout with High-Quality Development)," Xinhua News, December 15, www.xinhuanet.com/politics/2019-12/15/c_1125348940.htm, accessed on March 9, 2021.

regional economies follow distinctive development trajectories based on their core competencies: Whereas resource-rich regions follow resource-based development, others promote the development of other sectors such as manufacturing, IT, or heavy industries. As a result, the socioeconomic impacts of the resource economy pertain to the host regions only and have rather limited influence on other regions, even the neighboring ones.

Besides these structural factors that put natural boundaries to how far mineral resources can impact China, this research highlights the roles that the Chinese state plays in containing the extent of the resource curse. The Chinese state has been actively involved in the economy and deeply penetrated the society. Chinese local governments are a crucial stakeholder in the resource economy and interact extensively with the other two key stakeholders, capital and labor. The resource-based economic structure puts local governments of resource-rich regions in an intricate situation and forces them to strike a delicate balance between the mining businesses and local citizens. On the one hand, local governments are strongly motivated to foster the development of mining industries, which can contribute hugely to local economic growth and fiscal coffers, and to forge a symbiotic relationship with the mining businesses. On the other hand, local governments are aware of the negative externalities that the resource economy generates on local communities and are wary of the intensive conflicts between the mining industries and local citizens. Under the heavy top-down pressure to maintain regime stability, local officials acutely understand the serious threat that resource conflicts pose to social stability as well as their political careers. Therefore, the local governments in resource-rich regions are caught between the two foremost important yardsticks under China's cadre evaluation system, growth and stability, and have to find every means to balance the conflicting goals. Whereas they zealously promote the development of mining industries as an engine of growth, they have to cautiously address the negative impacts of mining industries on regime legitimacy and stability.

Toward this end, the Chinese state has devised a variety of coping strategies and mediated actively between the conflicting interests of mining businesses and local citizens. The coping strategies boil down to job creation that allows local labor force to share part of the resource wealth, redistributive mechanisms that transfer revenue from the mining industries to compensate local citizens who lose out in the resource economy, and industrial diversification to transition out of resource dependence.

Resource-Based Employment Opportunities

In view of the financial losses caused to local citizens due to mining, local governments of mining areas try to create economic opportunities based on the resource sector, so that local citizens can also share part of the resource wealth. Local authorities commonly require or encourage mining companies to hire local citizens. However, mining companies usually offer limited and dangerous jobs owing to increasing mechanization and the harsh working conditions in the mines. And for the less dangerous technician and managerial positions, local labor force is hardly equipped with the knowledge and expertise for the jobs. Thus, local governments have to scramble to identify alternative income sources for local citizens. The detailed practices vary widely across regions depending on local conditions and customs, but they can be categorized into two types of job creation.

One commonly used strategy is to create employment opportunities in derivative businesses such as catering, property management, environmental recovery, and transportation services that serve the mining sector. Local authorities in mining areas often encourage citizens, especially those who lost their land and became displaced, to engage in these service businesses as new income sources. However, there are often hurdles for rural residents to overcome. Many peasants lack the necessary skills or start-up funds. For example, in order to provide transportation services for mining companies, peasants have to learn driving and accumulate enough savings to buy trucks, given that it is very difficult for rural citizens to obtain bank loans. Even if they can secure enough start-up funds and start the business, small rural businesses have rather weak bargaining power against the mining companies they intend to serve, and they also face fierce competition from other service providers on the market.

Realizing these problems, some grassroots governments played active roles in organizing the labor force, providing vocational trainings and protecting their interests by collectively bargaining with the mining companies and fending off outside competition. In an innovative model I observed in a coal-rich Y Banner in Inner Mongolia, the village branches of the CCP set up village-based companies to provide various services such as transportation, environmental recovery, and catering to the mining companies operating within the territories of the villages. The village enterprises employed only their own villagers, and usually operated under the leadership of the village party secretaries. As legal entities instead of individual service providers, the village enterprises collectively bargained with the mining companies for better prices and terms of service and demanded timely payment for the services provided, which the villagers did not receive previously when working on individual bases. Because the mining companies needed to expropriate land from the villages, which necessitated the authorization by the village party secretaries, they tended to accommodate the village enterprises' requests. Meanwhile, the village enterprises could monopolize the local market by imposing various charges or set up administrative barriers on competing service providers from outside the villages. Furthermore, the village cadres mobilized their political connections with upper-level authorities to obtain policy support in the form of tax breaks or favorable land policies, which helped enhance the profitability of the village enterprises.

In addition to creating employment opportunities in derivative businesses that serve the resource sector, some resource-rich regions adopted a different approach by requiring mining companies to invest in non-resource sectors to create new jobs for local citizens. For example, starting in 2004, an X County in Shanxi Province launched a campaign to create job opportunities in non-coal sectors for local citizens. The county government required all coal mining companies operating on its territory to contribute 15 yuan for each ton of coal produced to set up a non-coal business (Zhang, 2008, p. 79). For a medium-size coal mine with annual production capacity of 1 million tons, this policy would translate into a required investment of 15 million yuan per year. Thanks to the investments by coal companies, new businesses and employment opportunities gradually emerged. Based on the pilot experiments in different localities following the initiative of X County, the Shanxi Provincial government issued a policy of "subsidizing peasants by coal (*yimei bunong* 以煤补农)" in 2006 and made it a province-wide requirement for coal-related companies to invest in non-coal businesses, which also functioned as an industrial strategy for Shanxi to transition out of heavy resource dependence and diversify its industrial structures. Under this formal policy, subprovincial governments in Shanxi all devised their own policies such as subsidies and favorable land and taxation policies to facilitate the investments in non-coal businesses, and received some enthusiastic responses from the mining companies (Zheng, 2011, pp. 31–32). To enlarge the employment of peasants, local governments particularly welcomed coal companies to diversify into agricultural production. According to a media report, 610 coal companies had set foot in the agricultural sector by 2008. As typical examples, one coal-turned poultry company claimed to employ more than 3,000 peasants, and another produce-processing company claimed to generate more than 50 million yuan of income for local citizens.[6] These cases suggest that when prompted by the government, mining companies could become a new source of job opportunities for local citizens.

Redistribution of Resource Wealth

Besides creating resource-based employment opportunities, many mining areas adopt various mechanisms to redistribute the resource wealth from mining companies to local citizens, some in the form of public goods provision and some through fiscal transfers and relief policies funded by resource revenue. First of all, it is fairly common for the Chinese government to require companies, state-owned or private, to provide various public goods for local communities. Mining companies are no exception. Especially for state-owned mining companies established during the Maoist era, they normally shoulder many social responsibilities not only for their employees but also for residents in neighboring areas. They provide a wide range of public goods such as water and electricity for local residents, and also finance all kinds of public infrastructure project. Some companies run their own elementary and secondary schools, hospitals, and even police stations for the neighborhood. These mining companies are closely intertwined with local communities and have become an essential part of local residents' daily life.

Similar to state-owned mining companies, private companies are also mobilized to provide various public goods such as paved roads,

---

[6] China News Net, 2009. "Shanxi Yimei Bunog, 'Meilaoban' Bianshen 'Nonglaoban' (Shanxi Subsidizes Peasants by Coal, 'Coal Bosses' Transform into 'Agriculture Bosses')," October 22, http://news.ifeng.com/mainland/200910/1022_17_1400633.shtml, accessed on February 12, 2020.

public facilities, and funding for schools. Based on the claim that mining companies profit from state-owned resources, Chinese local governments often require them to pay back to local communities. In the abovementioned policy initiative of subsidizing peasants by coal in Shanxi Province, on top of the required investment in non-coal businesses, Shanxi local governments also demanded coal companies to contribute certain amount of their revenue to public welfare projects. Driven by either a sense of social responsibility or a calculation to gain positive publicity and improve relations with the government and citizens, private entrepreneurs more or less accommodated these requests, willingly or reluctantly. Quite a number of private coal companies were deeply involved in government-launched campaigns on poverty alleviation, environmental protection, New Socialist Countryside Construction (*shehuizhuyi xinnongcun jianshe* 社会主义 新农村建设), etc. For example, Table 6.1 documents some financial contributions that L Company, a large private coal company in Shanxi

Table 6.1. *Selected financial contributions to public projects by L Company*

Year	Amount (million yuan)	Projects
2003	120	Established a middle school and a vocational school
2003–2013	12	Provided allowances for 1,200 orphans and elderly people with no family at the rate of 1,000 yuan per person per year
2003–2007	4	Built 5 wells, 4 water pools, more than 7,500 meters of water pipes for villages suffering water shortage
2005	5	Environmental recovery and planting 1.83 million trees
2007	10	Built a pagoda in a public park
2008	20	Donation to earthquake-affected areas in Sichuan Province
2010	12	Donation to earthquake-affected areas in Qinghai Province

Source: Chen Xiaoyan, 2016. *The Political Logic of Enterprise-driven Urbanization: A Case Study of Y Town in Shanxi Province*, pp. 79–80.

Province, made to charity and public projects before it went bankrupt in 2013. In return for these massive contributions, the owner of L Company was awarded multiple official titles and honors, including becoming a representative to Shanxi People's Congress and honorary vice president of the CPPCC of his county, and obtained substantial support from local governments including policy favors and bank loans (Chen, 2016, pp. 79–80, 101).

In ethnic minority areas such as Xinjiang Uygur Autonomous Region, which face high risks of interethnic contentions, the local governments pay special attention to mobilize state-owned and private enterprises, including mining enterprises, to participate in various redistributive schemes to address the needs of disadvantaged minority groups, especially in the underdeveloped and conflict-prone southern Xinjiang. For example, mining companies have been called upon to contribute to anti-poverty projects in southern Xinjiang by sponsoring schools, building infrastructure, fighting desertification and deforestation, providing job opportunities, etc.[7] As part of the Targeted Poverty Alleviation campaign (*jingzhun fupin* 精准扶贫) that the central government launched in 2016, Xinjiang local governments initiated a policy to pair 1,000 enterprises with 1,000 villages to help lift the villagers out of poverty (*qianqi bang qiancun* 千企帮千村). A copper mining company, as one of the participating enterprises, reportedly contributed more than 100 million yuan to help 3 ethnic minority villages, covering more than 1,000 peasants and herdsmen. Since 2016, the company helped the villages build a dam and irrigation systems, construct infrastructure to develop tourism as the staple industry, and offered financial aid to two primary schools. In addition to creating jobs for the paired villages, the company followed the instructions of local governments and made extra efforts to hire ethnic minority workers from southern Xinjiang.[8]

[7] Xiong Wenbing, 2020. "Yijia Henan Meiqi Zai Jiang Fazhan de Zeren yu Dandang (The Duties and Contributions of A Henan-invested Coal Company in Xinjiang)," *China Energy News*, May 25, http://paper.people.com.cn/zgnyb/html/2020-05/25/content_1988954.htm, accessed on March 10, 2021.
[8] Wu Yajing, 2020. "Ashele Tongye Huo Xinjiang 'Qianqi Bang Qiancun' Jingzhun Fupin Xingdong Xianjin Qiye (Ashele Copper Awarded the Title of '1000 Enterprises Aiding 1000 Villages' Model Enterprise under the Targeted Poverty Alleviation Campaign)," Zijin Mining, www.zjky.cn/about/zjhuodong-detail-118320.htm, accessed on March 10, 2021.

In addition to requiring the mining enterprises to participate in public welfare projects, local governments also redistribute resource wealth to citizens through the fiscal system. Apart from various taxes, governments of resource-rich regions collect from mining companies all kinds of nontax exaction such as environmental management fees, resource compensation fees, and land compensation fees. These fiscal revenues, which mostly go to local coffers, allow resource-rich regions to increase their coverage and standards of social welfare benefits such as low-income allowance, retirement pension, and medical insurance. As the data analysis in Chapter 5 shows, resource-rich regions spend notably more fiscal revenue on social security than non-resource regions. These expenses in flexible forms can meet different needs of citizens and offset some detrimental effects of the mining sector on local residents. For example, when mining-related environmental degradation such as pollution or water shortage decreased the productivity of farmland, some local governments offered the affected farmers low-income allowances to cover their losses. In some areas, medical insurance or low-income allowances are allocated to citizens suffering from health problems or incapacitation owing to mining-caused environmental hazards. Housing allowances are handed out to displaced peasants who lose their land and properties to mining. And other kinds of subsidy are also granted to residents in extreme financial difficulties. Such relief policies can vary widely across regions and take various formats, some through institutionalized channels and others on ad hoc basis, but they are all partially financed by the mining sector's tax and nontax contributions.

Although the public services and fiscal transfers generate extra financial costs for the mining sector, they partly compensate for the negative externalities imposed on local residents. Moreover, they create vested interests among local residents who, despite their many disputes with and grievances about the mining companies, in general still welcome the existence and prosperity of the mining companies, owing to the economic benefits they bring to the local communities. For mining companies that take their social responsibilities seriously and contribute to public welfare generously, they may well earn the trust and support of local citizens. For instance, the owner of the above mentioned L Company was a native of one town in Shanxi Province and continuously supported the infrastructural construction of his hometown and distributed jobs and welfare benefits to his country fellows. In view of his great contributions to local development and public welfare and in hope that he could help lift the villagers out of poverty, he was invited to run for the 2011 village elections and was successfully elected as the village committee head of 14 villages in his hometown, although it was against the law for one person to head more than one village. Unfortunately, his leadership ended abruptly in 2014 when he was arrested for financial misconducts and corruption-related charges. And L Company ceased supporting the villages financially as it went bankrupt in 2013 (Chen, 2016, pp. 94, 172). Indeed, this is a very rare and perhaps dramatic case, as most mining entrepreneurs can hardly be as devoted to local public affairs and as willing to take up so much social responsibility, and there are also many legal barriers to overcome in order for mining entrepreneurs to be directly involved in local governance.

Transitioning out of Resource Dependency

Besides addressing the problems associated with the resource economy, some resource-rich Chinese localities also try to diversify the local economic structure and transition out of resource dependency. As comparative studies suggest, industrial diversification is an important strategy for resource-rich countries to cope with the resource curse and transition out of resource dependency (International Monetary Fund, 2014; Ross, 2019). For Chinese localities witnessing massive socio-political problems caused by the mining industries or those foreseeing the exhaustion of their mineral resources in the near future, they see especially pressing needs for transition, and many have made serious efforts in diversification. As mentioned above, the policies of Shanxi Province that required mining enterprises to invest in non-coal sectors served this purpose and have to a certain degree promoted the growth of not only manufacturing industries such as food processing but also service industries including logistics and tourism. For instance, according to my field research in Shanxi, an L City has entered strategic partnership with Alibaba Group and tried to turn itself into an e-commerce logistical hub to serve the vast rural areas in China.[9]

[9] Also see Yellow River News Net, 2018. "Fang Alibaba Nongcun Taobao Shanxi Zongjingli Zhou Guodong (Interview with the Shanxi General Manager of Alibaba Rural Taobao)," July, https://m.sohu.com/n/459743012/ , accessed on February 17, 2020.

Some local governments also attempted to induce industrial upgrading and foster high-tech industries. For example, an H City, which hosts the largest coal base in Sichuan Province, set aside lands to establish industrial parks and offered supporting policies to attract electronics and IT companies, with the ambitious goal of transforming itself into the "Silicon Valley of West China."[10] Another case is the antimony-rich L City in Hunan Province. In the face of depleting antimony reserves, the city was forced to diversify its economic structure by developing non-resource industries such as new materials, electronic information, biomedicine, and produce processing. The local government specifically launched a campaign to attract leading scientists and high-caliber professional experts into the city to facilitate the transition.[11]

These diversification strategies appear to be partially effective, particularly for those resource-depleting areas with urgent needs for industrial transformation. Between 2001 and 2011, the Chinese government officially recognized 69 resource-depleting cities and offered a series of policies to support their transition out of resource dependency. For example, the central government offered financial subsidies and earmarked loans, established compensation schemes for mining industries to pay for their environmental damages, and encouraged these cities to identify and incubate replacement industries. Through the central support and local efforts, these 69 cities saw quite remarkable economic growth, despite the depletion of mineral reserves and declining contributions of the mining industries. Altogether, the total GDP of these 69 cities increased from 438.33 billion yuan in 2001 to 2.46 trillion yuan in 2012, and their share in national GDP increased from 4.0% in 2001 to 4.73% in 2012. Moreover, the industrial transformation brought new opportunities to the local labor force. Between

---

[10] National Development and Reform Commission, 2018. "Ziyuan Kujie Chengshi Peiyu Zhuangda Xin Dongneng, 'Meidu' Bian 'Dianzicheng' (City Facing Resource Depletion Cultivates New Engines of Growth: Turning the 'Coal Capital' into an 'Electronic City')," January 26, www.ndrc.gov.cn/fggz/dqzx/zyxdqzxfz/201801/t20180126_1084921.html, accessed on February 17, 2020.

[11] National Development and Reform Commission, 2019. "'Shijie Tidu' 10 Nian Qiubian, Jiakuai Zhuanxing Shengji ('The World's Antimony Capital' Seeks Change within 10 Years by Speeding up Transformation and Upgrading)," January 25, http://china.qianlong.com/2019/0125/3084983.shtml, accessed on February 17, 2020.

2008 and 2012, 2.96 million people received vocational training, and 3.18 million new jobs were created in these 69 cities. Their average annual urban income increased from 10,847 yuan to 15,080 yuan, with an annual growth rate of 11.6%.[12]

However, we have to realize that the transition out of resource dependency is a long, arduous process that does not guarantee success. The Chinese state's efforts in transforming local economic structures have encountered a fair amount of obstacles. First of all, because resource-dependent localities normally lack the basic infrastructure, supply chains, and more importantly, human capital necessary for industrial transformation and upgrading, the governments have to make huge efforts and spend large sums of money on training local labor force or attracting talents from elsewhere. Second, compared with the regions facing depleting resources, the other resource-rich regions that do not foresee the exhaustion of their resources in the near future have much weaker incentives to actively diversify their industrial structure. Partly because of the psychological dependence on resources, and partly due to the short tenure and thus time horizon of local officials, who are under strong pressure to maintain economic growth during their relatively short tenures, can hardly afford to give up the profitable mining industries. Third, the diversification policies of resource-dependent regions are more often than not arbitrary and transitory. The transformation plans may come out of the whimsical decisions of some leading officials. When the decision-makers leave office, the plans are very likely to be dropped by the successors. For example, one former leader of Shanxi Province devised a diversification strategy, which demanded each village in Shanxi to identify one staple produce and to make a brand name out of it. Following this policy, some villages focused on planting walnut trees. But before the peasants' hard work bore any fruit, a succeeding provincial leader changed the plan to planting Chinese herbs. Such abrupt policy changes not only led to financial losses for the peasants, but also undermined the credibility of the policymakers. Therefore, the industrial policies are very sensitive to political changes and tend to be

---

[12] Zhi Dalin, 2015. "Woguo Ziyuanxing Chengshi Zhuanxing yu Kechixu Fazhan de Kunjing ji Pojie Duice (The Difficulties and Solutions of the Transition and Sustainable Development of Resource-Based Cities in China)," *China Regional Economy*, September 25, www.cre.org.cn/list2/zy/9262.html, accessed on March 10, 2021.

unsustainable, especially given the high turnover rates of Chinese local officials.

Overall, despite the strong need of many resource-rich regions to diversify their economic structures and transition out of resource dependency, we have seen mixed pictures about the effectiveness of their strategies. After all, since the Maoist years, the Chinese state has constantly struggled in its relationship with the market. It has never successfully planned the economy in full but has largely relied on market forces to release the massive productive power of its population and to generate the remarkable economic growth since the late 1970s. Therefore, whether and how the Chinese state can wrestle with the invisible hand and lead resource-rich regions out of resource dependency remains a big question.

Explaining State Intervention: Capacity and Incentive

This research highlights the active roles that the state can play in mitigating the malaises of resource-based economy. But there are crucial preconditions for effective state intervention, namely strong state capacity and proper incentive structure. First, the Chinese state's intervening strategies, particularly the redistributive policies, depend on its strong capacity to mobilize resources from some social groups or industrial sectors and transfer them to some other groups or sectors. This is to a large degree attributable to the Chinese Communist Party-state's expansive intervention in the economy and deep penetration into the society. This makes it vastly different from the rentier states in many resource-rich developing countries, which tend to lack socially intrusive and elaborate bureaucracies and have limited capacity to carry out many functions (Fearon & Laitin, 2003; Lujala, 2010).

Although the decentralization and market reforms since the late 1970s have gradually emancipated the Chinese economy from the totalitarian control under the Maoist rule, a strong local state corporatism (Oi, 1992; Unger & Chan, 1995) has emerged and persisted that allowed the local state and the business sector to collaborate closely and exchange favors constantly. Chinese local governments, including the administrative departments and other government-sponsored bodies, maintain frequent contacts with enterprises for purposes of regulation, taxation, policy implementation, etc. Local governments can hand out favorable policy treatments and lucrative business opportunities in exchange for enterprises' cooperation on many issues. Bearing in mind future policy benefits and fearful of potential retaliation such as the imposition of unusually stringent regulations, companies tend to comply with the government's requests. The extensive ties with economic entities hence grant the Chinese state strong bargaining power against the business sector and help minimize resistance to the implementation of its policies.

In addition to the state–business ties at the organizational level, local officials also build up ties with mining entrepreneurs at the personal level. Personal favors and "face giving" (*gei mianzi*给面子) have long existed in China (Yang, 1994) and continued to flourish in state–business interactions under the market reform (Wank, 2002). Informal negotiations between officials and entrepreneurs, which are powerful tools of persuasion and resource mobilization, have been prevalently conducted on dining tables and after rounds of toasts. Even after Xi Jinping's high-profile anti-corruption campaign officially banned extravagant banquets, there are still ample venues and subtle ways such as business clubs and recreational activities for officials to mingle with business people. The personalized state–business ties allow local governments to solicit financial support from mining companies for public services, infrastructural projects, and welfare benefits for local citizens on an ad hoc basis. To give face to local leaders and cultivate a favorable environment for their businesses, mining entrepreneurs would normally accommodate these requests. Some mining entrepreneurs even proactively participate in charity work to build a reputation of a philanthropist, which not only generates good publicity for business purposes but also helps them to gain the support of local leaders when they pursue political positions in the local People's Congress or CPPCC. Basically, there are many informal channels through which local governments can mobilize resources from mining businesses.

On the other hand, partly as a legacy of the CCP's mass line, the party-state penetrates deeply in the Chinese society and maintains close contact with local citizens through its extensive grassroots government branches and party organs. In many Chinese localities, county- and township-level officials are required to regularly visit the villages in their jurisdiction and to acquaint themselves with the villagers and their needs. This interaction allows grassroots officials to forge personal connections with the villagers and gain their trust. In the Chinese society, where social networking still plays important roles and personal favors are highly valued (Yang, 1994), such personal ties and trust are essential tools for communication and persuasion, especially in rural communities. Moreover, village cadres, although not formally part of the *nomenklatura* system, are instrumental in extending the state's reach into rural communities and implementing policy tasks handed down by higher authorities. The deep reach into the society thus enables the party-state to accurately understand the citizens' needs and concerns, to devise redistributive schemes to address them, and to ensure the transfers reach their targeted social groups relatively effectively.

Second, the success of the Chinese state's intervening strategies also depends on local governments' incentives to implement them faithfully. As discussed in Chapter 4, there is a high risk of local state capture by resource interests in resource-rich regions. Since local officials' political careers benefit hugely from a thriving resource sector that can boost GDP and fiscal growth, and there are also ample rent-seeking opportunities for the officials to enrich themselves. Why would the local governments respond to citizens' needs and demands when they are at odds with those of the mining industries, especially in an authoritarian regime with no meaningful election and little accountability of local officials to the citizenry? The key lies in the party-state's personnel management system that tightly controls local officials and heavily emphasizes stability maintenance. Although not a democracy, the Chinese Communist regime is deeply concerned about its legitimacy and highly sensitive to social unrest that threatens regime stability. China's cadre management system prioritizes the prevention of mass protests and makes stability maintenance a hard indicator in the evaluation of cadres' performance from the provincial to the grassroots levels. The heavy pressure from top-down to maintain stability provides the ultimate incentive for local governments to respond to citizens' grievances so as to prevent the eruption of collective incidents, which may ruin the political career of local leaders.

Meanwhile, the party discipline and anti-corruption measures also put a cap on the collusion between local governments and resource interests in resource-rich regions. Driven by the need to maintain regime legitimacy and to strengthen central control over local agents (Cai, 2014; Keliher & Wu, 2016; Li, 2016), the Central Commission for Discipline Inspection, the supreme anti-corruption body of the

CCP, has frequently launched anti-corruption campaigns and dispatched inspection teams to clean up corruption at local levels. Although these top-down anti-corruption endeavors can hardly eliminate corruption, they confine the degree of illicit collusion between local governments and mining businesses by punishing and deterring corrupt officials. These anti-corruption measures arguably help ensure the loyalty of local agents and prevent local state capture by resource interests from going out of control.

In summary, both strong state capacity and proper incentive structure are necessary conditions for effective state intervention in the conflicts between resource capital and labor. The Chinese Communist Party-state's strong capacity to penetrate the economy and society allows it to implement policies to redress various negative sociopolitical impacts of the resource economy and to mobilize resources from the mining sector to the citizens. Meanwhile, political centralization and the CCP's tight personnel control construct the incentive structure for local officials to largely align their actions with the central policy goals and force them to devise concrete strategies to cope with the adverse impacts of resources according to local conditions.

What Lessons Can We Learn from China?

The empirical observations in China confirm that even in a country that is not heavily resource-dependent at the national level, there can be local resource curse in subnational jurisdictions, a phenomenon that deserves more careful examination from the scholarly and policy circles. Meanwhile, China's experiences also show possible ways for states to cope with the resource curse. The successes and pitfalls of the China model may well provide valuable lessons for other resource-rich developing countries to handle the adverse socioeconomic and political impacts of mineral resources.

The first lesson that we can learn from China is the importance of engaging mining industries in local public affairs and preventing the formation of enclaves that only extract resources but never pay back to local communities. As the Chinese experiences reveal, the resource economy can be characterized as pro-capital and anti-labor. Whereas resource capital rips huge benefits from the nature's gifts, common citizens as labor share only small fractions of the resource wealth but bear huge costs of the negative externalities of extractive activities. The imbalanced distribution of benefits and costs between capital and labor aggravates social inequality and injustice, which could become sources of regime-threatening social unrest. Wary of the threat to regime stability, the Chinese state strives to alleviate the conflicting interests between the resource capital and labor. One important remedial strategy is to establish formal and informal redistributive channels between mining businesses and local citizens. By creating resource-based job opportunities and handing out social welfare benefits financed by resource revenues, the Chinese state allows common citizens to share part of the resource wealth and partially compensate for their losses from the mining activities. But different from the normal redistribution through taxation, it is important to note that the Chinese state actively engages mining companies in the redistributive processes and encourages them to establish direct, benevolent ties with local communities. Mining businesses are pressured or induced to directly provide public services such as sponsoring schools and hospitals, paving roads, building irrigation systems, and financing other kinds of public welfare project. Moreover, successful mining entrepreneurs are invited to take up political leadership roles such as village heads to directly involve in rural governance, with the aim of leading local citizens out of poverty. These strategies essentially create multiple channels to embed the resource capital in the local communities and encourage or force them to compensate the victims of the resource economy.

Second, the state intervention requires strong state capacity to channel resources from the mining sector to citizens. An elaborate bureaucratic system with extensive contacts with the economy and society is a must. What rentier states can learn from China is that the state needs to build up extractive and redistributive capacity and strengthen its ties with the business sectors as well as the citizenry. Equally importantly, there must be sufficient incentives for the local agents to implement the redistributive policies effectively on the ground. In the case of China, the local state is susceptible to the influence of resource interests and tempted to side with them at the expense of local citizens. When local officials are not electorally accountable to the citizens, China's top-down cadre management system that tightly controls the political careers of local officials serves as an alternative monitoring and checking mechanism to make sure the local state does not completely ignore the citizens' interests and has to respond to their demands to a certain extent. Therefore, when accountability through democratic election is lacking, a higher layer of authority that is not captured by resource interests and is concerned about regime legitimacy and stability is necessary for making the local agents responsive to the citizens.

Nevertheless, the Chinese strategies to cope with the resource curse are not without flaws. One fundamental flaw is the lack of institutionalization. Without a sound and impartial legal framework to guide the redistribution of resource wealth, Chinese local governments all make their own policies in the form of administrative decrees or regulatory rules, which may not have sound legal foundation and may even transgress the legal rights of relevant parties. For example, Shanxi's policy of "subsidizing peasants by coal" was challenged regarding its legality. Although it may be morally sound for the government to require state-owned companies to shoulder more social responsibilities, forcing private mining companies to contribute to public welfare projects and invest in non-coal businesses obviously infringes on the property rights of mining companies, which have been legally recognized and protected since the revision of the Chinese Constitution in 2004. Similarly, interfering in mining companies' hiring or service purchase decisions so as to enhance local employment, despite the good intentions, lacks legal basis and impinges on market freedom. In this sense, many of Chinese local governments' redistributive strategies operate in gray areas outside the widely accepted legal norms. Without a sound legal foundation, these strategies can give rise to the abuse of administrative power as well as inefficient allocation and utilization of resources.

Relatedly, many local practices are based on bargaining instead of following clear and institutionalized laws and regulations. The resolution of resource conflicts between resource capital and labor often depends on the relative bargaining power of the involved parties. For example, when local governments face mining companies with stronger bargaining power, such as larger firms that carry more weight in the local economy or those with stronger political connections, the local governments may be more lenient toward the companies and sacrifice citizens' interests. Alternatively, if the citizens adopt highly disruptive means to advance their requests, local officials may put more pressure on mining companies to accommodate the requests in order to buy peace. Such bargaining-based solutions can be arbitrary, unfair, and incompatible with the rule of law.

Besides the lack of guidance by an impartial legal framework, the local strategies to cope with the resource curse vary hugely across regions and rely heavily on local state capacity. Although overall the Chinese party-state demonstrates remarkable capacity in mobilizing resources and manpower to achieve its prioritized policy goals, there is great heterogeneity among Chinese local governments in their ability to design and implement policies on the ground. Under the highly decentralized system of public goods provision in China, local governments' ability to devise redistributive policies is constrained by their financial capacity, which can vary vastly owing to different levels of economic development, industrial structures, resource endowments, fiscal transfers from higher-level governments, etc. Population density also significantly affects the costs of redistributive policies and the ability of local governments to accommodate citizens' needs. For example, during the resource boom, some resource-rich areas in Inner Mongolia and Xinjiang, thanks to their massive resource revenue and low population density, could afford to hand out very generous compensation packages to farmers and herdsmen who lost land, which included not only one-off subsidies, long-term pensions, and medical insurance but also settlement into spacious residential areas. By contrast, other more densely populated mining areas, such as in Jiangxi and Shanxi, were not as lucky and could hardly offer satisfactory compensation and relocation packages. The local governments had to scramble to finance their relief policies and to find lands to relocate the displaced residents. Without standardized policies and procedures across China, wide cross-regional gaps exist that greatly affect the equality and fairness of the treatment that local citizens receive.

Moreover, local policymaking and implementation are strongly affected by the personal capabilities and visions of those leaders in charge. Some local leaders appear more farsighted and competent than others when dealing with mining-related problems. For instance, at the height of the resource boom in the late 2000s, mining industries in Shanxi caused increasing environmental damages such as land subsidence, and social conflicts frequently broke out between displaced citizens and mining companies. Some local governments quickly made policies to relocate and compensate the affected citizens. As the coal prices were at the peak and local coffers and mining companies were flush with cash, the relocation policies were carried out smoothly. By contrast, other regions tabled this issue until several years later when the problem became too serious to ignore. Unfortunately, as the coal market was going down and mining companies were suffering financial losses, their relocation policies were greeted by immense resistance from both mining companies and grassroots policy implementers. Therefore, the variation in the vision and competence of local policy-makers further contributes to the cross-regional discrepancies in the effectiveness of local strategies.

Last but not least, the local policies more or less suffer from short time horizon and demonstrate a high level of volatility and instability. Local political leaders play key roles in designing and implementing major policies, the success or failure of which would critically affect their political careers and become their personal asset or liability. However, they commonly have short tenures and high turnover rates. When someone leaves office, the successor is commonly reluctant to continue the predecessor's policies, because he/she can hardly get credit from successfully implementing them but may bear the blame for policy failures. As a result, with each change of political leadership, there often comes significant revamping, if not complete abandoning, of major policies that have become the trademark of the predecessor. This mentality thus leads to frequent disruptions of mining areas' coping strategies. The instability and unpredictability of local policies may affect their effectiveness, especially those that need a relatively long period to bear fruits, such as the industrial transformation out of resource dependency. Therefore, how local states' coping strategies can endure political changes and continue to serve local citizens is a big issue that the Chinese authorities have to grapple with.

Overall, China's experiences provide valuable lessons for resource-rich countries and regions to cope with the resource curse. The China model demonstrates that the state, if equipped with strong capacity and proper incentive, can play important roles in containing the adverse sociopolitical impacts of resources and redressing the unequal and unfair distribution of the costs and benefits of the resource economy between capital and labor. In this sense, the resource curse is not incurable. However, we have to also realize that state intervention is a double-edged sword. While it may address certain malaises of the resource economy, it also generates side effects such as the infringement of market freedom and the violation of the rights of economic entities or individual citizens. These risks become especially perturbing as the Chinese state's coping strategies lack the support of a sound legal structure, which undermines their legitimacy, impartiality, and sustainability. From the pitfalls of the China model we may draw another important lesson. That is, while state intervention is crucial for coping with the resource curse, the policies need to be institutionalized instead of being driven by ad hoc bargaining, to be based on the rule of law rather than the rule of man, and to follow due procedure instead of impulsive political decisions.

Limitations and Future Work

I will close with some remarks on the limitations of this research. First, I take an aggregate approach to analyze the rich and diverse mineral resources in China, including coal, oil and gas, metals, and nonmetal minerals. Due to the nature of the available data, I cannot parse out the impacts of each and every mineral resource, such as oil, which many comparative studies on the resource curse focus on. Instead, I lump all the resources together in my data analysis. Since coal is by far the largest component of mineral resources and the most widely distributed mineral in China, a large part of the story told in this book is about coal and its impacts on state–capital–labor relations. Meanwhile, based on my observations in the field, other mineral resources, especially solid minerals, have qualitatively similar effects in terms of the unfair game between capital and labor, the environmental damages caused by mining, and the ensuing sociopolitical consequences. Therefore, the logic identified applies to most mineral resources actively explored in China. Nevertheless, there are probably heterogeneous effects of different minerals that can be more carefully examined. I will leave it to future research when more reliable and time-consistent data on specific types of mineral become available.

Second, this research adopts mixed research methods combining qualitative and quantitative analysis, but I put more emphasis on the qualitative discussion based on fieldwork and case studies, which reveals many interesting, untold stories and discerns the causal links behind my theory. I intentionally keep the quantitative parts light and limit the statistical analysis to only the last section in each of the substantive Chapters 2–5 (and the Appendices of these chapters for readers interested in learning more technical details). Although I have tried different statistical models and conducted robustness checks to ensure the reliability and validity of the statistical results, still more comprehensive and advanced econometric models can be employed and more robustness checks can be conducted to make the data analysis more sophisticated. I hope other researchers who find my causal hypotheses interesting will test them against more empirical data on China and even generalize the theory beyond China with empirical evidence from other countries.

Third, this research adopts a subnational approach to analyze the impacts of mineral resources on Chinese localities. One limitation of this approach is that the findings based on within-country observations and comparisons are conditional on national institutional settings. China's peculiar political regime and economic system are important preconditions for many empirical observations in this research. For instance, the Chinese Communist Party-state's strong capacity to intervene in the economy and penetrate in the society clearly sets it apart from the weak or failed states in some other resource-rich countries. And due to the Chinese government's restrictions on foreign investment in mineral exploration, the resource capital in China is largely Chinese, which is different from the foreign capital that controls much of the extractive industries in other resource-rich countries and may lead to divergent dynamics in the state–capital–labor interactions. Meanwhile, some causal mechanisms that work at the national level may not work at subnational levels, and vice versa. For example, the exchange rate mechanism of the Dutch disease theorem (Corden & Neary, 1982) obviously does not apply to subnational units that share the same currency – although resources may affect the prices of non-tradable goods such as real estate, arguably following a similar logic. Alternatively, subnational governments operate under the constraint of the national government, which significantly circumscribes local policies and sociopolitical outcomes. But such a constraint does not apply to the national government of resource-rich countries, which, as sovereign states, are not subject to any higher authority. Therefore, we must be cautious about the generalizability of the findings from subnational studies when extending them to cross-national comparisons.

Last, although I allude to the cross-regional variations in Chinese local practices to cope with the resource curse in the previous section, this book does not go in much depth to compare different regions in terms of the impacts of resources as well as local governments' coping strategies. It would be interesting and worthwhile to investigate how the resource-rich regions, although under the same national settings such as the political regime and bureaucratic structure, may differ from each other in terms of the state–capital–labor relations and what factors explain such cross-regional variations. For example, why do some mining areas experience more disruptive resource conflicts between the mining sector and local communities than the others? What kinds of redistributive scheme can more effectively help the citizens suffering from the adverse impacts of resources? And why can some local governments successfully transition out of resource dependency but others cannot? There are many important and intriguing questions arising from this research. Due to the limited scope of this book, they are left to future work.

References

Ades, A., & Di Tella, R. (1999, September). Rents, Competition, and Corruption. *American Economic Review*, 89(4), 982–993.

Ahmadov, A. K. (2014). Oil, Democracy, and Context: A Meta-analysis. *Comparative Political Studies*, 47(9), 1238–1267.

Alexeev, M., & Conrad, R. (2009). The Elusive Curse of Oil. *The Review of Economics and Statistics*, 91(3), 586–598.

(2011). The Natural Resource Curse and Economic Transition. *Economic Systems*, 35(4), 445–461.

Allcott, H., & Keniston, D. (2018). Dutch Disease or Agglomeration? The Local Economic Effects of Natural Resource Booms in Modern America. *The Review of Economic Studies*, 85(2), 695–731.

Andersen, J. J., & Aslaksen, S. (2008). Constitutions and the Resource Curse. *Journal of Development Economics*, 87(2), 227–246.

(2013). Oil and Political Survival. *Journal of Development Economics*, 100(1), 89–106.

Andersen, J. J., & Ross, M. L. (2014). The Big Oil Change: A Closer Look at the Haber–Menaldo Analysis. *Comparative Political Studies*, 47(7), 993–1021.

Ang, Y. Y. (2016). *How China Escaped the Poverty Trap*. Ithaca, NY: Cornell University Press.

Anthonsen, M., Löfgren, Å., Nilsson, K., & Westerlund, J. (2012). Effects of Rent Dependency on Quality of Government. *Economics of Governance*, 13(2), 145–168.

Aragón, F. M., Chuhan-Pole, P., & Land, B. C. (2015). *The Local Economic Impacts of Resource Abundance: What Have We Learned?* Washington, DC: World Bank.

Arezki, R., & Bruckner, M. (2011). Oil Rents, Corruption, and State Stability: Evidence from Panel Data Regression. *European Economic Review*, 55(7), 955–963.

Arezki, R., & van der Ploeg, F. (2011). Do Natural Resources Depress Income per Capita? *Review of Development Economics*, 15(3), 504–521.

Aslaksen, S. (2010). Oil as Sand in the Democratic Machine? *Journal of Peace Research*, 47(4), 421–431.

Auty, R. M. (1990). *Resource-Based Industrialization: Sowing the Oil in Eight Developing Countries.* Oxford: Oxford University Press.

(1993). *Sustaining Development in Mineral Economies: The Resource Curse Thesis.* London: Routledge.

(1994). Industrial Policy Reform in Six Large Newly Industrializing Countries: The Resource Curse Thesis. *World Development, 22*(1), 11–26.

(1995). *Patterns of Development: Resources, Policy and Economic Growth.* London: Edward Arnold.

(2001). *Resource Abundance and Economic Development.* Oxford: Oxford University Press.

Bannon, I., & Collier, P. (2003). Natural Resources and Conflict: What We Can Do. In I. Bannon & P. Collier, *Natural Resources and Violent Conflict: Options and Actions* (pp. 1–16). Washington, DC: World Bank.

Bardhan, P. (1997). Corruption and Development: A Review of Issues. *Journal of Economic Literature, XXXV,* 1320–1346.

Barro, R. J. (2009). Determinants of Democracy. *Journal of Political Economy, 107*(6), 158–183.

Basedau, M., & Lay, J. (2009). Resource Curse or Rentier Peace? The Ambiguous Effects of Oil Wealth and Oil Dependence on Violent Conflict. *Journal of Peace Research, 46*(6), 757–776.

Bhattacharyya, S., & Hodler, R. (2010). Natural Resources, Democracy and Corruption. *European Economic Review, 54,* 608–621.

Blanco, L., & Grier, R. (2012). Natural Resource Dependence and the Accumulation of Physical and Human Capital in Latin America. *Resources Policy, 37*(3), 281–295.

Bodin, J. (1967). *Six Books of a Commonwealth* (Vol. 5). (M. J. Tooley, Ed. & M. J. Tooley, Trans.) New York: Barnes & Noble.

Brautigam, D., Fjeldstad, O.-H., & Moore, M. (2008). *Taxation and State-Building in Developing Countries: Capacity and Consent.* New York, NY: Cambridge University Press.

Breslin, S. (2012). Government-Industry Relations in China: A Review of the Art of the State. In A. Walter & X. Zhang, *East Asian Capitalism: Diversity, Continuity, and Change* (pp. 29–45). Oxford: Oxford University Press.

Brunnschweiler, C. N. (2008). Cursing the Blessings? Natural Resource Abundance, Institutions, and Economic Growth. *World Development, 36*(3), 399–419.

Brunnschweiler, C. N., & Bulte, E. H. (2008). The Resource Curse Revisited and Revised: A Tale of Paradoxes and Red Herrings. *Journal of Environmental Economics and Management, 55*(3), 248–264.

Bulte, E. H., Damania, R., & Deacon, R. T. (2005). Resource Intensity, Institutions, and Development. *World Development, 33*(7), 1029–1044.

Butkiewicz, J. L., & Yanikkaya, H. (2010). Minerals, Institutions, Openness, and Growth: An Empirical Analysis. *Land Economics, 86*(2), 313–328.

Cai, R. (2014, October 9). Su Rong An Yubo Buduan: Jiadai Wenti Huoshe Shushi Ming Jiangxi Guanyuan (Dozens of Jiangxi Officials May Be Involved in Su Rong's Case). *Zhongguo Xinwen Zhoukan (China Newsweek), 679,* http://news.sina.com.cn/c/sd/2014-10-09/172730964529.shtml, accessed on December 27, 2014.

Cai, Y. (2014). *State and Agents in China: Disciplining Government Officials.* Palo Alto, CA: Stanford University Press.

Caselli, F., & Cunningham, T. (2009). Leader Behaviour and the Natural Resource Curse. *Oxford Economic Papers, 61,* 628–650.

Caselli, F., & Michael, G. (2009). Do Oil Windfalls Improve Living Standards? Evidence from Brazil. NBER Working Paper No. 15550, www.nber.org/papers/w15550.pdf, accessed on July 21, 2012.

   (2013). Do Oil Windfalls Improve Living Standards? Evidence from Brazil. *American Economic Journal: Applied Economics, 5*(1), 208–238.

Chen, N., & Wang, R. (2006). Woguo Meikuang Anquan Shigu Jili Fenxi Ji Duice (Coal Mine Safety Accidents in China: Reasons and Solutions). *Beifang Jingji (Northern Economy),* (9), 34–35.

Chen, X. (2016). *Qiye ZhiZao Chengzhen de Zhengzhi Luoji: Yi Shanxi Y Zhen Weili (The Political Logic of Enterprise-driven Urbanization: A Case Study of Y Town in Shanxi Province).* Beijing: Chinese Social Science Press.

Chen, X. (2017). Origins of Informal Coercion in China. *Politics and Society, 45*(1), 67–89.

Collier, P. (2003). The Market for Civil War. *Foreign Policy, 136,* 38–45.

Collier, P., & Hoeffler, A. (1998). On Economic Causes of Civil War. *Oxford Economic Papers, 50*(4), 563–573.

   (2004). Greed and Grievance in Civil War. *Oxford Economic Papers, 56* (4), 563–595.

   (2005). Resource Rents, Governance, and Conflict. *Journal of Conflict Resolution, 49*(4), 625–633.

Corden, W. M. (1984). Booming Sector and Dutch Disease Economics: Survey and Consolidation. *Oxford Economic Papers New Series, 36* (3), 359–80.

Corden, W. M., & Neary, J. P. (1982). Booming Sector and De-Industrialisation in a Small Open Economy. *The Economic Journal, 92*(368), 825–848.

Côte, M., & Korf, B. (2018). Making Concessions: Extractive Enclaves, Entangled Capitalism and Regulative Pluralism at the Gold Mining Frontier in Burkina Faso. *World Development, 101,* 466–476.

Cotet, A. M., & Tsui, K. K. (2013). Oil and Conflict: What Does the Cross Country Evidence Really Show? *American Journal of Microeconomics, 5*(1), 49–80.

Cust, J., & Poelhekke, S. (2015). The Local Economic Impacts of Natural Resource Extraction. *Annual Review of Resource Economics, 7,* 251–268.

Cust, J., & Viale, C. (2016). *Is There Evidence for a Subnational Resource Curse?* New York, NY: Natural Resource Governance Institute.

Dauvina, M., & Guerreiro, D. (2017). The Paradox of Plenty: A Meta-Analysis. *World Development, 94,* 212–231. doi:10.1016/j.worlddev.2017.01.009.

Davis, G. A. (1995). Learning to love the Dutch disease: Evidence from the mineral economies. *World Development, 23*(10), 1765–1779.

Dickson, B. J., & Chen, J. (2010). *Allies of the State: China's Private Entrepreneurs and Democratic Change* (First ed.). Cambridge: Harvard University Press.

Dickson, B. J., Landry, P. F., Shen, M., & Yan, J. (2016). Public Goods and Regime Support in Urban China. *The China Quarterly, 228,* 859–880.

Discipline Inspection Commission of Jiangxi Province. (2010). Zhongdian Lingyu Yufang Fubai Gongzuo Tanxi (Anticorruption in Key Areas). *Zhongguo Jiancha (Supervision in China), 5,* 40–42.

Dittmer, L. (2017). Xi Jinping's 'New Normal': Quo Vadis? *Journal of Chinese Political Science, 22*(3), 429–446.

Dong, J. (2016). *Meikuang Chanquan Zhidu Gaige yu Ziyuanxing Xiangcun Zhili Yanjiu (Reform of Coal Mining Property Rights System and Governance of Resource-Rich Villages).* Beijing: China Social Science Press.

Du, Y. (2000). *Jiaoyu Fazhan Bupingheng Yanjiu (Study on the Unbalanced Development of Education).* Beijing: Beijing Normal University Publishing Group.

Dunning, T. (2005). Resource Dependence, Economic Performance, and Political Stability. *Journal of Conflict Resolution, 49*(4), 451–582. doi:10.1177/0022002705277521.

(2008). *Crude Democracy: Natural Resource Wealth and Political Regimes.* New York, NY: Cambridge University Press.

Edin, M. (2003). State Capacity and Local Agent Control in China: CCP Cadre Management from a Township Perspective. *The China Quarterly, 173,* 35–52.

Elfstrom, M. (2017). *China Strikes.* https://chinastrikes.crowdmap.com, accessed on March 21, 2021.

Englebert, P., & Ron, J. (2004). Primary Commodities and War: Congo–Brazzaville's Ambivalent Resource Curse. *Comparative Politics*, 37(1), 61–81.

Fan, C., Shao, S., & Jiang, C. (2013, April 18). Fawai Zhidi: Ziyuan Zuzhou xia de Gejiu Gongrencun (Land of the Outlaws: Gejiu Worers' Village under the Curse of Resource Depletion). *Nanfang Zhoumo (Southern Weekend)*, www.infzm.com/content/89728, accessed on April 21, 2013.

Fearon, J. D. (2004). Why Do Some Civil Wars Last So Much Longer Than Others? *Journal of Peace Research*, 41(3), 275–301.

Fearon, J. D., & Laitin, D. (2003). Ethnicity, Insurgency, and Civil War. *American Political Science Review*, 97(1), 75–90.

Feng, X. (2004). *Dangjian Yanjiu Neibu Wengao 2000-2004 (Internal Documents on Party Building Research 2000–2004).* Shanghai: Shanghai Jiaotong University Press.

Franke, A., Gawrich, A., & Alakbarov, G. (2009). Kazakhstan and Azerbaijan as Post-Soviet Rentier States: Resource Incomes and Autocracy as a Double 'Curse' in Post-Soviet Regimes. *Europe-Asia Studies*, 61(1), 109–140.

Friedman, T. L. (2012, March). Pass the Books. Hold the Oil. *New York Times*, www.nytimes.com, accessed on March 10, 2012.

Fu, L., & Wang, Z. (2010). "Ziyuan Zuzhou" yu Ziyuanxing Chengshi ("Resource Curse" and Resource-Rich Cities). *Chengshi Wenti (Urban Problems)*, 184, 2–8.

Geissdoerfer, M., Savaget, P., Bocken, N., & Hultink, E. J. (2017). The Circular Economy: A New Sustainability Paradigm? *Journal of Cleaner Production*, 143(1), 757–768.

Gerelmaaa, L., & Kotani, K. (2016). Further Investigation of Natural Resources and Economic Growth: Do Natural Resources Depress Economic Growth? *Resources Policy*, 50, 312–321.

Guthrie, D. (1998). The Declining Significance of Guanxi in China's Economic Transition. *The China Quarterly*, 154, 254–282.

Gylfason, T. (2001a). Natural Resources, Education, and Economic Development. *European Economic Review*, 45, 847–859.

(2001b). Lessons from the Dutch Disease: Causes, Treatment, and Cures. Institute of Economic Studies Working Paper Series.

Gylfason, T., Herbertsson, T. T., & Zoega, G. (1999). A Mixed Blessing: Natural Resources and Economic Growth. *Macroeconomic Dynamics*, 3, 204–225.

Haber, S., & Menaldo, V. (2011). Do Natural Resources Fuel Authoritarianism? A Reappraisal of the Resource Curse. *American Political Science Review*, 105(1), 1–24.

Havranek, T., Horvath, R., & Zeynalov, A. (2016). Natural Resources and Economic Growth: A Meta-Analysis. *World Development, 88,* 134–151. doi:10.1016/j.worlddev.2016.07.016.

Ho, P., & Yang, X. (2018). Conflict over Mining in Rural China: A Comprehensive Survey of Intentions and Strategies for Environmental Activism. *Sustainability, 10*(5), 1–18.

Hong, J. Y., & Yang, W. (2018). Oilfields, Mosques and Violence: Is There a Resource Curse in Xinjiang? *British Journal of Political Science, 50*(1), 45–78. doi: 10.1017/S0007123417000564.

Hu, Y., & Xiao, D. (2007). Jingji Fazhan Menkan yu Ziran Ziyuan Zuzhou —Jiyu Woguo Shengji Cengmian de Mianban Shuju Shizheng Yanjiu (The Threshold of Economic Growth and the Natural Resource Curse). *Guanli Shijie (Management World), 4,* 15–23.

Huang, D. (2014). Siying Qiyezhu yu Zhengzhi Fazhan: Guanyu Shichang Zhuanxing zhong Siying Qiyezhu de Jieji Xiangxiang jiqi Fansi (Private Entrepreneurs and Political Development in China: Theoretical Imagination of Private Entrepreneurs in the Marketization as a Class and Its Reflection). *Shehui (Chinese Journal of Sociology), 34*(4), 138–164.

Huang, D., & Chen, M. (2020). Business Lobbying within the Party-State: Embedding Lobbying and Political Co-optation in China. *The China Journal, 83,* 105–128.

Humphreys, M. (2005). Natural Resources, Conflict, and Conflict Resolution. *Journal of Conflict Resolution, 49*(4), 508–537.

International Monetary Fund. (2014). Sustaining Long-Run Growth and Macroeconomic Stability in Low-Income Countries – The Role of Structural Transformation and Diversification. *IMF Policy Paper.*

Isham, J., Woolcock, M., Pritchett, L., & Busby, G. (2005). The Varieties of Resource Experience: Natural Resource Exports Structures and the Political Economy of Economic Growth. *World Bank Economic Review, 19*(2), 141–174.

James, A., & Aadland, D. (2010). The Curse of Natural Resources: An Empirical Investigation of U.S. Counties. *Resource and Energy Economics, 33*(2), 440–453.

Jensen, N., & Wantchekon, L. (2004). Resource Wealth and Political Regimes in Africa. *Comparative Political Studies, 37*(7), 816–841.

Ji, K., Magnus, J. R., & Wang, W. (2013). Natural Resources, Institutional Quality, and Economic Growth in China. *Environmental & Resource Economics, 57,* 323–343.

Jiang, F. (2016). *Yundongshi Fan Fubai Gongzuo Yanjiu (Campaign-Styled Anticorruption Work: A Case Study of Anticorruption Work in Coal and Coking Industries of Shanxi Province). Dissertation.* Central Party School, Beijing.

Jiang, J., Meng, T., & Zhang, Q. (2019). From Internet to Social Safety Net: The Policy Consequences of Online Participation in China. *Governance*, 32(3), 531–546.

Johnson, R. N. (2006). Economic Growth and Natural Resources: Does the Curse of Natural Resources Extend to the 50 US States? In R. Halvorsen, & D. F. Layton (Eds.), *Explorations in Environmental and natural Resource Economics* (pp. 122–136). Cheltenham: Edward Elgar.

Karl, T. L. (1997). *The Paradox of Plenty: Oil Booms and Petro-States.* Berkeley: University of California Press.

Kaufmann, D., & Siegelbaum, P. (1996). Privatization and Corruption in Transition Economies. *Journal of International Affairs*, 50(2), 419–458.

Keliher, M., & Wu, H. (2016). Corruption, Anticorruption, and the Transformation of Political Culture in Contemporary China. *The Journal of Asian Studies*, 75(1), 5–18.

Kennedy, S. (2005). *The Business of Lobbying in China.* Cambridge: Harvard University Press.

Klare, M. T. (2001). *Resource Wars: The New Landscape of Global Conflict.* New York, NY: Metropolitan Books.

Koech, J., & Wang, J. (2012). China's Slowdown May Be Worse Than Official Data Suggest. *Economic Letter*, 7(8).

Kolstad, I., & Søreide, T. (2009). Corruption in Natural Resource Management: Implications for Policy Makers. *Resources Policy*, 34, 214–226.

Landry, P. F. (2008). *Decentralized Authoritarianism in China: The Communist Party's Control of Local Elites in the Post-Mao Era.* Cambridge: Cambridge University Press.

Laowu, & Jingfei. (2011). *Meilaoban Zishu Sanshi Nian (Thirty Years as A Coal Mine Owner).* Beijing: Culture and Art Publishing House.

Lederman, D., & Maloney, W. F. (2008). In *Search of the Missing Resource Curse.* Policy Research Working Paper (4766). Washington, DC: World Bank.

Leite, C., & Weidmann, J. (1999). Does Mother Nature Corrupt? IMF Working Paper 99/85.

Li, H., & Zhou, L.-A. (2005). Political Turnover and Economic Performance: The Incentive Role of Personnel Control in China. *Journal of Public Economics*, 89, 1743–1762.

Li, L. (2016). The Rise of the Discipline and Inspection Commission, 1927–2012: Anticorruption Investigation and Decision-Making in the Chinese Communist Party. *Modern China*, 42(5), 447–482.

Li, Y., & Lu, X. (1999). *Guotu Ziyuan yu Jingji Buju—Guotu Ziyuan Kaifa Liyong 50 Nian (Mineral Resources and Economic Structure – Fifty Years of Mineral Resource Exploration).* Beijing: Geology Press.

Libman, A. (2013). Natural Resources and Sub-National Economic Performance: Does Sub-national Democracy Matter? *Energy Economics, 37*, 82–99.

Litvack, J. M., & Oates, W. E. (1971). Group Size and the Output of Public Goods: Theory and Application of State-Local Finance in the United States. *Public Finance, 25*(2), 42–58.

Liu, Z. (2009). *Xin Qunti Shijian Guan: Guizhou W Xian 6.28 Shijian de Qishi (New Perspective on Collective Incidents: Lessons from the June 28 Incident of Guizhou W County)*. Beijing: Xinhua Press.

Lü, X. (2014). Social Policy and Regime Legitimacy: The Effects of Education Reform in China. *American Political Science Review, 108*(2), 423–437.

Lujala, P. (2010). The Spoils of Nature: Armed Civil Conflict and Rebel Access to Natural Resources. *Journal of Peace Research, 47*(1), 15–28.

Lujala, P., Gleditsch, N. P., & Gilmore, E. (2005). A Diamond Curse?: Civil War and a Lootable Resource. *Journal of Conflict Resolution, 49*(4), 538–562, doi: 10.1177/0022002705277548.

Luong, P. J., & Weinthal, E. (2010). *Oil Is Not a Curse: Ownership Structure and Institutions in Soviet Successor States*. New York, NY: Cambridge University Press.

Mahdavy, H. (1970). The Patterns and Problems of Economic Development in Rentier State: The Case of Iran. In M. A. Cook (Ed.), *Studies in Economic History of the Middle East*. London: Oxford University Press.

Markus, B., Ciccone, A., & Tesei, A. (2012). Oil Price Shocks, Income, and Democracy. *Review of Economics and Statistics, 94*(2), 389–399.

Martinez-Vazquez, J., & McNab, R. M. (2003). Fiscal Decentralization and Economic Growth. *World Development, 31*(9), 1597–1616.

Mauro, P. (1995, August). Corruption and Growth. *The Quarterly Journal of Economics, 110*(3), 681–712.

Mbaku, J. M. (1992). Bureaucratic Corruption as Rent-Seeking Behavior. *Konjunkturpolitik, 38*(4), 247–265.

Meng, X., & Zhang, J. (2001). The Two-Tier Labor Market in Urban China: Occupational Segregation and Wage Differentials between Urban Residents and Rural Migrants in Shanghai. *Journal of Comparative Economics, 29*(3), 485–504.

Michaels, G. (2011). The Long Term Consequences of Resource-Based Specialisation. *The Economic Journal, 121*(551), 31–57.

Mill, J. S. (1843). *A System of Logic, Ratiocinative and Inductive : Being a Connected View of the Principles of Evidence and the Methods of Scientific Investigation* (Vol. 1). London: John W. Parker.

Norman, C. S. (2009). Rule of Law and the Resource Curse: Abundance versus Intensity. *Environmental and Resource Economics, 43*, 183–207.

Nye, J. S. (1967). Corruption and Political Development: A Cost-Benefit Analysis. *American Political Science Review, 61*(2), 417–427.

O'Brien, K. J., & Li, L. (1999). Selective Policy Implementation in Rural China. *Comparative Politics, 31*(2), 167–186.

Oi, J. C. (1992). Fiscal Reform and the Economic Foundation of Local State Corporatism. *World Politics, 45*, 99–126.

Ong, L. (2018). Thugs and Outsourcing of State Repression in China. *The China Journal, 80*, 94–110.

Parris, K. (1995). Private Entrepreneurs as Citizens: From Leninism to Corporatism. *China Information, X*(3–4), 1–28.

Pearson, M. M. (1997). *China's New Business Elite: The Political Consequences of Economic Reform*. Berkeley: University of California Press.

Petermann, A., Guzmán, J. I., & Tilton, J. E. (2007). Mining and Corruption. *Resources Policy, 32*, 91–103.

Pineda, J., & Rodríguez, F. (2010). *Curse or Blessing? Natural Resources and Human Development*. New York, NY: United Nations Development Programme.

Qian, Y., & Xu, C. (1993). The M-form Hierarchy and China's Economic Reform. *European Economic Review, 37*, 54.

Ren, J., & Du, Z. (2008). Institutionalized Corruption: Power Overconcentration of the First-in-Command in China. *Crime, Law and Social Change, 49*(1), 45–59.

Reno, W. (1998). *Warlord Politics and African States*. Boulder, CO: Lynne Rienner.

Ricardo, D. (1817). *On the Principles of Political Economy and Taxation*. London: John Murray.

Robinson, J. A., Torvik, R., & Verdier, T. (2006). Political Foundations of the Resource Curse. *Journal of Development Economics, 79*, 447–468.

Rose-Ackerman, S. (1999). *Corruption and Government: Causes, Consequences and Reform*. New York: Cambridge University Press.

Ross, M. L. (1999). The Political Economy of the Resource Curse. *World Politics, 51*(2), 297–322.

(2001). Does Oil Hinder Democracy? *World Politics, 53*(3), 325–361.

(2003). The Natural Resource Curse: How Wealth Can Make You Poor. In I. Bannon, & C. Paul (Eds.), *Natural Resources and Violent Conflict: Options and Actions* (pp. 17–42). Washington, DC: World Bank.

(2012). *The Oil Curse: How Petroleum Wealth Shapes the Development of Nations*. Princeton, NJ: Princeton University Press.

(2015). What Have We Learned about the Resource Curse? *Annual Review of Political Science, 18*, 239–259.

(2019). What Do We Know About Export Diversification in Oil-Producing Countries? *The Extractive Industries and Society, 6*, 792–806.

Sachs, J. D., & Warner, A. M. (1995). Natural Resource Abundance and Economic Growth. NBER Working Paper 5398.

Sala-i-Martin, X., & Subramanian, A. (2013). Addressing the Natural Resource Curse: An Illustration from Nigeria. *Journal of African Economics, 22*(4), 570–615.

Schubert, G., & Heberer, T. (2017). Private Entrepreneurs as a "Strategic Group" in the Chinese Polity. *China Review, 17*(2), 95–122.

Sexton, R. (2020). Unpacking the Local Resource Curse: How Externalities and Governance Shape Social Conflict. *Journal of Conflict Resolution, 64*(4), 640–673.

Shao, S., & Qi, Z. (2008). Xibu Diqu de Nengyuan Kaifa yu Jingji Zengzhang (Energy Exploration and Economic Growth in Western Regions). *Jingji Yanjiu (Economic Research Journal), 4*, 147–160.

Shirk, S. (1993). *The Political Logic of Economic Reform in China*. Berkley: University of California Press.

Smith, B. (2004). Oil Wealth and Regime Survival in the Developing World, 1960–1999. *American Journal of Political Science, 48*(2), 232–246.

Spengler, J. J. (Ed.). (1960). *Natural Resources and Growth*. Washington, DC: Resources for the Future.

Stijns, J.-P. C. (2005). Natural Resource Abundance and Economic Growth Revisited. *Resources Policy, 30*, 107–130.

Su, B., Heshmati, A., Geng, Y., & Yu, X. (2012). A Review of the Circular Economy in China: Moving from Rhetoric to Implementation. *Journal of Cleaner Production, 42*, 215–227. doi:10.1016/j.jclep ro.2012.11.020.

Sun, Y. (2004). *Corruption and Market in Contemporary China*. Ithaca, NY: Cornell University Press.

Switzer, J. (2001). Armed Conflict and Natural Resources: The Case of the Minerals Sector. Minerals, Mining and Sustainable Development Project, London: International Institute for Environment and Development.

Tan, J., & Hu, J. (2011). Kuangchan Ziyuan Lingyu Fubai Diaocha (Investigation of Mineral Resource-Related Corruption). *Jiancha Fengyun, 4*, 26–29.

Teets, J. C., Hasmath, R., & Lewis, O. A. (2017). The Incentive to Innovate? The Behavior of Local Policymakers in China. *Journal of Chinese Political Science, 22*(4), 505–517.

Treisman, D. (2000). The Causes of Corruption: A Cross-National Study. *Journal of Public Economics, 76*, 399–457.

(2007). What Have We Learned about the Causes of Corruption from Ten Years of Cross-National Empirical Research? *Annual Review of Political Science, 10*, 211–244.

Tsui, K. K. (2011). More Oil, Less Democracy: Evidence from Wolrdwide Crude Oil Discoveries. *The Economic Journal, 121*, 89–115.

Unger, J., & Chan, A. (1995). China, Corporatism, and the East Asian Model. *The Australian Journal of Chinese Affairs, 33*, 29–53.

van der Ploeg, F. (2011). Natural Resources: Curse or Blessing? *Journal of Economic Literature, 49*(2), 366–420.

van der Ploeg, F., & Poelhekke, S. (2010). The Pungent Smell of 'Red Herrings': Subsoil Assets, Rents, Volatility, and the Resource curse. *Journal of Environmental Economics and Management, 60*, 44–55.

Varangis, P., Akiyama, T., & Mitchell, D. (1995). *Managing Commodity Booms and Busts.* Washington, DC: World Bank.

Vicente, P. C. (2010). Does Oil Corrupt? Evidence from a Natural Experiment in West Africa. *Journal of Development Economics, 92*(1), 28–38.

Wang, M.-X., Zhang, T., Xie, M.-R., Zhang, B., & Jia, M.-Q. (2011). Analysis of National Coal-mining Accident data in China, 2001–2008. *Public Health Report, 126*(2), 270–275.

Wang, W., Zheng, X., & Zhao, Z. (2012). Fiscal Reform and Public Education Spending: A Quasi-natural Experiment of Fiscal Decentralization in China. *Publius: The Journal of Federalism, 42*(2), 334–356.

Wang, X. (2014). Meiye Xunzu Toushi (Rent Seeking in the Coal Industry). *Shidai Zhoubao (Time Weekly).* May 22, www.time-weekly.com/html/20140522/24847_1.html, accessed September 24, 2021

Wang, Y. (2007). Kuangshan Kaicai "Gengshang" Chu (The Wound of Mines). *Hunan Anquan yu Fangzai (Safety and Disaster Prevention in Hunan), 8*, 19–23.

Wank, D. (1999). *Commodifying Communism: Business, Trust, and Politics in a Chinese City.* New York, NY: Cambridge University Press.

(2002). Business-State Clientelism in China: Decline or Evolution. In T. Gold, D. Guthrie, & D. Wank, *Social Connections in China: Institutions, Culture, and the Changing Nature of Guanxi* (pp. 97–115). New York: Cambridge University Press.

Wedeman, A. (2012). *Double Paradox: Rapid Growth and Rising Corruption in China.* Ithaca: Cornell University Press.

Whyte, M. K. (2010). *Myth of the Social Volcano: Perceptions of Inequality and Distributive Injustice in Contemporary China.* Stanford: Stanford University Press.

(2016). China's Dormant and Active Social Volcanoes. *The China Journal*, 75, 9–37.

Whyte, M. K., & Dong-Kyun, I. (2014). Is the Social Volcano Still Dormant? Trends in Chinese Attitudes toward Inequality. *Social Science Research*, 48, 62–76. doi: 10.1016/j.ssresearch.2014.05.008

Wick, K., & Erwin, B. (2009). The Curse of Natural Resources. *Annual Review of Resource Economics*, 1, 139–156.

Womack, B. (2017). Xi Jinping and Continuing Political Reform in China. *Journal of Chinese Political Science*, 22(3), 393–406.

Wooldridge, J. M. (2013). *Introductory Econometrics: A Modern Approach*. Mason, OH: South-Western, Cengage Learning.

Wright, J., Frantz, E., & Geddes, B. (2015). Oil and Autocratic Regime Survival. *British Journal of Political Science*, 45, 287–306.

Wright, T. (2009). Rents and Rent Seeking in the Coal Industry. In T.-W. Ngo, & Y. Wu, *Rent Seeking in China* (pp. 98–116). New York: Routledge.

Wu, A. M., & Wang, W. (2013). Determinants of Expenditure Decentralization: Evidence from China. *World Development*, 46, 176–184.

Xie, Y., & Zhou, X. (2014). Income Inequality in Today's China. *Proceedings of the National Academy of Sciences*, 111(19), 6928–6933.

Xu, K., & Wang, J. (2006). Ziran Ziyuan Fengyu Chengdu yu Jingji Fazhan Shuiping Guanxi de Yanjiu (An Empirical Study of the Linkage Between Natural Resource Abundance and Economic Development). *Jingji Yanjiu (Economic Research Journal)*, 1, 78–89.

Yang, K., & Niu, X. (2009). *Resource Curse in Resource Dependent Provinces in China*. 2009 International Conference on Management Science & Engineering, http://ieeexplore.ieee.org/stamp/stamp.jsp?arnumber=05318214, accessed on May 12, 2011.

Yang, L., Shao, S., & Cao, J. (2014). Ziyuan Chanye Yilai dui Zhongguo Shengyu Jingji Zengzhang de Yingxiang jiqi Chuandao Jizhi Yanjiu–Jiyu Kongjian Mianban Moxing de Shizheng Kaocha (The Effects of the Dependence on Resource-Based Industries on Provincial Economic Growth in China and Its Transmission Mechanism: Empirical Analysis Based on Spatial Panel Model). *Caijing Yanjiu (Journal of Finance and Economics)*, 40(3), 4–15.

Yang, M. M.-H. (1994). *Gifts, Favors, and Banquets: The Art of Social Relationships in China*. Ithaca: Cornell University Press.

Yang, X., Zhao, H., & Ho, P. (2017). Mining-Induced Displacement and Resettlement in China: A Study Covering 27 Villages in 6 Provinces. *Resources Policy*, 53, 408–418.

Yu, J. (2006). *Business Associations and Local Government: A Study Based on Wenzhou, Zhejiang Province.* Beijing: Economic Science Press.

Yuan, Z., Bi, J., & Moriguichi, Y. (2006). The Circular Economy: A New Development Strategy. *Journal of Industrial Ecology, 10*(1–2), 4–8. doi:10.1162/108819806775545321.

Zeng, M., & Xia, Y. (2013). The Resource Curse in Stability Maintanance: A Case Study of X Mining Zone (Shehui Wending zhong de Ziyuan Zuzhou Xianxiang: Yi X Kuangqu Weili). *Wuhan Daxue Xuebao (Wuhan University Journal), 66*(5), 60–66.

Zeng, M., & Zhan, J. (2013). *Caizheng Zhuanyi Zhifu yu Difang Zhengfu Gonggong Zhichu Qingxiang: Lilun, Shizheng yu Zhengce Jianyi (Fiscal Transfer and Local Public Expenditure: Theories, Empirics, and Policy Suggestions).* Beijing: People's Publishing House.

Zeng, M., & Zhan, J. V. (2015). Sharing Resource Wealth for Peace: A Chinese Strategy to Cope with the Resource Curse. *The Extractive Industries and Society, 2*(2), 302–309.

Zeng, X., Ali, S. H., Tian, J., & Li, J. (2020). Mapping Anthropogenic Mineral Generation in China and Its Implications for A Circular Economy. *Nature Communications, 11*(1544), 1–9. doi:10.1038/s41467-020-15246-4.

Zhan, J. V. (2009). Undermining State Capacity: Vertical and Horizontal Diffusions of Fiscal Power in China. *Asian Politics & Policy, 1*(3), 390–408.

(2013). Natural Resources, Local Governance, and Social Instability: A Comparison of Two Counties in China. *The China Quarterly, 213,* 78–100.

(2017). Do Natural Resources Breed Corruption? Evidence from China. *Environmental & Resource Economics, 66*(2), 237–259.

(2021). Repress or Redistribute? The Chinese State's Response to Resource Conflicts. *The China Quarterly,* 1–24. doi:10.1017/S0305741021000047.

Zhan, J. V., & Zeng, M. (2017). Resource Conflict Resolution in China. *The China Quarterly, 230,* 489–511.

Zhan, J. V., Duan, H., & Zeng, M. (2015). Natural Resources and Human Capital Investment in China. *The China Quarterly, 221,* 49–72.

Zhang, H. (2008). *Shanxi Meitan Ziyuan Zhenghe he Youchang Shiyong (Consolidation and Paid Use of Coal Resources in Shanxi).* Taiyuan: Shanxi People's Publishing House.

Zhang, Q., & Brouwer, R. (2020). Is China Affected by the Resource Curse? A Critical Review of the Chinese Literature. *Journal of Policy Modeling, 42,* 133–152.

Zhang, W. (2015). The Institutionalized Political Participation. In W. Zhang (Ed.), *Market and Politics: To Lift the Veil of Chinese Private Entrepreneurs.* Beijing: Central Compilation & Translation Press.

Zhang, X., Gu, S., & Wang, X. (2011). Xinjiang Kuangchan Ziyuan Kaifa Xiaoying Jiqi dui Liyi Xiangguanzhe de Yingxiang (Mineral Resource Exploration in Xinjiang and Its Impacts on Stakeholders). *Ziyuan Kexue (Resources Science)*, *33*(3), 441–450.

Zhang, X., Xing, L., Fan, S., & Luo, X. (2007). Resource Abundance and Regional Development in China. International Food Policy Research Institute Discussion Paper 00713.

Zheng, Y. (2011). *Quanfu Jipin: Jujiao Lvliang Shijian (Poverty Relief by the Wealthy: Focusing on the Practices in Lvliang).* Beijing: China Social Science Press.

Zhu, J., & Wu, Y. (2014). Who Pays More "Tributes" to the Government? Sectoral Corruption of China's Private Enterprises. *Crime, Law and Social Change*, *61*(3), 309–333.

Index

219

For EU product safety concerns, contact us at Calle de José Abascal, 56–1°, 28003 Madrid, Spain or eugpsr@cambridge.org.

www.ingramcontent.com/pod-product-compliance
Ingram Content Group UK Ltd.
Pitfield, Milton Keynes, MK11 3LW, UK
UKHW020328140625
459647UK00018B/2071

*9 7 8 1 0 0 9 0 4 8 9 8 9 *